SCHOOLS AS LEARNING COMMUNITIES

Also available from Cassell:

G. Allen and I. Martin: *Education and Community*
D. Atkinson: *Radical Urban Solutions*
M. Barber and R. Dann (eds): *Raising Educational Standards in the Inner Cities*
M. Bottery: *The Morality of the School*
G. Claxton: *Teaching to Learn*
P. Fisher: *Education 2000*
M. Fullan: *The New Meaning of Educational Change*
I. Lawrence: *Education Tomorrow*
P. Lunneborg: *OU Women*
S. Ranson: *Towards the Learning Society*
P. Walsh: *Education and Meaning*
P. Whitaker: *Managing to Learn*

Schools as Learning Communities

Transforming Education

David Clark

CASSELL

To my students

Cassell

Wellington House
125 Strand
London WC2R 0BB

PO Box 605
Herndon
VA 20172

First published 1996
Reprinted 1997

British Library Cataloguing-in Publication Data
A catalogue record for this book is available from the British Library.

ISBN 0-304-33075-2 (hardback)
     0-304-33073-6 (paperback)

Typeset by Action Typesetting Ltd, Gloucester
Printed and bound in Great Britain by
Redwood Books, Trowbridge, Wiltshire

Contents

Preface

This book is born out of a deep conviction that the future of our planet increasingly pivots on two key concepts – that of 'community', and that of 'education'. The survival of the human species depends on community because without the emergence of new forms of association which can offer identity and solidarity, civilization will explode. Our survival depends on education because unless such communities can become open and not closed to one another, civilization will implode. The stakes have never been higher.

The task that we face, therefore, is the creation and nurture of learning societies encompassing a diverse range of learning communities. In this undertaking, our education systems are of paramount importance. Their new role must be as catalysts for the transformation of all systems, family and neighbourhood, business and commerce, health and welfare, law and order, and government itself, into learning communities.

This cannot happen unless education systems are themselves transformed. It is a transformation which must embrace learning institutions of all kinds, from the nursery to the university. But in all societies, the school remains of critical importance. Here, if anywhere, are laid the foundations of what a learning community should be like. So this book focuses attention particularly on schools, though only as a paradigm of what the whole education system should be about.

Running throughout our exploration of the nature of the learning society is the concept of 'community education'. It is a dynamic concept which could give immense impetus to the task before us. But community education has become increasingly marginalized. It has been largely ignored because of the inability of its exponents to recognize and demonstrate the power that can be generated when genuine community and real education fuse.

This book explores what genuine community and real education, true community education, have to offer to the creation of a learning society. It is written from an English perspective. But the core material is of vital importance to all other societies and all other education systems. For if we are to live and to live well through the next millennium, learning societies have to bring into being a learning world.

March 1995
David Clark

Glossary

Communal dilemma (p. 48)   The problem of how social systems can become more open to one another without weakening their own sense of community or destroying that of others.

Community (p. 45)   The strength of community within any social system is revealed by the degree to which its members experience a sense of security, of significance and of solidarity within it.

Community education (pp. 90–91)   The creation of an increasingly strong sense of security, of significance and of solidarity within and across systems through the learning process (or) The creation of learning communities.

Conflict – communal (p. 50)   Conflict where the ultimate interests and basic norms which integrate and support systems remain respected and intact.

Conflict – non-communal (p. 50)   Conflict which undermines the very existence of social systems because it is between final values and ultimate convictions.

Education (p. 83)   The process of learning to learn.

Interests – like (p. 35)   Interests which we have distributively, privately, each to himself or herself.

Interests – common (p. 35)   Interests which we have collectively, which are not divided up.

A learning community (p. 91)   A social system engaged in the process of community education.

Partnership (p. 131)   A sense of community created across social systems.

Symbolic universe (p. 53)   An all-encompassing system of beliefs and values which offer a coherent picture of the universe.

Synergy (p. 49)   Working together in a way that produces a whole greater than the sum of the parts.

Synergistic code (p. 93)   A curriculum code embracing a common quest for a richer experience of community by two or more social systems working together in partnership.

System – connecting (p. 101)   A social system which links together other social systems in a way which strengthens the sense of community within and across them.

System – focal (p. 67)   A social system for which the focal task is focal.

System – resource (p. 103)   A social system which offers assistance or support to focal systems, but which does not operate with the focal task as its major concern.

System – social (p. 28)   A human collective whose members fulfil a diversity of roles within a recognisable and sustainable whole.

Task – communal (p. 52)   To create an increasingly strong sense of security, of significance and of solidarity within and across social systems.

Task – community educator's (p. 99)   To create an increasingly strong sense of security, significance and solidarity within and across social systems through the learning process (or) To create learning communities.

Task – educational (p. 83)   To further the process of learning to learn.

Task – focal (p. 29)   That task which a social system must perform in order to survive.

Introduction

My grandfather worked as a booking clerk on the Great Western Railway. Though associated with transport all his life, he never left England because of work or for pleasure. In a life of over ninety years, he lived entirely in middle England – Ludlow, Birmingham and Nottingham. My father, now well over ninety, also lived mainly in central England. However, his work as the first personnel manager for a large pharmaceutical company often took him to the continent and occasionally, by boat, to the USA. As a boy, an army officer, a student, a Methodist minister and a lecturer, I have already lived in nine different locations from London to the Lake District. I have travelled around four continents. Our son, married to a Swiss girl, works in the field of artificial intelligence and has lived in both Canada and now resides in the USA.

Whether this increasing generational dispersion can technically be called a move from the 'modern' to the 'post-modern' might be debated. But at least it illustrates that over a few generations 'mobility' has transformed human experience in a quite dramatic way. If this were mere physical movement then perhaps the modern world would have changed more slowly. But alongside spatial mobility has also gone both cognitive and cultural mobility.

My mother was a remarkable correspondent, so much so that we always said that a logo of pen and paper should have appeared with any epitaph to her. I have produced many thousands of words; but it was only a few years ago that I put my battered old typewriter aside to struggle with a word processor. Our son lives by the computer. He regularly accesses Internet and his 'e-mail' traverses the globe. We have well and truly entered what Peter Drucker, the management guru, calls 'the knowledge society' (1993, p. 2). This not only means that more than ever before 'information is power', but that every person with a telephone or television, let alone computer facilities, is offered instant access to world-wide contacts and global experiences. Such cognitive mobility has profound implications for human relationships, formal and informal.

Spatial and cognitive mobility inevitably bring with them what can be termed 'cultural mobility'. It may not be true that 'You can always tell a Brummie by the shamrock in his turban', but living in Birmingham I can empathize with the sentiment. Cultures are in transition more rapidly than ever before because people, spatially and cognitively, are on the move. Mobility means the emergence of pluralism and together they are bringing into being a new era, call it 'post-modern' or what you will, in the history of humankind.

Mobility, and the pluralism which accompanies it, lie at the heart of two other dynamic forces now dramatically impinging on every society world-wide. These forces have been present throughout the whole of human history but what was once limited or latent is now unleashed and manifest. The one force is centrifugal. It dislodges people, their beliefs, values and relationships, from traditional foundations, and thrusts them outwards into a bewildering cosmopolitan world (Merton, 1957, pp. 387–420). The other force, often in reaction to it, is centripetal. Here people are impelled inwards to attempt to retain or reclaim their physical and human roots, their common heritage, a localized and distinctive identity.

Both forces are essential for the future viability of human life on this planet. But both also have the potential to destroy it. It is discovering how these two movements can become complementary, and not mutually destructive, that is the most critical task facing us at the turn of this millennium.

'MOVING OUT'

Centrifugal forces at work in our world are shifting people around, spatially, cognitively and culturally, in unprecedented ways. There can be no doubt that the resulting transformation of human relationships is often hugely creative.

We are now aware, as never before, how the rest of the world lives. It has become almost a cliché that many people still remember exactly what they were doing when news of President Kennedy's assassination reached them, whether English or Indian, German or Japanese. Knowledge of, indeed empathy for, those who suffer through human violence or natural disaster, is now a world-wide phenomenon.

Some, like Ferguson (1982), argue that this ability to network across the globe, this opportunity to communicate horizontally rather than hierarchically, heralds the beginning of a totally new era. Such an era, she claims, will revolutionize our approaches to health, to education and to religion. Though the scenario she paints is essentially Utopian, the centrifugal forces now evident within our world are certainly raising awareness to possibilities and potentialities never dreamt of before.

Moving out means that the opportunity to share knowledge, skills, experience, ideas, values and beliefs is now available, not just to the powerful and the great but to billions of people across the globe. Our generation has access to a storehouse of human resources, past and present, as no generation before it. From finance to films, from cooking to sport, from architecture to wildlife, from fashion to property, all now constitute a world-wide 'exchange and mart'.

The centrifugal forces currently at work also bring massively enhanced opportunities for scientific and technological innovation and change. Medical skills, commercial experience, engineering know-how, computer expertise, together with many other scientific and technical resources, can now be passed around the globe at immense speed. The potential for all to benefit from such advances promises a vastly enhanced quality of life for millions of people in every continent.

This movement out is also one which offers the possibility of a more humane and responsible international ethic for economic and political affairs. Organizations such as the United

Nations and the Commonwealth, however far they fail in practice, symbolize a commitment to human rights, social well-being and ecological stewardship. And alongside the international search for a just and sustainable world order now exists the myriad of 'special issue' groups, from Amnesty International to Green Peace, themselves networking globally for humane causes.

Moving out brings an immense enrichment of our quality of life world-wide. But moving out is about far more than 'enrichment' – it is about the preservation of life on earth. Ecologically, economically and politically, the centrifugal forces evident today offer us the means to make human interdependence a reality and not a dream, to build a world working for the common good and not for self-destruction. Hugely difficult as this task is, we now have a chance to get our human act together for the sake of future generations.

Yet the centrifugal forces at work on our civilization today also contain within them the seeds of potential disaster. Accompanying threats such as the misuse or mishandling of nuclear power and the ecological collapse of our planet through pollution or the wasteful use of finite resources, can only be overcome if we learn to live in harmony. But mobility can wrench people away from their territorial, mental and cultural roots and profoundly weaken those human bonds which previously held life together. Two words sum up this potentially destructive shaking of the foundations – 'anonymity' and 'amorality'.

Our cosmopolitan world is one in which we now relate to people through role rather than personal relationships. I do not want to know the life-history of the mechanic who services my car, the telephonist who deals with my insurance claim or even my secretary at work. In a society of such immense numbers and variety, we cannot cope with more than a handful of intimate and continuing relationships. This is why 'bureaucracy' is essential; effective organizations can no longer operate on the basis of interpersonal affinities which get in the way of the job to be done. Such anonymity can be a liberating experience, as the young person leaving home for the first time to study or work elsewhere knows full well. But it is a high-risk equation, with loneliness, isolation and loss of identity lurking on the other side. 'The homeless mind', as Berger *et al.* (1974) called this loss of our moorings, this getting lost in 'the lonely crowd' (Riesman, 1950) can become a highly dangerous phenomenon. Its outcome can be a deep sense of alienation from the world of real people.

Centrifugal forces threaten to bring anonymity, or what Beck (1992) calls 'individualisation', at all societal levels. The demise of the extended family in the western world, the emergence of 'organisation man' (Whyte, 1956), who must be trained in the art of constant uprooting, and the huge rise in the number of migrant workers across the world, are but indicators of forces steadily weakening sustainable personal relationships and affecting all of us. A great enhancement of choice 'moving out' may bring us; but increasing exposure to insecurity and isolation are also part of the package.

Accompanying anonymity is the threat of amorality. Mobility of mind and culture are key factors in the emergence of 'the vertigo of relativity', as Berger (1980, p. 9) terms it. 'Never before', he states, 'has "the pluralisation of meaning and values" [been] experienced as massively by as many people' (p. 58).

Among the first casualties of this situation are the great religious traditions of the world. Their claims to embody codes of ethics based on absolute values are now openly exposed to questioning and often summary dismissal. As these traditional repositories of morality are cast adrift, the opportunities for other mechanisms of social control to take their place, economic and political, and often a good deal more soulless, are greatly enhanced.

The emergence of amorality has been given an immense boost by the emergence of 'the market' as a key player in the shaping of human affairs. The very credibility of the market rests on the assumption that it is ethically neutral, that it lifts economics from the mire of contested values on to firm and universally reliable ground. The market attempts to raise amorality to the status of a virtue. But the problem with amorality is that it has much in common with what Emile Durkheim (1951) called 'anomie', a state of normlessness wherein the roles and rules clarifying human relationships and giving people a sense of identity and purpose simply collapse. Durkheim found that the result could sometimes be suicide. In our world today such amorality and anomie are often at the heart of the threat to identity and meaning experienced not only by individuals but many ethnic, religious or social groupings whose values hitherto have been rooted in a long heritage and strong cultural tradition.

The centrifugal forces affecting our world have much to commend them – a new openness and enrichment of experience, greater choice, the chance to learn from one another and share resources, and the hope of tackling critical global problems with at least some chance of success. But these forces have their darker side. They threaten to atomize relationships, foster anonymity and amorality where a cultural identity and shared values have previously given meaning and purpose to life. No wonder, therefore, that there now exists an urgent concern to regain a new sense of cohesion, to find forms of social integration which can hold together what seems like a rapidly fragmenting world. Thus, in tension with the centrifugal forces impinging on our world are those of a centripetal kind working against dispersal and apparent disintegration. It is the latter in particular that are bringing a renewed impetus to 'the quest for community'.

THE QUEST FOR COMMUNITY

Some argue that concern about community is unfounded. The issue is not the breakdown of human society but a displacement of cultures, something that has gone on throughout history. Centrifugal tendencies have always been there, though now they exist across the whole of our planet. The wizardry of modern technology, in fact, offers us a unique opportunity to build a *world-wide* community. 'Massification' is not to be feared, but welcomed as the harbinger of a new 'global embrace' which overcomes the barriers of 'both space and time' (McLuhan, 1973, p. 11). And if such a global community is not yet fully in place, we are at least halfway there through the emergence of new continent-wide identities, economic and social, rapidly taking shape in the East as well as the West. Are we not all Europeans (or North Americans, or Africans) now?

The potential, and indeed the need, for 'world citizenship' will be a theme underlying the whole of this book. But it has to be acknowledged that the countervailing strength of centripetal forces would be far less if there were not huge question marks over the benign nature of the so-called global village. The track-record of 'world powers' is as horrific as beneficent, and their power seems to corrupt absolutely, the more absolute it becomes. In this century alone, imperialism, fascism, Marxism and Maoism have all manifest the immense potential of 'massification' for evil. And the more recent growing economic domination of a handful of transnational companies gives cause for as much concern as hope. The new centripetal energies now evident are giving the quest for community fresh impetus because totalitarianism, in its many and varied forms, is known from bitter experience to be utterly destructive of a human and humane society.

'MOVING IN'

The quest for community is thus as much about depth as breadth. It is inward as well as outward. It seeks to retrieve 'the human scale' in terms of both the size and intimacy of groups.

The James Bulger affair in which two young boys battered a toddler to death in Liverpool in 1993, led to agonizing debates as to the consequence of the breakdown of one such community – the family. 'Are not the forces of fragmentation at work on this fundamental community, undermining the very foundations of society?' was a question many asked after this event.

The explosion of communes in the 1960s on both sides of the Atlantic, the growth of the human potential movement and its many forms of group therapy, the vast expansion of 'special interest' associations and support groups (Wuthnow, 1994) (political, professional and leisure), the emergence of what Drucker (1993, pp. 152–61) calls 'citizenship through the social sector' (the latter made up of 'autonomous community organisations'), and the steady dispersion away from cities in the West into towns and villages, are all more recent signs of the search for genuinely human relationships that can give a renewed sense of belonging and identity. They are indicators that the primary group has to remain an essential building block in the new world order on the horizon.

Such groupings often emerge out of the new freedom of choice which mobility and plurality has brought. But many are born out of moving in (and 'moving back') to recover a common heritage which has been latent or suppressed. So we have the attempted resurrection of historic cultures such as those of the Indians in North America, the Maoris in New Zealand and the Aborigines in Australia. The strengthening cultural retrenchment in places such as Canada, Kurdistan and the old Russian states, which Ignatieff (1993) calls the resurgence of 'blood and belonging', also features here.

But as with centrifugal forces, those of a centripetal kind likewise have their darker side. If fragmentation threatens to be the cost of 'moving out', fundamentalism and the ghetto can be the price paid for 'moving in'. The quest for community can become circumscribed by rigid boundaries which foster paranoia by persuading those engaged in the search that beyond lies a hostile and evil world. The tragic siege of the religious sect at Waco in Texas in 1993 was only a symbol of how incestuous and destructive such a restrictive understanding of community can be.

The incestuous form of this search for community is evident where there is wealth as well as poverty, privilege as well as marginalization, good fortune as well as disadvantage. There is just as great a danger of more elite and articulate groupings who have attained a 'culture of contentment' (Galbraith, 1992) carving out for themselves impenetrable niches in order to secure their status and ensure their influence.

Just as destructive is a moving in which takes history with it and locks groups into an anachronistic tribalism in the name of past victories or defeats. The Afrikaner in South Africa and the Jew in Palestine, for example, have frequently championed the concept of 'the chosen people' and their 'promised land' in a way that has brought inevitable conflict and suffering to millions. Protestant and Catholic in Northern Ireland have for years entrenched themselves in a past as degrading as glorious, and the horrors of the conflict between Serb, Croat and Moslem in the former Yugoslavia only underline the terrible potential for evil of a quest for community which becomes culturally and historically entrenched.

BREAKING THE MOULD

> Universalism is destroying the particularity needed to nourish it; particularity, especially in the political order, is threatening the universalism needed for human survival, not just for progress. Can the two be reconciled? Where lies the basic identity of a person or social entity? At the universal or particular level?
> (Davis, 1994, pp.133–4)

Where, then, do we go from here? The challenge is by no means a new one, but it has become in our time even more urgent than when Simpson (1937, p. 39) summed it up nearly sixty years ago.

> The challenge facing humankind is that of communalising those who are in conflict. That is a large problem. It is the problem of carrying over the ideal of the primary or face-to-face group which is most easily communalised, to the larger group, and ultimately to nations and international action ... What is needed is a return to the ideals of the primary group in such a shape and so adjusted as to be capable of application to cosmopolitan conditions. Otherwise, a sort of return to the communal womb is being urged, a nostalgia for the infantile.

It is a sentiment echoed in more recent times by Vaclav Havel (*Guardian*, 20 September 1990, p. 19), then President of Czechoslovakia: 'We must not be ashamed that we are capable of love, friendship, solidarity, sympathy and tolerance but just the opposite', he writes. 'We must set these fundamental dimensions of our humanity free from their "private exile" and accept them as the only genuine starting point of meaningful human community.'

Communalizing the cosmopolitan as well as the local, secondary as well as primary groupings, cannot be achieved without a deep awareness that the creation of 'one world' is not a Utopian vision but a social, political and economic necessity. 'Community', writes Palmer (1987, p. 15) 'means more than the comfort of souls. It means, and has always meant, the survival of the species.'

Such awareness is about a vision without which 'the people perish', as the Book of Proverbs puts it (ch.29 v.18), and about a commitment to putting that vision into practice. But it is also about education. It involves a profound learning process which enables people to realize that utilizing the experiences, insights and resources of each and all, past and present, is essential to the quest for a quality of community which will not only rescue our world from oblivion but create a future life on earth worth living. 'The real community of man, in the midst of all the self-contradictory simulacra of community', writes Bloom (1988, p. 381) in his attack on 'the closing of the American mind', 'is the community of those who seek the truth, of the potential knowers, that is, in principle, of all men to the extent they desire to know'. We would add, 'and to learn'.

OPEN LEARNING

Education, as a learning process which opens the mind to the richness of human diversity and difference in the search for the common good, is a far cry from culturally conditioned nurture, subject specific instruction or skills dominated training. Education involves whole persons and whole systems; it embraces learning of a cognitive, expressive and normative kind (Davis, 1994, p. 48f). It is about a leading out and moving on (*educere*) not about a moulding and a formal shaping (*educare*). Genuine education is about questioning the status quo, being open to 'the new and the strange'. It is about the search for a fresh understanding and appreciation of others. Not least, it is about a quest for new forms and expressions of community.

On an education of this kind depends our ability to challenge those centripetal forces that would revive self-destructive tribalism, entrench elitism and drive us into ghettos. On a process of 'open learning' which treasures the diverse cultures, experiences and insights of others, past and present, depends our hope of challenging all forms of communal fundamentalism which threaten to implode our world.

One of the major achievements of the past half-century is that 'open learning', and, even more important, the opportunity of 'learning to learn', have become available not just to the wealthy and privileged but to millions of people of ordinary means. Barriers and boundaries have been crossed and recrossed, assisted by the modern technological advances already touched on. The college in which I work has, in the past few years, had student exchanges with Israel, Germany, Italy, Poland, Northern Ireland, France, Hungary and the USA. And the wider federation of colleges to which we belong often has as many as seventy-five nationalities represented on its campus.

Of course, the value of such boundary-hopping in challenging the centripetal forces of communal fundamentalism cannot be gauged by simply tracking who goes where. How increasing mobility and exposure of one society to another can enhance, and not undermine, open learning is a particular concern of this book. But there is certainly abundant evidence that open learning, rooted in the definition of education outlined above, is an essential and powerful force in challenging incestuous and destructive centripetal forces and the tribalism they can produce.

Yet massive problems remain as our daily news bulletins ever remind us. Open learning, still on offer to only a minority of the world's population, and this mainly in the West, is now profoundly conditioned and constricted by so-called 'market forces'. Our world, with all its potential for a new openness, with previously undreamt of opportunities to share and learn from the riches of diverse cultures and faiths, remains embroiled in a battle between the 'haves' and 'have nots' which threatens to tear it apart. 'The culture of contentment' (Galbraith, 1992) faces head-on those forces demanding economic justice for all nations, and its triumph could mean the final obliteration of any hope of a global community. Open learning is, too, still circumscribed by those religious, ethnic and political systems which down the years have insisted on their own primacy and which are sustained more by indoctrination than education. Even if the numbers associated with such systems are slowly declining, their tenacity threatens the urgent need for the creation of one world.

Open learning, however, cannot be the answer to all our problems. For, as we have seen, there are also centrifugal forces at work, potentially as destructive of genuine community as centripetal ones. A world in which open learning simply led to fragmentation, to anonymity and the collapse of norms, would destroy the foundations of human distinctiveness and identity, and community along with them. The challenge we face is discovering how to break free of the excesses of the centripetal without being flung out into the void by the excesses of the centrifugal.

LEARNING COMMUNITIES

Our response to this impasse is the contention that the very future of the planet depends on our discovering and learning to live with distinctive forms of community which are continually and creatively open. These must be real communities engaged in real learning. Those centrifugal forces, which at their best can widen our horizons yet which threaten to atomize and alienate, have to be tempered by a quest for community which can offer security, significance and belonging. Those centripetal forces which at their best can foster human and humane collectives, yet can also bring retrenchment and retreat into tribalism and fundamentalism, have to be tempered by an openness to learning as an adventurous and transforming experience. Our future survival depends on a dynamic synthesis of centripetal and centrifugal, of cohesion and openness, of community and learning – in short on 'community education'.

It is the synthesis of community and learning that gives birth to 'the learning community'. We shall be looking at the latter's distinguishing features much more fully in subsequent chapters. Here, what needs to be emphasized is that to prevent our world exploding or imploding, every region and every sector of society needs to be saturated by such learning communities. Families, associations, organizations and nations have increasingly to become learning communities, a manifestation of community education in action, if our world is to avoid the fragmentation of the centrifugal and the fundamentalism of the centripetal.

But learning communities are not just a messy compromise. At best, they are a source of immense energy and a means of radical transformation. They are life-giving and liberating groupings which offer their members the excitement of a journey into the unknown, as well as the companionship to make it worth the risk. They are the source of friendship and faith, of freedom and fun. They are interdependent not incestuous, mutually supportive not sectarian.

Throughout history, there have been many attempts to cash out this 'ideal type' community, often through the creation of relatively small 'intentional communities' and cells. I was closely associated, from a Christian perspective, with such a phenomenon, the communes movement, from the late 1960s onwards. I have written at some length (Clark, 1977; 1984; 1987) about a wide range of initiatives which, albeit on a microcosmic scale, are strongly cohesive yet experientially open, and many of which are at least indicators of what learning communities can look like. Such are the Corrymeela Community in Northern Ireland working for reconciliation, the Iona Community in Scotland concerned with the welfare of the unemployed as well as with the issues of justice and peace, and the l'Arche communities serving the mentally disabled across the world.

One lesson to be learnt from such microcosms of a better world order is that community building of this quality is no easy or short-term affair. Both staying with and opening up relationships is a long and demanding undertaking, however great the long-term rewards. Bringing into being and sustaining such creative forms of human life requires not just commitment but experience, skill and wisdom. Community building is an art which has to be learnt.

But the kind of human communities required to sustain life on earth in the next century cannot be only microscopic and marginal. They have to be major and mainstream. It is not just small groups which have to be communalized. Our ultimate destiny depends on the communalizing of institutions and whole societies. What in the past could be regarded as 'Utopian' experiments now have to be implemented for real in a cosmopolitan and large-scale world.

Equipping ourselves for this task, therefore, has to be undertaken on a scale and with resources never deliberately utilized for this task before. Thus, if learning communities of sufficient quality and resilience are to emerge, then whole societies must give top priority to this task. Indeed, the creation and sustaining of learning communities is ultimately dependent on the creation of learning societies; the undertaking is so important and so demanding that it must be an 'all-in' affair.

All societies have one sector, that formally responsible for 'education', which must lead the way if the whole is to be transformed. Though by no means the only player on the pitch, it is education systems which bear the major responsibility for helping or hindering the emergence of learning communities. It is thus to educational institutions that we must first turn to see what can be achieved.

THE SCHOOL AS A LEARNING COMMUNITY

At the heart of all education systems is the school. Colleges and universities of further and higher education, and the wider adult education service, are also key players. But it is re-forming the attitudes and aspirations of the child and young person that will lay the foundations of a society which epitomizes what it is to be a learning community. Our schools, or their equivalent in years to come, will in large part decide our future. It is no wonder, therefore, that the battle for their control rages as fiercely as ever before in many places across the world.

Schools cannot exist at all without embracing at least some features of a 'learning community' (and we shall always mean *open* learning community when we use this term in future). The real issues relate more to how far schools have genuinely embraced the char-acteristics of such a community and what must be done to develop such qualities further. It is the contention of this book that if schools do become fully fledged learning communities then education will be transformed, and it is nothing less than this that can suffice for 'the survival of the species'.

The history of English education, as elsewhere across the world, shows that schools have moved towards becoming open learning communities in ways never dreamt of a century or more ago. In the nineteenth century, schooling for the young was founded on rigid and often elitist divisions of wealth, class, religion and gender. For those involved in 'popular education', the physical context of learning was immovable desks which resembled sheep pens, windows too high to give even a glimpse of the outside world and a school building surrounded by prison-like iron railings. The content of teaching was largely determined by the desire to socialize pupils into the idealized and formalized aspects of the prevailing culture, 'gentling the masses' as it has been called. Education was strictly subject based and subject bound, in elementary schools around 'the three Rs'. The learning process was instructional and didactic, formal and largely passive, with teachers assuming the role of 'elders' and guardians.

Most schools today would be unrecognizable to a child from the Victorian era. Divisions of social class and even wealth are far less obvious and clear-cut, religion usually separates schools in only a nominal way, and girls now formally enjoy 'equal opportunities', as do those from different ethnic backgrounds. Pupils with 'special needs' previously ignored or rejected, are in receipt of a range of skilled support services. The educational environment is now more mobile and less insular, with pupils frequently moving beyond the school to learn about the neighbourhood, the region and the wider world.

The curriculum today is not so culture-bound and, in spite of recent moves back into narrower subject areas, learning now embraces a real diversity of experiences and cross-curricular themes. Teaching is a much more interactive affair with teachers exercising a range of styles, and frequently cast in roles such as resource person, parent or friend.

However, such advances towards schools becoming learning communities can easily give a false impression. All countries started from a very low 'base' in this respect. The transformation that has occurred has simply revealed the distance there is to travel. The broad sweep of changes outlined above hide many situations where growth and development have been far less in evidence. Nor has development been evolutionary in the linear sense. There have been periods of regression, of increased divisiveness and of considerable insularity. Some would argue that, in England at the present time, we are experiencing a period just like this.

What is more, we are still fumbling our way to grasping what we mean by 'community education'. Many changes across the education system over the past century have taken us in that direction. But our understanding of 'community' and of 'education' appears often grossly superficial. Thus our awareness of the real potential of schools as learning communities, able to transform education so that it can match the needs of the twenty-first century, is also superficial and fails to stimulate excitement or commitment. Schools and society beyond remain content with parochial and circumscribed expectations.

This will not do. As we enter the era of 'the risk society' (Beck, 1992) we have to prepare ourselves – and our young people – for a world radically different from that within which even post-war generations have been schooled. It is an era in which the gains of the past century cannot suffice to ensure that we are well-equipped to face the 'brave new world' of the future. Nor can we be all that confident, as we look at the policies of governments around the world, that the clock will not go backwards. Not all are agreed about, or even want, the emergence of schools as open learning communities, for learning communities are always about challenge and change.

If, however, the survival of our species does depend on a synthesis of community and education then schools, above all, are the places where such a task must be addressed. It is this conviction that gave impetus to, and has sustained, the so-called 'community education' movement in England and elsewhere across the world (Poster and Krüger, 1990; Poster and Zimmer, 1992). It is to an examination of whether or not this movement has fulfilled its early promise that we now turn.

Chapter 1

The Community Education Project

HENRY MORRIS

Henry Morris, appointed County Education Secretary (today's equivalent of a Chief Education Officer) for Cambridgeshire in 1922, is seen, at least in an English context, as the founder of community education, even though he never called it by that name.

He appeared on the scene when the English education system, as was the case with many other social institutions, was experiencing a period of rapid transition. The Education Act (1902) had opened up a new era with centrifugal forces gathering momentum. School boards had been abolished and their responsibilities taken over by county councils and county boroughs. The church, though still very influential, was beginning to lose ground as the Board of Education, set up in 1899, took increasing responsibility for the funding and direction of the public system. The 'payment by results' approach of the later nineteenth century was on the wane, and the first decade of the twentieth century saw elementary education steadily adopting a more liberal and child-centred curriculum. The Education Act (1918) raised the school-leaving age, for now compulsory education, to fourteen.

At the same time, adult education was changing its complexion. The major voluntary initiatives of the nineteenth century – adult schools, Mechanics Institutes, socialist and union initiatives, the inauguration of the Workers' Educational Association in 1903 and other such ventures – were being overtaken by university extension classes and, from 1919, the rapid expansion of extra-mural classes in large part under the auspices of local authorities.

Many of these trends were given increased impetus by the upheavals of the First World War, in which Henry Morris himself served as a young officer. Yet, when he took up the senior educational post in Cambridgeshire a few years later, there remained many vestiges of a nineteenth-century world, as well as new problems of the twentieth, with which he had to deal.

In Cambridgeshire, Morris inherited a county in which three-quarters of the schools, and these 'all-age' ones, remained church schools. He was also faced with a multitude of small elementary schools (114 with less than 100 children, and only 21 with over 100 children attending), most of whose pupils were housed in a single room within an inadequate and often insanitary building. Inevitably, in such circumstances, the curriculum remained narrow, teaching was highly formalized and control rigid. At the same time, Morris, a champion of local government, was unhappy about the growing power of the central state in shaping the character and structure of a universalized education system in post-war England.

Other broader shifts in the nature of English society also presented Morris with a daunting challenge. The countryside was experiencing a time of economic decline as the population, including children, drifted inexorably towards the cities, not least London. There was a dearth of leadership on the rural scene. The knowledge and skills needed to sustain farming and agriculture were held in low esteem, while the inhabitants of rural Cambridgeshire remained so scattered and isolated that shared recreational and especially cultural facilities were a rarity. Nor did the economic depression sweeping the whole of the country in the early 1920s make things any easier.

It was in response to this situation that Morris, in late 1924, produced his 'Memorandum' on *The Village College* (Rée, 1985, pp. 143–57). This document, together with its physical embodiment in the slow emergence of the Cambridgeshire village college, became the bench-mark for much described as 'community education' in future decades. Morris' plan was to provide 'about ten ... village colleges' across the county (p. 148) combining primary, secondary, further and adult education, together with social and recreational facilities.

Morris rarely used the term 'community' and when he did, it usually referred to the local neighbourhood. But he implied that community meant much more than this and, in a broader sense, he associated with it five qualitative features: community was indigenous, all-age, holistic, 'aesthetic' and 'popular'.

Morris believed that community should, almost literally, be rooted in the land, for which he personally had great affection. It should be intensely indigenous. Education should give expression to 'the spirit of the English countryside ..., [to] something of its humaneness and modesty, something of the age-long and permanent dignity of husbandry' (p. 153). His concern was to 'fit boys and girls for life ... as countrymen and country women' (p. 153). Thus for Morris, the concept of 'the village' remained normative and his colleges, with their long central corridors and side-rooms, can be seen as villages with a roof on. For all his personal experience and love of the wider world, Morris wanted his colleges to be 'local' before they were 'cosmopolitan'.

Community for Morris was in consequence an all-age affair. 'We must do away with the insulated school', he argued (p. 20). Thus we needed to 'shift the bias of education from childhood to youth and maturity' (Rée, 1973, p. 60). 'There would be no "leaving school" – the child would enter at three and leave the college only in extreme old age' (p. 62).

At the same time, the school should become a socially holistic community: 'the environment of a genuine corporate life' (Rée, 1985, p. 154). It should become the focus of a wide range of groupings which catered for more than the educational needs of a rural population. Morris longed for 'an educational institution that at one and the same time provided for the needs of the whole family and consolidated its life – its social, physical, intellectual and economic life' (Rée, 1985, p. 154). And beyond that he listed in his 'Memorandum' a whole range of voluntary and statutory agencies arguing that 'all the activities and facilities that already exist in the countryside, and all those which by statute could be provided, should be brought together in and around one institution' (p. 148) in a 'remarkable synthesis' (p. 153). Thus, 'the village college would change the whole face of the problem of rural education. As the community centre of the neighbourhood it would provide for the whole man, and abolish the duality of education and ordinary life' (p. 254).

Morris saw this new 'communal synthesis' as having a strongly aesthetic flavour. Indeed, he was called 'the beauty man', his love of art, literature, music, architecture and things religious permeating all he did. He set out to make his schools 'fine and worthy public buildings' (p. 153). After Sawston had been opened, he persuaded Walter Gropius, the famous German architect, and others like him, to offer their vision and expertise. He sought to round off his colleges with works of art, often lending his own artefacts for the purpose, and he wanted every aspect of school life, from classroom decor to school dinners, to be aesthetically pleasing. Though he never achieved it, he stated that he would have welcomed in the village colleges 'places for worship, silence and meditation, where the sense of the sacred and eternal could be nourished' (Rée, 1973, p. 59).

Morris wanted his village colleges to be 'popular'. This did not just relate to who used them but how they were run. Their governing body consisted of county council and parish council representatives, a representative from the Senate of Cambridge University as well as 'representatives of other interests' (Rée, 1985, p. 152). The head of the village college, called a 'warden', was to be country-bred and have a love of rural life. But Morris intended that responsibility would fall on the shoulders of many people within the locality (p. 155).

Morris, however, did not view his village colleges as all communal form and no learning process. He saw them as places within which a new style of education would develop. For him, education was about life with a capital 'L'. He hated educationalists with 'no apprehension of light and delight, of impulse and passion; of Art at once sensuous and sensual; of the satisfaction of pure intelligence; of food and wine; of the imperious demands of the body; of love encounters most vehement and prodigal' (Rée, 1984, pp. 5–6). He viewed education as a liberating force and change-agent in human affairs. He saw the village college as not 'committed irrevocably to any intellectual or social dogma or to any sectional point of view ... [but as] one of the freest of our English institutions' (Rée, 1985, p. 155)

Within the village college, Morris asserted that 'the conditions would be realized under which education would be not an escape from reality, but an enrichment and transformation of it. For education is committed to the view that the ideal order and the actual order can ultimately be made one' (p. 154). Morris believed that 'the great task of education is to convert society into a series of cultural communities ... where every local community would become an education society, and education would not merely be a consequence of good government, but good government a consequence of education' (p. 21). In this sense, for Morris, the village college was meant to be 'the training ground of a rural democracy realizing its social and political duties' (p. 155).

The curriculum deriving from such an educational philosophy was to be all-embracing. It 'would provide for the whole man, and abolish the duality of education and ordinary life'. It would be 'the training ground for the art of living' and remove 'the dismal dispute of vocational and non-vocational education' (p. 154). It would encompass 'all those activities which go to make a full life – art, literature, music, festivals, local government, politics' (p. 20).

This kind of learning was a far cry, for Morris, from 'our state education institutions and particularly our schools [which] are classroom ridden, lesson ridden, textbook ridden, information ridden and given over to incessant didactic discourse and discursiveness' (Rée, 1973, p. 63). 'It is only in a world where education is confined to infants and adolescents', wrote Morris, 'that the teacher is inclined to become a pundit or a tyrant' (Rée, 1985, p. 20).

Henry Morris was one of those rare breed of reformers who not only possess a vision of a better world but have the will and tenacity to make their vision become a reality. His first village college was opened at Sawston in 1930. Then came Bottisham and Linton in 1937, and Impington in 1939. The Second World War put paid to further immediate developments but by the time the last of the village colleges was opened at Benwell in 1966, the total number had reached twelve (two more than Morris had originally suggested). At the same time, Morris gave a good deal of attention to implementing many aspects of his vision among the elementary and, later, primary schools of Cambridgeshire, not least with regard to their physical design and natural resources.

Inevitably, however, a gap remained between the ideal and the practice. Communally, as Baron comments (1989, p. 90), 'Morris fell prey to a version of the "Golden Age" myth [of] ... the organic village way of life which was (as ever) just disappearing.' Not only did such a phenomenon never exist, but there was little chance of any lasting resurrection of what had been communally significant within old rural England. Like many social architects, Morris failed to realize that it was extremely difficult to plan a community. Although he 'weighed the politics of access up to a fine degree' (p. 90), he simply had to assume that when people entered the same building, 'community' would somehow automatically be (re)created. But such a view neglected the fact that where in the past the rural village had been communally strong, this was the result of factors to do with a common heritage, common land and extensive kinship bonds, and not of occasional brief encounters in a special interest group.

Even 'access' was not as wide as Morris hoped. Figures do not exist for the early life of the village colleges but, in 1970, a review of their use found daytime attendance to be minimal and attendance at other times unexceptional (Jones, 1978, p. 16). Nor did Morris, as far as is known, overcome the tendency for middle-class, rather than working-class residents to make most use of such facilities.

Morris' attempt to give his colleges a more 'popular' form of management likewise yielded only half-a-loaf. He certainly succeeded in undermining the influence of '"filleted" parsons with their fluted voices' (Rée, 1973, p. 57), as he called them, within the sphere of rural education. Indeed, in the early 1970s, the Rector of Stresham, Ely, asserted in a letter to the press that Henry Morris had quite cold-bloodedly set out to destroy the influence of the church in village life (Rée, 1985, p. 133). But Morris' attempts to popularize the governance of his colleges was limited by two factors. One was his mistake in equating 'the Parish Council and the County Council with "representing local interests" (Baron, 1989. p. 91). The other was his own benevolent despotism, or 'sponsorship' as Martin (1994, p. 7) calls it, which meant that innovation was often imposed rather than negotiated, especially on the staff of his schools, and was not infrequently more the façade than the substance of everyday school life.

It is even harder to assess the lasting impact of Morris on the learning process that went on in his village colleges. Much of the evidence here comes from the experience of those who once taught in his schools. Morris' ideals about content and method are outlined at length in his writings and recorded comments, and there is ample evidence that his influence enriched the curriculum of his schools with regard to the vocational and aesthetic aspect of education. He sincerely believed that education could free people from a narrow view of community and prepare them to play an active part in the social and political life of the nation. His own enthusiasm for learning, and for the role of the arts within it, was certainly infectious. But whether all this turned the classroom practice of his colleges into the anti-didactic and anti-textbook world he hoped for, liberating young and old to explore new personal and public horizons, is difficult to ascertain. Indeed, Martin (1994, p. 11) suggests that 'the reform of the school curriculum [seems] to have amounted to little more than a combination of traditional subjects with some basic skills training for rural life' attached.

Nevertheless, Morris did succeed in giving expression to a view of schools and schooling which not only encompassed an innovative and exciting approach to what community and education were about, but brought the two ideas together in a way which went a long way to transforming especially secondary schooling in Cambridgeshire. His village colleges were a potent symbol, not least architecturally and in the facilities they possessed, of what 'community education' might be. Despite the huge problems of shifting control to local people, 'the village colleges represented an ambitious and brave attempt to advance popular educational interest at the limits of the [growing] statist strategy' (Baron, 1989, p. 87). Morris was also a powerful advocate for a learning process which both affirmed what was indigenous, yet liberated people for richer experiences and greater responsibilities within wider society.

In this context we cannot agree with Baron that Morris espoused 'radicalism without struggle' (p. 91). The struggle to earth this vision in practice was a lifelong, arduous and lonely affair, provoking powerful opposition and much antagonism for those whose vested interests were threatened. 'I gave my blood for Sawston; not my sweat, my blood', he once said (Rée, 1984, p. 5). He summed up his own commitment: 'As to being constructively communal, in the belief that only a communal world order, in which every single being is significated in the economic and cultural order, [can suffice], I can equal you any day, and I work at it every day, and at nothing else' (Rée, 1985, p. 16).

SECONDARY EDUCATION

Overtly, the legacy of Henry Morris to education can be regarded as limited. His most creative work was restricted to one county and later contributions to the New Town Commission made little impact. But Morris laid the foundations of what later became known as 'community education' through two major bequests. One was a model, distinctive and tangible, of what the synthesis of community and education might look like – his village college. Here, quality was more important than quantity. The other bequest was people imbued with his visionary zeal – those who worked with him in local government or on the staff of the village colleges who were later promoted to positions of major responsibility across the country.

Elmslie Philip, for example, the Chief Education Officer for Devon after the Second World War, who presented a plan for a village college approach to that county in 1945, had worked for a year with Morris in the 1930s. Stewart Mason, who as Chief Education Officer for Leicestershire launched that county on the path of community education with his own memorandum in 1949, had worked for a time with Morris before 1939. The principals of Glinton, Peterborough, the first village college outside Cambridgeshire, founded in 1949, and of Ivanhoe, the first such venture in Leicestershire, established in 1954, had been on the staff of Linton and Bottisham respectively. Numerous other chief education officers or principals of community colleges in later years had direct links with Morris or his influential colleagues.

The impact of Morris on the educational scene in post-war England was thus far more pervasive and long lasting, even though gradual, than might at first sight appear. However, his influence was much more clearly recognizable at the secondary than primary level of the educational scene. We consider first, therefore, the emergence and nature of community education in the secondary context.

The diffusion of Morris' ideals and practice among secondary schools over the fifty years since the Second World War have gone through four distinct phases.

Phase one

First came the development of the rural village (or community) college in counties beyond Cambridgeshire. Many of these were modest affairs, being simply secondary schools with limited facilities for neighbourhood use incorporated when built or at a later date. In the 1950s, Leicestershire and Derbyshire opened such 'colleges', although Stewart Mason chose 'community college' rather than 'village college' as the name for his Leicestershire schools, as he foresaw their development in urban as well as rural areas (Rée, 1985, p. 136). Devon opened its first community school at South Molton in 1952 (Poster, 1982, p. 33). In the 1960s, such schools were opened in Cumberland (Wyndham School being purpose-built), with Somerset's community schools taking off in the 1970s.

Phase two

Though such rural growth continued, in the 1980s, notably in such places as Derbyshire and Staffordshire, the second phase of post-Morris development was in more urban areas. Here there was a movement from schools with added facilities, through schools with 'community associations' attached, to the fully integrated 'school and community college', notably on the Leicestershire scene where Bosworth College, Countesthorpe College and Wreake Valley College (opened between 1969 and 1971) were of the last kind (Poster, 1982, p. 29).

The urban growth of community schools/colleges occurred in two types of area – in well-established cities and in new towns. Development of schools/community colleges in the former were led by Coventry and Walsall in the West Midlands, Coventry's Sidney Stringer Community School, opened in 1972, being purpose-built and right in the heart of the city. A year later, two other elaborate complexes, integrating a host of recreational and welfare facilities with a secondary school, were opened at Sutton-in-Ashfield in Nottinghamshire and Cheetham Crumpsall (the Abraham Moss Centre) in Manchester. From this time onwards, the growth of urban community schools/colleges continued apace well into the 1980s, notably in Dudley, St Helens, Rochdale, Newcastle-upon-Tyne and in a number of London boroughs, such as Newham and Waltham Forest.

The other type of urban area in which community schools/colleges took root was the new towns. In 1971, Madeley Education and Recreation Centre was opened in Telford. The early 1970s saw Stantonbury Campus in Milton Keynes developing along similar ambitious lines and, in 1977, Bretton Woods School was opened as part of the

Peterborough New Town development with The Gressit, a social and administrative recreational complex, linked to it.

Phase three

Although the 1970s did not quite see the end of the often emporium-like community school (e.g., the Dukeries Complex in Nottinghamshire was opened in 1985), the 1980s ushered in the third phase of the post-Morris era which might be called 'diffusion'. As the financial stringencies of the mid-1970s began to bite, purpose-built community schools or facilities attached to them rapidly became a thing of the past. At the same time, a growing number of secondary schools added the title 'community' to their name, some euphemistically, others because of a determination to create new linkages with their neighbourhood and the agencies operating therein. Furthermore, many schools though not taking the title 'community' were themselves becoming increasingly open to external links and liaisons. The 1980s also saw a number of new local authorities, notably Dudley, Waltham Forest and Derbyshire, launch extensive community education development programmes.

Phase four

This phase was ushered in by the Education Reform Act (1988) and the subsequent spate of government legislation. This seemed to threaten the development of the community secondary school in a number of ways and might, therefore, be called a time of potential retrenchment. Such threats arose from three developments in particular:

- an increasingly dominant focus on education as being about subjects and examinations defined in narrow academic terms;
- a form of local management which could make extra resources for 'community' initiatives, in respect of staff or facilities, seem an expensive luxury; and
- competition between schools which might prevent the sharing of experience, expertise and resources of value to a wider constituency.

However, there were contrary trends bringing secondary schools into closer contact with parents, sponsors and other sectors such as industry and commerce, upon which the school's 'market' image increasingly depended. Whether these more 'communal' forces have prevented a major retreat from the movement which Morris initiated we shall explore in subsequent chapters.

PRIMARY EDUCATION

Henry Morris' claim to fame justifiably rests on the development of the village college. Though this was associated with the education of children 'from 10 to 15 or 16 years', Morris also planned for his colleges to contain 'a nursery schoolroom' and 'a primary school for children of 5–10 years of age in the central village' (Rée, 1985, p. 149). Furthermore, Morris sought to apply his educational philosophy to all the Cambridgeshire elementary (primary) schools under his jurisdiction, achieving many material and professional advances in this sphere. Nevertheless, Morris' influence on the future of primary education was relatively modest. It was not until well into the 1960s that 'community education' principles began directly to be applied in any significant way at the primary level, and then without explicit reference to Morris.

The national catalyst here was the Plowden Report (1967) *Children and their Primary Schools*, the first major enquiry into the state of primary schooling in England and Wales since the early 1930s. The Plowden Report was a response to a rapidly changing national scene, showing a steep rise in the number of children in education, the first signs of an explosion of a young immigrant population in urban schools and a growing awareness that the provisions of the welfare state had not broken 'the cycle of deprivation' in inner-city areas.

Two key concepts emerged from the Plowden Report which were to guide the development of the primary community school for many years to come: 'positive discrimination' and 'parental involvement' (Rogers, 1980, p. 85).

Positive discrimination

Positive discrimination was a concept based on the principle that the education of children in 'deprived' areas was such a fundamental factor in bringing about long-term change for the better that additional resources must be channelled in this direction. The philosophy echoed that of the Head-Start Programme launched in the USA in the mid-1960s, an initiative then still riding high on a wave of optimism about managed change of this kind.

The Plowden recommendations led to a range of 'special provision' for schools deemed to be in 'educational priority areas' (EPAs), though the resources injected were nowhere very substantial. At the same time, the government established five action-research projects in EPAs, under the direction of A.H. Halsey, with four objectives:

to raise the children's educational performance;
to improve the teachers' morale;
to increase parental involvement in their children's education, and
to increase people's sense of community responsibility.
(Rogers, 1980, p. 124)

The EPA Research Project adopted a much more radical stance than Plowden. Whereas Plowden defined 'the community school' as 'a school which is open beyond the ordinary school hours for the use of children, their parents and, exceptionally, for other members of the community' (Halsey, 1972, p. 134), the research project workers wanted 'to obliterate the boundary between school and community' (Rogers, 1980, p. 127). They saw the school not only as a place of educational encounter and exchange for all kinds of local residents and groups, but as a catalyst for social and political change. As Eric Midwinter, who led the continuation of the Liverpool EPA Project, put it, 'The aim of community education is to serve community development' (Keeble, 1981, p. 48).

The emphasis on community education as intimately linked to that of 'community development' played a major role in shaping the function of the primary community school over the next two decades. In practical terms, this often took the form of the provision of special facilities and staff earmarked to serve neighbourhood needs. For example, the brochure commemorating the opening of Belfield School in Rochdale in 1973 by Lady Plowden herself carried the message that it was to be 'a community school in the fullest sense … It should become a focal point of all activities in the Belfield area of a community nature and not necessarily just those which would usually be described as educational' (Keeble, 1981, p. 55). In the 1970s, the school housed a public library, a baby clinic and chiropodist, a pre-school playgroup and a community hall available for public functions. At this time, the school had 'a full-time community worker and "two-and-a-half" teachers available for community work' (p. 55). Another of the many primary schools across the country adopting an ambitious community development approach was Birchills in Walsall. The 1970s saw the building of a community centre on this primary school's campus together with a coffee bar, a committee/quiet room and squash courts. In 1975, Birchills appointed its first Director of Community Activities.

The role of the primary school as an agent of community development, often with a major emphasis on adult education in inner city areas where a large immigrant population exists, has continued to the present day. Work at this level has been notable in Coventry, Cheshire, Birmingham, Newcastle, as well as Cambridgeshire and Leicestershire, many of these also being pioneering local authorities at the secondary level. In all these situations, a strong emphasis on the primary school as an active agent of neighbourhood regeneration was always to the fore.

Parental involvement

The Plowden Report also stressed the importance of parental involvement with the school as a means of enhancing the child's education. This required a planned programme of contact with the home, including personal visits where necessary. But, whereas Plowden saw the link with parents as an attempt to 'compensate' disadvantage, the EPA Research Project believed that the parent–teacher relationship should be a much more 'complementary' one (Jones, 1978, p. 3). The two decades since that time have seen an enormous development in the linkage of parents and teachers, along the whole compensatory–complementary continuum, or, as Long (1986, p. 2) describes it, from 'peripheral involvement' through 'collaboration' to 'partnership'. Research carried out by the National Foundation for Educational Research (NFER) found that from 1976 to 1978, 55 per cent of the primary schools investigated (1700) had seen an increase in parental involvement and 63 per cent of heads believed 'that parental attitudes have changed markedly as a result' (Cyster *et al.*, 1979, p. 50). Since then parental involvement has moved from being noteworthy to normative with virtually all primary schools taking such links increasingly seriously, not least as the result of the Education Act (1988) with its emphasis on parental choice of school and parental influence in school management.

However, the nature and intensity of parental involvement remains uneven. At the 'peripheral' end, parents are usually taken note of, but demarcation lines remain and they are not encouraged to participate directly in the educational process. At the 'partnership' end, a wide range of complementary roles have been developed over the years. These include such initiatives as Belfield School's nationally famous home-reading project (Long, 1986, p. 36), Harringay's similar venture with immigrant parents (p. 35), Coventry's volunteer parent home visiting scheme (Karran, 1985) and Liverpool's long-standing home–school initiative consisting of 31 'teacher key workers', 31 'outreach workers' and 400 'accredited parents as educators' (Bastiani and Bailey, 1992, p. 17).

The community curriculum

Alongside 'positive discrimination', with its spin-off into community development, and 'parental involvement', has run one other less well-documented initiative, that of 'the community curriculum'. Plowden paid little attention to this concept believing that in general 'English primary education was "very good indeed"' (Rogers, 1980, p. 85). The EPA Research Project, however, brought the concept to the fore. Halsey (1972) put it as follows:

> However 'open' the school may become in relation to parents, residents and other members of the community, it cannot validly claim the title of a fully developed community school until it has a community curriculum. There is much work to be done in this field.
> (pp. 143–4).

Interpretations of 'the community curriculum' at the primary (and often secondary) level have, since the early 1970s, taken two main forms. One has been that initially associated with the name of Eric Midwinter (1972) in which the 'social environment' becomes 'the leading directive' (p. 7). Midwinter advocated that the child's learning should be rooted in the local environment, a classroom without walls, and that therein lay a huge resource for all subjects and topics. He believed such an approach would not only be experientially attractive for the child but raise the latter's awareness to a whole range of social issues and concerns of wider educational significance. Liverpool's 'Priority' venture, a national centre for urban community education set up after the EPA Research Project had finished, became for a good number of years the focus of this approach, producing a wide range of promotional materials.

The other interpretation of the community curriculum has been more along the lines of curriculum 'enrichment'. Here the classroom and the school have remained more central and there has been less emphasis on local issues. But a range of 'resources' embracing parental expertise, 'adults other than parents' with special skills, professionals outside education, local agencies and organizations, as well as the physical environment as such, have been used to enrich the largely classroom-based work of the school. One of the most effective exponents of this approach was Birmingham which in the late 1980s appointed a team of ten 'community education development officers', each serving some twenty schools, primary and secondary, with a brief which included the harnessing of neighbourhood resources for curriculum development purposes. But many other local authorities and schools have moved, and continue to move, in this direction despite constraints imposed by the National Curriculum.

The emergence of the community school at the primary level has thus moved on apace since the Plowden Report. Its rootedness in the local neighbourhood, its immediate links with parents at a particularly formative age for their children, its continuing flexibility in terms of curriculum and its human scale, have in many ways enabled it to adopt a more dynamic model of community education than the secondary school. Nevertheless, primary schools as well as secondary schools have encountered major problems in developing the concept of community education and to these we now turn.

'SCHOOL' AND 'COMMUNITY' – THE FATAL DIVIDE

The history of community education from the founding of Henry Morris' first village college at Sawston in 1930 to the present day has shown imagination and energy, as well as diffusion and diversity. It has been a hyperactive movement, strong on pragmatic experimentation and initiative. Its leaders have been educational entrepreneurs of considerable vision and ingenuity. But high on inspiration and action, it has been weak on analysis and theory, and thus particularly rich in anomalies and contradictions. The consequence has been that as a project – for many of its exponents from Morris onwards, a project concerned with the radical transformation of education – it has painted itself into a corner. At the same time, others, stealing its clothes, have forged happily on. Why then has community education, and the community school in particular, lost its way?

The fundamental problem has been an inability to define its core concept, that of 'community', in a way that both transforms education and makes education transforming. For, in the end, what has community education to offer to education other than the keyword 'community'?

The history of the community school shows that even the most perceptive of its advocates have fallen into the trap of divorcing the concept of community from that of the school. Morris himself did not explicitly make this mistake, in large part because he used the term 'village' college. But even in his Memorandum, Morris speaks of schools as providing 'a community centre for the neighbourhood' (Rée, 1985, p. 148). In other words, the school as an entity is regarded as different in kind from 'the community' beyond its gates.

The separation of the concepts of 'school' and 'community' has permeated the whole history of community education since Morris, at both secondary and primary levels. As with Cambridgeshire, Leicestershire's community colleges took the word 'community' to mean colleges open to serve the needs of the surrounding neighbourhood. In Walsall, a community school was defined as one with additional facilities provided for the use of a local neighbourhood community association. The first community school to be opened in Coventry was called Sidney Stringer School *and* Community College. Likewise, the primary community schools developed throughout the country since the 1960s have defined 'community' predominantly in terms of the locality in which the school is situated, their 'community rooms' and facilities being for the use of local residents.

That community education has succumbed to the commonplace practice of talking about school and community as separate entities has led to a kind of communal schizophrenia. 'They', the community, are 'out there', to be educated, served, resourced, supported or used by 'us', the school, 'in here'.

Community education as community development

One consequence of regarding community as 'out there' is that it has encouraged both primary and secondary schools to become actively engaged in 'community development' (usually defined as some form of neighbourhood regeneration). Some community schools, not least in areas of urban deprivation, have fulfilled a useful role in offering facilities and expertise to local residents, in raising awareness to social and economic injustices, in boosting low morale, and in providing advice and counselling services. Community schools have also played an important part in promoting inter-agency links. Their facilities have been given to provide meeting places for neighbourhood organizations, and they have often promoted and provided hospitality for inter-professional forums of one kind or another. Community schools have actively engaged in adult education. At secondary level, they have offered a wide variety of courses and classes to a large catchment area of participants. Primary schools have focused more on the needs of their parents and, especially in inner-city areas, on ethnic minorities with a need to learn English as a second language.

But seeing community education as about community development 'out there' has created a range of problems for would-be community schools.

How to define the territorial boundaries of 'the community'

This problem has been especially difficult for secondary schools with their wide pupil catchment areas. Both secondary and primary schools have also had to be careful that they are not encroaching on 'patches' claimed by other schools.

How to define 'the community' in relation to those served

Many secondary schools openly acknowledge that their facilities are used mainly by the more articulate and mobile adults often from beyond even their large catchment areas. Women predominate. At the primary level, the scene is even more gender specific with young mothers (and sometimes old-age pensioners) being the main users.

This situation has led critics such as Baron (1989, pp. 95–6) to argue that some community education projects (he was referring to the Birmingham Experiment in Community Education in the 1970s) simply reproduce and cement 'class structures with their gender and race based inflections'. Thus, community schools reinforce traditional class, race and gender stereotypes and do little to promote real change in favour of the disadvantaged. Martin (1994, p. 15) believes that such an approach is in reality a 'surveillance of deprived communities' designed to ensure that they are 'co-opted' into the existing economic and political structures.

How to acknowledge and address the dysfunctional nature of neighbourhood life

The limited range of neighbourhood groups which most community schools remain content to serve and, with some notable exceptions such as in Liverpool in the 1970s, their general readiness to accept the social and economic status quo, has led many community educators to adopt a model of 'the community' far more homogeneous and conflict-free than it actually is. 'The community' is thus talked and written about as a harmonious whole. Its diversity and differences, often very divisive, are rarely recognized or acknowledged. The fact that neighbourhoods can be made up of a complex range of often antagonistic communities, and that fostering co-operation is a daunting task, are issues never openly faced.

How to provide appropriate resources and skills

Because genuine community development is in reality a demanding task, community schools have always been stretched to provide the resources and expertise required. The provision of premises has been the least problematic, although the cost of these to the school, especially at primary level, has sometimes been high. The introduction of the local management of schools (LMS) could make such costs even harder to absorb.

Offering personnel with the necessary skills to undertake community development has been far more difficult. In general, schools have relied on extra resources from their local authorities so that community workers, youth workers or home–school liaison teachers could be appointed. But the professional suitability of educational personnel for community development has not always been self-evident. Even in the field of adult education, community schools have sometimes struggled. Relating to and supporting children has not necessarily fitted teachers for working with adult groups, especially from ethnic minorities, in such fields as parenting skills or the teaching of English as a second language.

It is not surprising, therefore, that the demands on time, energy and skills of meeting the needs of 'the community' have frequently led many teachers to contract out of 'community education', gratefully leaving the task to special appointees wherever possible. Thus at both secondary and primary levels, there have been frequent reports of only a small part of a school's staff being actively involved in these 'extramural' responsibilities.

How to maintain continuity

The demands of working with the community 'out there' have meant that even committed schools and keen staff, sometimes specially recruited for such work, as in the purpose-built secondary schools of the 1970s, have not found it easy to maintain their impetus over the long term. Local authorities, from Leicestershire to Somerset, from Rochdale to Birmingham, are littered with once active community schools which have now returned to 'normality'. Not least, where external funding has been withdrawn, for whatever reason, initiatives have foundered and petered out. The once famous pioneers now have other concerns to preoccupy them.

How to serve rather than 'use' 'the community'

A further problem facing community schools in the 'out there' aspect of their performance has been that of how much they exist for 'the community' and how much 'the community' exists for them. Henry Morris was accused of destroying the parish church as a social entity (Rée, 1985, p. 133). In the early days of the Abraham Moss Centre in Manchester, a letter appeared in *New Society* from a local youth leader complaining that his club had been destroyed by the attractions of the rival facilities provided at the new community school. Of late, the economic need for schools to recruit pupils as well as attract sponsorship has inevitably tempted many to see 'the community' as a means to further their own development, or sometimes ensure their survival, and not as an end in itself.

Neglecting the curriculum

The problem of separating the concepts of school and community is, however, not just that schools are thereby tempted to take on the complexities and demands of community development. If the expertise and resources were available one might argue, as the EPA Research

Project did, that serving 'the community out there' is a wholly admirable role for schools to play. The real danger is that if schools define 'community' as only 'out there', they can easily ignore what goes on 'in here', not least with regard to the vital business of the school as 'a learning community'.

A good deal of what follows is about what it means to take seriously the idea of the school as a learning community. Our thesis is that though lip-service may be paid to this idea, it is in practice universally neglected. And defining community 'out there', as always beyond the school gates, has simply made matters worse. Our conviction is that if schools really took community into their system, education would both be transformed and itself become transforming. Indeed, the school as a prototype learning community would play a role of paramount importance in helping organizations in other sectors, as well as society itself, to develop into learning communities. And this, we have argued, is what we urgently need to equip us for the century to come.

At the heart of the school as a learning community lies the curriculum. It is the school's failure to relate the concept of community to its own curriculum that has been the great weakness of community education so far witnessed down the decades.

It is true that Morris' hope was to bring a new impetus to the preparation of young people for rural life, that he wanted to end the vocational–non-vocational divide, and that he had a passion for a curriculum which gave high culture a prominent place. It is true, too, that he believed the role of the teacher should be a much less didactic one. Yet his village colleges remained more renowned for open access and the provision of facilities for adults than for curriculum reform. Likewise with those secondary schools which followed the Cambridgeshire model. A few, such as Countesthorpe (Watts, 1977; 1980) and Sutton Centre (Fletcher, 1984) engaged in innovative curriculum developments but, by and large, the secondary model was one of 'dual use' of premises and programmes for adults rather than curriculum innovation.

Community education at the primary level brought the school curriculum more to the fore, especially through the EPA Research Project and the work of Eric Midwinter in Liverpool. Here, the environment of the school was used to enhance pupils' education. This was sometimes as a means for raising critical awareness of what needed to be changed, more often as a way of enriching the curriculum with experientially stimulating material. At primary level, too, curriculum delivery was of a much more 'progressive' nature than in most secondary schools with children actively engaged in the learning process. Even so, the contribution of 'community' to curriculum development was still defined largely in terms of the interest or the resources which the local neighbourhood could provide. And these could be drawn on or ignored as inclination, time and energy permitted.

Overall, then, the nearest that the history of community education comes to revealing a genuine engagement with the school curriculum is, on the one hand, through offering the neighbourhood as a resource for teachers to tap and, on the other, through some initiatives in the pursuit of 'progressive' methods of delivery. Many outside community education have thus quite properly asked what is so special about the 'community school'? In the early 1980s, for example, Wallis and Mee (1983) submitted a check-list of some 150 communal features (as they defined them) to 32 'community schools' and '32 secondary schools without an identified community function' (p. 37). They concluded that there was little evidence that the former were more communal than the latter and that, in particular, 'community schools will have to overcome somewhat intractable obstacles to change in the curriculum' (p. 65). In the early 1970s, I taught at a London comprehensive school where a new social education department introduced curriculum reforms as innovative as any within the community schools mentioned in this chapter, with the possible exception of Countesthorpe. It never even considered calling itself a community school.

Surveying the whole project since Morris, therefore, we have to conclude that community education has allowed its pre-occupation with community development to localize and imprison its key concept. Although community education has moved 'concern for the local neighbourhood' up the school's agenda, although it has stimulated schools to establish links with local groups, parents in particular, and although it has made a major contribution to lifelong learning and adult education, it has not offered a concept of 'community' large enough and dynamic enough to transform education itself. The equating of 'community' with the school's geographical catchment area and its residents, 'the retreat into localism' as Martin (1994, p. 17) puts it, has led to the captivity and taming of 'community' and allowed educationalists to ignore or marginalize community education.

The real challenge thus remains, evident in the ideals of more than a few community educators down the years who have tried, with limited success, to put their vision into practice. Can we discover and introduce into schools an understanding of community which can transform education and enable it to meet the needs of a world now striving to manage those immensely powerful centrifugal and centripetal forces likely to make or break the lives of future generations?

Chapter 2

What is Community?

Though rich in pragmatic initiatives and innovations and, as Cowburn (1986, p. 215) puts it, involved in 'an endless drive to engage in and publicize examples of "good practice"', the history of community education reveals a project which has painted itself into a corner. It has lost its sense of direction by neglecting to address and interpret its key concept of 'community' in more than a parochial and superficial way.

This is a tragedy because the real journey has only just begun. As our world struggles to turn the centrifugal and centripetal forces so powerfully evident within it to creative and not destructive ends, a deeper understanding of and engagement with community remains the key to a meaningful future. Boswell (1990, p. 1) puts it this way.

> In advanced western societies, our consciousness of community has become threadbare. There is an impoverishment in our sense of what it is to be social beings and members one of another, and builders of community.

This failure to take community seriously Boswell calls 'a gigantic omission' (p. 3). It is an omission which the community education project has had every opportunity to tackle but so far has failed to address with any enduring success.

The inadequacy of the community education project has also deprived education of a transforming role in contemporary society. The project's failure to give the concept of community real depth, and to demonstrate the latter's critical importance for the whole of the education system, has allowed others to subvert the learning process in the name of utilitarian philosophies which can never hope to prepare us for the challenges of the next century. At present, therefore, community education is agonizing as to whether or not it has any future. In reality, neither world nor education can do without it.

Any reappraisal of the role of community education in the years ahead has to begin with a readiness to address yet again, but in much greater depth, the question 'What is community?'. Rennie's (1990, p. 3) complaint that 'its definition is still, increasingly tediously, the subject of long debate during the conference seasons' is understandable. But this is simply because very few so far have done their preparatory homework on a concept so rich in meaning. This is not to pretend or even hope that universal agreement about a definition will emerge. But unless the potential of this 'gigantic omission' is recognized, there is no possibility of the reframing and reinstatement of community education.

A few involved in the community education project have grasped the nettle. Cowburn (1986, p. 11) believes that community education 'can no longer be allowed to escape the attention of critics by being all things to all people'. Martin (1987, p. 13) argues that community educators 'must be about recognising the negative implications of a functional ambiguity that allows so much of the debris of social and economic policy to be swept under the carpet of "community"'. Baron (1989, p. 82) states that 'the literature on community education is remarkable for its repetitive disavowal of precise definitions or for its proposal of tautological definitions'. The problem is, however, that even those who do realize that the end of the cul-de-sac has been reached have so far been unable to suggest ways of getting out of it.

The person who has unwittingly done the greatest disservice to community education is the otherwise little known G.A. Hillery who, in 1955, produced an article which in analyzing 94 definitions of community found that less than a quarter produced anything like a common formula and that at least 16 mutually exclusive elements were evident overall. Instead of goading community educators into a search for quality, rather than quantity, this remote article has been used *ad nauseam* as conclusive proof that 'community' is a redundant word. Nothing could be further from the truth.

The concept of community has a hugely rich pedigree dating back many years before Hillery put pen to paper. Williams (1976, pp. 65–6) reveals that the word has been in use in the English language since the fourteenth century and has moved through a number of clear and important stages in the development of its meaning (as have all words, of course). It was, however, not until the late nineteenth century that the first major framework for a sociological understanding of community was laid down when, in 1887, Ferdinand Tönnies produced his classic study entitled *Gemeinschaft und Gesellschaft* (see Tönnies, 1955, for the English edition). Since then, the concept of community has been addressed, interpreted and applied in a variety of ways and contexts, all of which have enriched, not detracted from, its meaning and operational potential.

The task that faces us, therefore, is to examine the major approaches to the concept of community which have been made from Tönnies onwards. Our purpose is to discover which has the most to offer in addressing the needs of the twenty-first century and to begin to remedy the 'gigantic omission' to which Boswell refers.

MODELS AND THE SOCIAL SYSTEMS

In order to give coherence to the wealth of writing on the concept of community over the years (Clark, 1969), we shall approach our task through a process of model building. This is a fine art. It can take many and often complex forms, e.g. Morgan (1986). For our purposes, however, the comment of Richard Titmus is the most apt (quoted in Martin, 1987, p. 23).

> Model building is not to admire the architecture of the building but to help us to see some order in all the disorder and confusion of facts, systems and choices.

All models have limitations. The greatest danger is that of mistaking the image for 'the real thing'. The uniqueness and diversity of human life mean that no model can adequately 're-present' it. And the constant flux of human experience makes it inevitable that at different times and in different situations one model will be more adequate than another. On the other hand, to abandon model building because of the dangers involved is rather like refusing to build a house because it might fall down. We would then have nowhere to live and would become homeless wanderers. Better, therefore, to establish some structure, which can be examined, tested and improved on, than to have no structure at all.

The model that we are looking for is, in the first instance, not one of community itself. Before we can hope to define the latter adequately we need to come to terms with the fact that human life and living, to which the concept of community must relate, is made up of a bewildering array of collectives – groups, associations, organizations, institutions, societies – all of which embrace a huge diversity of both formal and informal interactions and relationships. Unless we are to beg the question by assuming at the outset that community is synonymous with one or other of these collectives, then we first have to find a means of handling the multitude of human aggregates all around us.

We address this challenge by means of another concept, 'the social system'. It was Talcott Parsons, the American sociologist, who first put the concept of the social system on the map. But from the 1950s onwards a reaction against the 'functional' and supposedly static nature of this analytical approach gained momentum. Of late, however, the collapse of the communist bloc and a growing disillusionment with sociological analysis of a dominantly Marxist kind have led to a new concern with the potential of functionalism, or 'neofunctionalism' as it is now called. With this has come a revived interest in the concept of the social system and its potential for handling both stability and flux in human affairs (Colomy, 1992).

We, thus, put forward our model of the social system as a first stage in getting to grips with the concept of community. The *social system* we define as:

> A *human collective whose members fulfil a diversity of roles within a recognizable and sustainable whole.*

For us, a social system is a human collective (though intimately linked with its physical environment) made up of people having distinctive parts to play, but who operate together as an integral whole. Such a collective must be identifiable – culturally, socially and economically – and have 'boundaries' that make this possible. Such a collective must also be sustainable, in that its members' life together continues long enough for them to recognize themselves and be recognized as an enduring collective.

All groups may be regarded as social systems. Thus it is commonplace to use the word 'group' as a synonym for 'social system'. But groups are usually assumed to be small collectives. We require a term which can also embrace large organizations (like schools) and major institutions (like the education system), as well as ranging from the family to the nation.

An important feature of social systems is that they are inter-related. They form an interlocking network of human collectives which, rarely without tensions or conflict, impact on and influence one another. To clarify the complex nature of this inter-relatedness is a task high on the agenda of the neofunctionalists. It is one not merely of academic importance for sociologists but of direct relevance to the potential, for good or ill, of those centrifugal and centripetal forces described in our Introduction.

We depict the social system (See Figure 2.1) as made up of a number of concentric circles, or segments (as we shall call them). Another, and perhaps more accurate way of describing these segments is as a series of plates each laid one on top of the other.

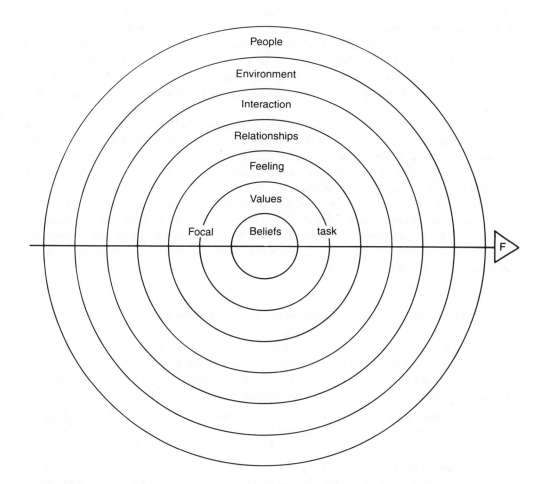

Figure 2.1 *The social system*

For it should be recognized that each segment of the social system impinges on and influences the rest.

We place 'people' on the boundary as we see this segment as most accurately defining the parameters of the system although, as we shall discuss below, some would regard 'the environment' (in terms of place or locality) as most clearly marking the system's circumference. Moving 'inwards' come 'interaction' (embracing the activities in which people participate), and 'relationships' (including the roles people play and the status accorded to these). The 'centre' of the social system we show as featuring 'feeling' (or morale), 'values' and 'beliefs'. These three segments are 'the heart of the matter' and their significance will be discussed in the next chapter.

Our diagram shows that all segments of the social system are crossed, bound together and given direction by the *focal task*. It is a task similar to that of Rice's 'primary task' (1965, p. 17).

The focal task is that task which the social system must perform in order to survive.

Systems which meet to address a particular focal task sometimes find, over time, that 'slippage' or 'displacement' occurs and what was originally a secondary concern begins to dominate the scene. Thus, for example, a religious group which originally met in order to convert others into becoming believers could, over time, grow more concerned with the pastoral care of its own members. This means that the original social system then has to accept (consciously or unconsciously) a new focal task, or fragment and disappear.

It is very important for systems to gain impetus from task achievement. Indeed, if in the long run, systems fail to achieve their focal task participants will become disillusioned and drop away. Provided, however, that a social system is clearly engaged in seeking to attain its focal task, and that related objectives are attained *en route* then, other things being equal, the system is likely to remain intact.

This model of the social system is a simple representation of a highly complex human phenomenon. But it offers us a helpful way of introducing the various interpretations of community that have appeared since the time of Tönnies. We shall pursue this undertaking by asking a key question and examining the ways in which those investigating the concept of community have sought to answer it.

By what criteria do we judge a social system to be a community?

This question is one which has concerned many writers since Tönnies, who have never assumed that community could be simplistically equated with this or that specific human collective. For example, Homans (1951, p. 367) makes this pertinent comment about the New England settlement (population 1000) he was investigating:

> Because Hilltown still has a name, geographical boundaries, and people who live within the boundaries, we assume that it is still a community and therefore judge that it is rotten. It would be wiser to see that it is no longer, except in the most trivial sense, a community at all.

We shall, therefore, take nothing for granted and will pursue the task of examining each segment of the social system in turn, to assess its potential for a deeper understanding of what community is all about. We have stressed above that no segment of the social system can exist in isolation from other segments. However, for analytical purposes we shall here treat the segments separately. In this review, we shall be drawing on the work of an important cross-section of community studies undertaken over many years.

THE SOCIAL SYSTEM AS A COMMUNITY

People

The members of any social system cannot be treated en masse as a segment of that system divorced from other segments. Yet there exist community studies which almost achieve this. One famous investigation of this kind was of Muncie in Indiana in the 1920s, given the pseudonym of 'Middletown'. It was undertaken by the Lynds (1929) and followed up by a volume entitled *Middletown in Transition* (1937). The first volume, in particular, was a wide ranging account of almost everyone and everything in Muncie. Its approach to community was very much a descriptive 'getting at the facts' approach with little attempt at any kind of critical analysis.

A number of British writers who produced a wealth of community studies which appeared during the period after the Second World War also major on detailed but unstructured descriptions of participants in the social system concerned. For example, Dennis and his colleagues (1969) writing about the life of Ashton, a small mining town in the West Riding of Yorkshire, and a book which virtually brought the era of British community studies to an end, that of Blythe (1969) writing about Akenfield in Suffolk, fall into this category of wide-ranging people-centred portraits.

This designation of loosely defined collectives as 'communities' has continued both in academic studies and in common speech to this day. But we have to ask whether or not such an understanding of community is appropriate or adequate for our purposes. For example, do the following phrases which define 'community' as people in general, help or hinder our attempts to put the concept on the wider map?

- '*The community* should have a voice in where the new road goes'
- 'Industry should have a responsibility to *the community*'
- 'Representatives from *the community* should be on the governing body of the school'

Defining 'community' as a loose-knit human collective of this kind has its attractions. The community studies referred to are lively and interesting to read. They have all the zest and fascination of what Madge (1962, p. 146) once called 'raw empiricism'. But the problem is that, with no clear indication of what actually makes Middletown or Ashton or Akenfield a community, it is very hard to compare or contrast one collective with another. There are clues all the way along the line as to why these authors believe they are presenting a 'community' study. But what features make these human collectives more or less communities is a question never adequately addressed. While distinctive features of the social system viewed as a community remain undefined (e.g. in terms of such matters as boundaries, lifestyle or sentiments), it remains very hard to know why we are talking about a community at all.

Because of these problems of vagueness, most of those writing about community have engaged with more than the people segment of the social system. They have taken at least one further step – into the segment of the social system concerned with the physical environment.

Environment

Those writers who have opted to define community in terms of the social system's physical environment have, if anything, a longer pedigree than those who have focused on people in general.

The story of the environmentalists really begins with Robert Park who, in 1916, produced his famous essay on Chicago entitled *The City* (Timasheff, 1955). The full breadth of Park's vision is demonstrated in a series of edited articles spanning the years 1916–39 under the title *Human Communities* (1952). Park and his colleagues at Chicago University were leading figures in the so-called 'human ecology' movement which sought to translate the insights of biological science into human affairs. The theme of the interdependence of plants and animals, and their natural habitat, was applied to human beings and their physical surroundings.

Park's human ecology model is not a simple one. He believed human life operated at two intimately connected levels: a cultural level, which formed the superstructure of society; and a biotic level which was the substructure. The latter was described as 'community'. He also believed that the ties which united individuals at the societal level were 'based on a natural division of labour' (1952, p. 158); those at the communal level were more intimate and rested on 'communication, consensus and custom' (p. 259). Park was convinced that the most significant research into human life could be made at the communal level. This was because it formed 'the habitat in which alone societies grow up' (p. 182), and because it was easier to map and statistically analyse in terms of territory and population than the cultural level.

Burgess (1961), a colleague of Park's, took a number of ecological concepts and integrated them into his well-known 'zonal theory' concerning the shape and growth of the city. He defines five successive areas of urban spread, from the central business district to the commuters' zone. Like Park, Burgess believed that 'the city ... is ... a product of natural forces, extending its own boundaries more or less independently of the limits imposed upon it for political and administrative purposes' (p. 219).

An understanding of community based on the relation between human groups and their environment has been prominent in many studies since the days of 'the Chicago school', even though the links with biological concepts and models have weakened considerably. Those investigations which have focused on geographical, architectural or economic features, fall into this category.

In Britain, the association of community with environment was very much in evidence during the classic post-war period of community studies, such as those of Gosforth in Cumbria (Williams, 1956), Aberdaron in North Wales (Jenkins *et al.*, 1960) and Ashworthy in the West Country (Williams, 1963), although this form of investigation petered out in the 1970s. Interest in the city as a community, however, has never flagged and studies range from Pahl's (1964) examination of the metropolitan fringe in Hertfordshire to Donnison and Middleton's (1987) detailed description of the regeneration of Glasgow's Eastern Area.

Closely related to these more ecological studies was the pioneering work of Perry (Herbert, 1963) who, in the late 1920s, set out his famous ideal type 'neighbourhood unit'. By the appropriate construction of such features as size, boundaries, open spaces, institutional sites, shops and street systems, Perry believed relationships of a communal kind could be firmly established. British interest in the idea of the neighbourhood unit remained limited until after the Second World War when a huge programme of urban reconstruction, notably of residential estates, got underway. In the 1950s and 1960s, it was taken for granted by many that Perry's formula, plus 'community facilities' and a community association, would go a long way to ensuring 'a caring community'. As White (1950, p. 41), writing at this time, put it:

> All evidence suggests that there are certain fairly well-defined limits of size, population and density within which neighbourliness is easily fostered, and outside which the community tends to disintegrate.

And as Herbert (p. 162), commenting a little later, concluded, there was little questioning of the assumption:

> ... that the community is geographically based, that is, that it is identified with the area in which its residents are located and, consequently, it is important to maintain the identity of the

community, by making it introspective, locally self-contained, and especially by the clear expression of its boundaries; and that the city is a federation of neighbourhood units together with specialised units such as industrial areas and the town centre.

Despite the huge amount of work done, and still continuing on these environmental aspects of community life, there remains overall a nagging doubt, even among the more ardent advocates of the importance of this segment of the social system, that they are delivering only half-a-loaf at most. This uncertainty is revealed by the title of a more recent book by Harloe *et al.* (1990): *Place, Policy and Politics – Do Localities Matter?* Their investigation of seven diverse locations and the environmental features impacting on community life therein reaches no easy answer to their own question.

What then is the potential of 'community as environment', inevitably linked closely with 'community as people', for our purposes? To put the question in everyday language, how meaningful and adequate is it to use the following common phrases:

- 'The aim of urban renewal is to regenerate *community*.'
- 'This area will be given a new lease of life by the *Community* Development Corporation.'
- 'Notting Hill is a very diverse *community*.'
- 'We live in a pleasant suburban *community*.'

The environmental approach to community has much to commend it. The environmentalists are absolutely right to stress the significance of the geographical and physical context of community life. Whether it be the more natural environment of a Gosforth or an Aberdaron, or the man-made surroundings of a Chicago or Glasgow, the physical environment clearly has a huge impact on the quality of life.

The human ecologists have perhaps offered most food for thought with their interpretation of community as akin to a biological organism. Thus community is deeply affected by growth and change, as well as evolutionary competition as seen in the shifting 'zonal' patterns of city life. This school of writers insist on the importance of statistical data to help track such changes; this is also important.

The champions of neighbourhood unit theory, from Perry onwards, have also offered useful pointers to the environmental features of community, not least in terms of size, physical structure and utilities.

Yet the environmentalists still leave a big gap in our understanding of the concept of community. On the more technical level, many critics have found it hard to accept the Chicago School's biological analogy, not least the division between 'community' supposedly operating at a 'biotic level' and society at a 'cultural level'. The model raises major questions not only about how the two levels can be distinguished, but how they relate and which is the more influential. The spectre of social Darwinism ever lurks in the background.

The use of communal indicators both by the human ecologists and the neighbourhood unit exponents also has limitations. The major problem here is not the indices as such but what they presume to indicate. Is, for example, a population of 5000, as Perry defined his ideal-type neighbourhood, always synonymous with a community? It is clear that certain quantifiable indicators have a bearing on the social well-being of residents in a neighbourhood, but it is not at all obvious which of these will be the most significant for the people concerned.

In the environmental approach to a definition of community, there is a constant danger of putting the cart before the horse. However influential the environment may be, it is people in all their complex patterns of interacting and relating, not place, that must define community. The ecological approach is too deterministic, and neighbourhood unit theory too simplistic, to offer us an adequate understanding of what community is really all about.

Interaction

Can we, therefore, get nearer 'the heart of the matter' by focusing not just on people and place, but what people do together? Do the activities in which people engage offer us a more comprehensive understanding of community?

As with every segment of our social system, interaction overlaps all the others. Here, however, we focus on those writers who have sought to approach an understanding of community in two main ways: on the one hand, through the study of common *interests* which people share; and, on the other, through a consideration of important *issues* of a collective nature.

It has been commonplace for community studies to assemble their material around the various interests and concerns of people. In my own investigation of Woodhouse (near Sheffield) in the 1960s (Clark, 1969), I found it helpful to group my material under such headings as work, government, health and welfare, family and neighbourhood, education, religion, and leisure, albeit within a wider communal framework which I shall touch on in subsequent chapters. For when people speak of such things as 'the business community', the 'medical community', 'the school community' or 'the church community' they are usually homing in on a concept of community defined largely by common interests and activities.

Other writers have explored common interests in their more intensive manifestations. For example, Frankenberg, in his book *Village on the Border* (1957), engaged in a detailed examination of the circumstances which led to football being replaced by the local carnival as the external symbol of the cohesive nature of life in Glynceiriog (near Llangollen). Frankenberg went on to pin-point four types of what he called 'dramatic events' which, for him, were examples of community in action. These Frankenberg (1966, p. 146) distinguished as:

- ceremonies surrounding individual and family life crises – such as christenings, weddings and funerals;
- reactions to individual tragedies such as 'whip rounds' after fire, flood, and accident;
- perennial occurrences such as Christmas, Easter, bank holidays, holidays in general, elections and meetings; and
- occasional celebrations such as coronations, victory parades, etc.

Frankenberg's highlighting of certain ritual or symbolic forms of interaction as warranting special attention by students of community, although a major theme for anthropologists working in primitive societies, has not been taken up by many on the British or American scene. One notable exception here is Cohen (1985) who in more recent years has focused on 'the symbolic construction of community' in a UK context.

The other major approach to an understanding of community through interaction is that which focuses on problems and their possible resolution. Such problem-centred studies cover an enormous range:

- rural decline and decay (aspects of Frankenberg's study of Glynceiriog),
- the demolition of old neighbourhoods and the difficulties of resettlement for urban populations, e.g. Barton Hill, Bristol, written about by Jennings (1962),
- the challenge of life on large estates like Dagenham in Essex (Willmott, 1963), and more recently,
- investigation of the ongoing fortunes of New Towns like Stevenage (Mullan, 1980) and of the British city in general (Lawless and Raban, 1986).

These studies overlap the next segment of the social system – relationships. But here our concern is with 'community action' in relation to a range of specific issues.

The equating of community with common interests offers a focused and lively approach to analysis. It enables the observer to gain a clear picture of those concerns which draw people closely together, as well as those which do not. Analysis would be helped, however, by a clearer distinction between what MacIver (1924, p. 103) terms 'like interests' and 'common interests'. These he distinguishes as follows:

> When each of a number of beings pursues an interest like or identical in type to that which every other pursues, say a livelihood, or reputation, or wealth, or any other interest which is for each discrete and personal, we may call the interests they severally pursue like interests ...
>
> When, on the other hand, a number of people pursue one single comprehensive interest of them all, say the welfare or reputation of town or country or family, or again the success of some business in which they are all concerned, we may call that interest a common interest.

Elsewhere, MacIver and Page (1950, p. 32) comment that 'the *like* is what we have distributively, privately, each to himself. The *common* is what we have collectively, what we share without dividing up.' Like interests 'do not necessarily involve any community, and social relationships, between the beings who will them, however like the interests are' (MacIver, 1924, p. 103). Thus we must beware of automatically ascribing communal quality to every kind of shared interest.

Evaluating the communal strength of a system through either symbolic events, as Frankenberg suggests, or through problems shared by a particular population, certainly provides a valuable means of penetrating beneath the surface of what could seem mundane and low-key. However, a number of difficulties arise here. As commented by myself (Clark, 1973a, p. 400):

> There could be a tendency to lay too much stress on actions witnessed or views expressed when group members are obviously tense (dramatic event) or acting in accordance with communal traditions (dramatic ceremonial or custom). The question raised is the extent to which these occasions accurately represent the 'real' sentiments of the group.

Such events sometimes reveal and even deliberately encourage behaviour and practices that are quite untypical, and even taboo, during the normal course of daily life.

One further problem here is how it can be decided on which dramatic occurrence or social problem to focus. It may well be that the more manifestly dramatic events are not those that most deeply affect the social system as a whole. Great care must be taken, therefore, not to equate community with unusual forms or periods of interaction. Can we, therefore, get nearer the heart of the matter by aligning community with certain kinds of human relationships, the next segment of our social system?

Relationships

As we move into the realm of community defined in terms of relationships, the stakes are raised. We are now dealing with an aspect of people's lives more important than territory or common interests can ever be. Relationships focus on what can be termed the normative aspects of community, embracing rules and regulations, roles and status, and various forms of social stratification.

Sociologists of community approach the issue of community and relationships in three broad ways: those commentators who focus on typical forms of human relationships associated particularly with kinship or class; more theoretical studies which are concerned with contrasting, and often conflicting, types of collectives; and a more recent concern with 'ethnic communities'.

In the first category would come the classic study by Young and Willmott (1962) of *Family and Kinship in East London*. Here the authors examined the social relationships existing among residents of Bethnal Green in the 1950s and the effect on family ties of removal to London County Council's estate of Greenleigh. This approach characterized a large number of other studies in the 1950s and 1960s as indigenous rural settlements continued to break up and massive movements of the urban population went on apace, notably from inner-city areas to large peripheral estates complete with high-rise housing. Josephine Klein's two volumes on *Samples from English Cultures* (1965a; b) drew together much of that era's work in exploring the impact of such mobility on social relationships.

Other British community studies of kinship and class employed a more dichotomous framework reflecting clashes of lifestyle or culture resulting from the post-war upheavals and resettlement of populations. Thus Brennan and his colleagues in their study, *Social Change in South-West Wales* (1954), portrayed the old residents there struggling to maintain their traditional way of life against, on the one hand, that represented by the 'unoriented working class (p. 182ff) who had little interest in the trade unions or chapels and whose associational participation was limited to loosely knit and less formal groupings and, on the other hand, that way of life typified by the "anglicised middle class" moving into the region with the influx of new industry'. Stacey, in her study of Banbury (1960), at that time experiencing the influx of newcomers to work at the large local aluminium factory, not only used the categories of class, but of 'traditional' and 'non-traditional' residents. Elias and Scotson (1965) entitled their study of a suburban development on the outskirts of a Midlands town, *The Established and the Outsiders*.

These post-war British studies in many ways reflect a second larger and broader sociological approach to community as relationships and one which has exercised a major influence in this field. Those involved have been termed 'the theoreticians' (Reissman, 1964).

The outstanding characteristic of the theoreticians is that they apply highly analytical concepts to the study of community. A key feature of this group of sociologists is that they deal in 'polar types' of a more global nature than those already mentioned above in an attempt to contrast one form of social system with another. Redfield, for example, in his study of *The Folk Culture of Yucatan* (1941), a Mexican peninsula where he undertook research from 1927 until 1936, pin-pointed four kinds of 'community': the tribal settlement, the peasant village, the town and the city. Becker (1950), some years later, took a broader approach dividing societies into 'sacred' and 'secular', and Merton (1957) forged the seminal concepts of 'locals' and 'cosmopolitans'.

But the founding-father of the theoreticians was Ferdinand Tönnies who, in the late nine-teenth century, was deeply influenced by the steady industrialization of rural Schleswig-Holstein where he was born and brought up. His reflections on the great upheavals he saw led him to suggest that an irreversible change was taking place from 'Gemeinschaft' to 'Gesellschaft' or, as Loomis (1955) translates it, from 'community' to 'association'. Tönnies' typology is extremely detailed and complex, and owes as much to social psychology as sociology proper, but, in broad terms, he is plotting the move from 'natural', close-knit and continuing forms of relationship to those which are 'rational', impersonal and often of a temporary or sporadic kind. Many writers since Tönnies, including some of those mentioned above, have made use of similar contrasting types to assist in their analysis of communal change.

A third and more recent contribution to the construction of community in terms of rela-tionships is that which has stressed ethnic ties. Thus we often speak of 'the ethnic minority community', 'the expatriate community' or, more specifically, 'the Jewish community' or 'the Moslem community'. The features of close-knit social systems encountering upheaval and enforced confrontation with other systems, which attracted the attention of the theo-reticians, apply to ethnic communities also. But the forces of contemporary life referred to in our Introduction have now brought matters to a head, deeply threatening the identity if not extinction of ethnic systems as cultural entities. It is little wonder that a strong political reassertion of cultural differences has resulted (Cohen, 1985, pp. 104–8).

Michael Ignatieff (1993) has vividly documented this current struggle for ethnic identity and survival in such places as Yugoslavia, the Ukraine, Kurdistan, Quebec and Northern Ireland. His analytical model distinguishes between 'civic nationalism' which 'maintains that the nation should be composed of all those – regardless of race, colour, creed, gender, language or ethnicity – who subscribe to the nation's political creed' (p. 3) and 'ethnic nationalism' which 'claims, by contrast, that an individual's deepest attachments are inher-ited, not chosen' (pp. 4–5). I myself have set out a typology of how such ethnic systems might relate to their 'host community' through a process of expulsion, assimilation, segre-gation, pluralism (closed and open), synthesis, revolution or withdrawal (Clark, 1982).

Those who seek to interpret community in terms of human relationships and their diverse forms have added great depth to the concept. Who can doubt that family, kinship, class, tribe or ethnicity are not key ingredients of communal life? It is ties such as these which so often determine the quality of life within social systems, and the latter's identity in relation to other systems.

Such studies also give new insight into what divides one community from another and open up the issues of change and conflict. We here see how 'community' is a phenomenon which can set one system against another and become as powerful a force for closure as openness.

Yet herein lies one of the limitations of constructing community largely in terms of rela-tionships. With which aspect or form of relationships are we equating it? Is the key communal ingredient family or class or ethnicity or something else? This is the question with which Cohen (1985) wrestles throughout his book, *The Symbolic Construction of Community*, yet without coming to a clear conclusion.

A major problem which the approach of the theoreticians in particular raises is whether the transition from one type system (such as Gemeinschaft) to another (such as Gesellschaft) means the obliteration of community altogether. Tönnies, for example, makes his ideal types so 'concrete' that the distinct impression is left that as Gemeinschaft is destroyed by urbanization, so is community. Does this mean, then, that in a world of asso-ciational, or secular (Becker, 1950) or cosmopolitan (Merton, 1957) relationships, there is no such thing as community?

Equating community with the relationships dimension of the social system does give a deeper and richer quality to our analysis, and usefully embraces potential conflict as well as co-operation. But it still leaves us unclear as to what is really at the heart of the matter.

The focal task

There is a large literature related to social systems where the focal task (defined as the task a system must address in order to survive) is regarded as the creator, builder or maintainer of 'community' as such. Throughout history many groupings, from the monastic movement (Knowles, 1969) to the millenarians (Cohn, 1970), from economic or political Utopias (Armytage, 1961; Hardy, 1979) to the more recent communes movement (Rigby, 1974; Clark, 1977; 1984; 1987), not to mention a whole gamut of therapeutic communities (Goffman, 1968; Vanier, 1979), have pursued community itself as their focal task.

This concern has also been high on the agenda of the spate of urban 'Utopias' (from Saltaire to Bournville), neighbourly neighbourhoods (such as Perry's ideal type units described above), and the host of post-war new towns. Other issues such as population explosions and hygienic housing have motivated these initiatives, but it is the belief that community as such can be deliberately manufactured that has been the major driving force.

Have these initiatives borne fruit? Can community building itself be sustained as the focal task for social systems?

My own experience of the Christian community movement, given impetus by the secular communes movement of the 1960s, bears witness to both the glories and hazards of pursuing community as an end in itself (Clark, 1977; 1984; 1987). Many impressive and creative 'intentional communities' emerged from that time onwards, often involving their members in considerable self-sacrifice. Some ventures were simply about community building for the benefit of the founder members. But others – such as the l'Arche commu-nities for the mentally handicapped, the hospice movement, the Cyrenian houses for the homeless, or residential homes for drug abusers (Clark, 1977, pp. 167–77) – existed to provide a community for many in deep need. In this context, community as focal task produced examples of human living of real quality.

However, tackling community building direct has also witnessed inglorious failures. Over the centuries 'Utopianism' has had a chequered history. The notable attempts in this century to plan urban villages and communal neighbourhoods have rarely managed to sustain their 'first generation's' enthusiasm. The Bournville Estate in Birmingham, where my own family has lived for the past twenty years, is widely regarded as an environmen-tally very pleasant but often impersonal place in which to live, with such communal facilities as public houses and fish and chip shops among the 'prohibited' amenities. And the communes movement of the past few decades has seen as much anguish as accom-plishment.

Community building pursued as focal task encounters at least four problems. First, it places very high (often Utopian) expectations on the shoulders of participants, frequently their being unable to clarify or agree what the end 'product' might look like. To espouse community as an end in itself is rather similar to the pursuit of happiness; it disappears mirage-like the nearer you get to it. The vision of community, though inspiring enthusiasm or yearning, is often too vague or elusive to offer a clear destination or even common purpose.

In the second place, and in contrast to many a Utopian vision, community building is an extremely demanding undertaking. The experts, such as the religious orders or those involved in the more recent community movement, record time and again that intentionally to live as a community requires a whole range of human skills and qualities much less necessary in the normative affairs of the daily round. Jean Vanier (1979), for example, the founder of the l'Arche communities, has written penetratingly about what such community building requires. Not least it demands 'staying with relationships', as George Ineson of the Taena Community puts it. Ineson writes (Clark, 1977, p. 49):

> Whatever the difficulties are, a solution will emerge if you can contain the problem and live through it. Once the community divides into two or more separate organisms, the heat escapes and the meal is uncooked – leaving only partial surface solutions instead of a radical transformation. Living in a town or city offers so many possibilities of escape that it is hardly possible to contain a problem in this way except in the limited sphere of the family; this is one reason why so many of us today never pass beyond adolescence, the spirit imprisoned in a surface adaptation to a particular external context.

In the third place, community as focal task suffers from the hubris of the social engineer. It is always easier to plan community for others than to live it oneself. Our urban society is littered with the failures of what Pahl calls 'architectural determinism' (1970, p. 106), from estates where nobody uses the proper footpaths to high-rise blocks of flats which have proved such a communal disaster for many. Fostering community has proved a far more complex task than the planners – social or physical – ever dreamed. One fears that even now we have failed to comprehend the real challenge that lies ahead.

Finally, the problem of seeking to pursue community as focal task is that 'slippage' easily occurs. Because of the difficulties of the direct approach, other focal tasks soon appear to displace the original one. There are many examples, from the monastic movement to modern rehabilitation communities (such as Synanon, the drug-abusers reformatory community in the USA), where communal living has been economically so 'successful' that the group has become affluent, ending up as a thriving commercial but communally compromised undertaking. Other groups have moved into agriculture or manufacturing, into welfare work or healing centres. Gradually, the focal task has shifted from community building as such to a more instrumental one, with fewer and fewer participants committed to the original vision. This does not mean that 'community' disappears but that it becomes more a latent than manifest concern.

This chapter has explored how over the years the concept of community has been aligned with different segments of our social system and defined largely in the context of these segments. All such definitions have made a contribution to the potential meaning of the term. But all have had their limitations, at times very restrictive.

We now turn our attention to those less easily observable segments of the social system – feeling, values and beliefs – in the conviction that, as far as the concept of community is concerned, these are really 'the heart of the matter'.

Chapter 3

The Heart of the Matter

The segments of the social system we have examined so far – people, the environment, interaction and relationships, as well as the focal task – have all been employed at one time or another to define particular dimensions of community. Such contributions to an understanding of the meaning of community have been valuable. But it is our contention that none of them goes far enough if we are to lay hold on a concept which can match the needs of a world trying to find the means of handling creatively those powerful centrifugal and centripetal forces described in our Introduction.

Over the course of this century, the more perceptive of writers have sought to remind us that our understanding of community is too small. 'Life is essentially and always communal life. Every living thing is born into community and owes its life to community', wrote MacIver (1924, p. 209). Simpson (1937, pp. 21 and 11), in a classic discussion of community between the two world wars, asserted: 'Men need community as they need nothing else ... Without the presence of community men could not will associational relations.' Nisbet (1969, p. 73), writing in the 1950s, maintained: 'The quest for community will not be denied, for it springs from some of the powerful needs of human nature – needs for a clear sense of cultural purpose, membership, status and continuity.' While Vaclav Havel (1990, p. 19) speaking much more recently comments:

> We must not be ashamed that we are capable of love, friendship, solidarity, sympathy and tolerance, but just the opposite ... We must set these fundamental dimensions of our humanity free from their 'private exile' and accept them as the only genuine starting point of meaningful human community.

COMMUNITY AS FEELING

In the light of these reflections, therefore, it is not surprising that community is often described in terms of feeling or sentiment, that phenomenon which draws its energy from the emotional nature of human beings. This is the expressive dimension of community. In everyday parlance, for example, such commonplace phrases as the following focus largely on community as sentiment:

- The sense of *community* in this neighbourhood leaves a lot to be desired.
- Christmas generates a real *community* spirit for many people.
- The head may call this a *community* school but it doesn't feel much of a *community* to me.
- The *community* spirit in this business has always been good.

Behind these everyday phrases, however, lies a wealth of commentary from many academic disciplines, including English literature and history as well as psychology and sociology, which leaves no doubt that community as feeling is one of the most potent emotions experienced by human beings.

Simpson, for example, in his major study, *Conflict and Community* (1937), takes community as feeling to be central to his thesis. He writes (pp. 97; 71):

> Community is no circumscribed sphere of social life, but rather the very life-blood of social life. Community is not simply economic, nor simply political nor simply territorial, nor simply visceral. Nor is it all these special elements added together. Ultimately, it is a complex of conditioned emotions which the individual feels towards the surrounding world and his fellows ... It is to human beings and their feelings, sentiments, reactions, that all look for the fundamental roots of community.

Fifty years later Vaclav Havel, in the words quoted above, echoes Simpson's view that community is rooted in people's emotions. On the British scene, Kingdom (1992, p. 86), refuting Margaret Thatcher's assertion that 'There is no such thing as society', argues: 'The sense of community gains its highest justification not as a means to an end, but as an end in itself, an indispensable component of the good life which we all seek.'

Following these and other writers, therefore, we place community as feeling in a key position within our social system. It lies between and links the more ostensible manifestations of community – people, environment, interaction, relationships and focal task – to those vital but less easily definable segments encompassing values and beliefs.

Community defined as feeling at last offers us a concept dynamic enough to match the needs of today's world. As the quotations above indicate, we are not here dealing with some superficial phenomenon of a 'take it or leave it' kind but an aspect of human experience without which social life falls apart. Community as feeling is an ingredient so important in human affairs that we ignore or devalue it at our gravest peril.

THE COMPONENTS OF COMMUNITY AS FEELING

Three major objections are raised to the definition of community as feeling. The first is that it reduces the concept to a purely psychological one. As such, a sense of community might be important for individuals but cannot be applied to or have relevance for the social system as a whole.

It is true that to define community as a feeling emphasizes what Homans (1951, pp. 37–8) calls the various 'internal states of the human body'. And MacIver and Page, in their seminal study, *Society* (1961), acknowledge that to stress community as sentiment is to major on its 'psychological configuration' (p. 291). But Homans goes on to employ community sentiment as essential to his study, *The Human Group* (1951). Likewise, for MacIver and Page, it is an indispensable ingredient of *Society*. Feelings do not occur in a vacuum. All sentiments are sparked off or strengthened by the experiences of everyday life.

To argue that feelings of horror at the atrocities of a Bosnia or a Rwanda, of frustration at the political state of the nation, or of elation at sporting triumphs, are purely psychological and private is quite clearly erroneous. Many such emotions are as powerfully group as personal sentiments.

It is quite possible, therefore, to regard 'the psychological configuration' of community, as MacIver and Page define it, as a corporate as much as an individualistic phenomenon, while at the same time distinguishing this emphasis from its more ostensibly sociological expression through interaction and human relationships. Our argument is in fact that much confusion has arisen because so much attention has been focused on the sociological expression of community without its psychological components having been clearly recognized.

A second criticism of community as feeling comes from those who ask, 'Which feelings?' This question is a quite proper one for any researcher within the human sciences, but because it can give rise to problems of complexity does not mean that distinguishing key communal features is impossible. Our contention is that distinguishing those feelings of greatest communal significance is a matter best dealt with by reflection on the work of the most perceptive researchers and writers described in this and the previous chapter. Given that our attention is at present on the psychological configuration of community, the question we must address is: 'What are the communal components which dominate the more psychological forms of analysis?' Such components will, of course, continue to be open to re-examination and potential adaptation as part and parcel of the ongoing quest for a deeper understanding of the meaning of community.

The third criticism levelled at community as feeling is that this dimension of community can never be measured objectively. Plant (1974, p. 79) argues this point stressing that 'the relativity of culture' makes any external assessment of the nature or strength of human feelings a hazardous undertaking. Our response is similar to that of Plant. While maintaining our argument that the essential components of community as feeling are distinguishable, we would still agree with him that their strength or weakness can be most accurately assessed by the members of the social system concerned. In this sense, community is a psychological, a sociological, as well as a culturally conditioned phenomenon.

In the light of these comments, we set out our first *communal proposition* as follows:

> *The degree to which any social system can be regarded as a community depends on the degree to which its members experience a sense of community within it.*

Such a proposition, although focusing on community as feeling, could be taken as tautologous, unless an attempt is made to clarify the essential components of 'a sense of community'. We shall, therefore, follow the trail blazed by MacIver and Page (1961, pp. 291–6) when they did just that, pin-pointing three key components of community sentiment described by them as 'we-feeling', 'role-feeling' and 'dependency-feeling'. Here, we shall talk about a sense of solidarity, a sense of significance and a sense of security.

Solidarity and significance

Solidarity is a sentiment akin to what MacIver and Page (1961, p. 293) call 'we-feeling' and which they define as: 'The feeling that leads men to identify themselves with others so that when they say "we" there is no thought of distinction and when they say "ours" there is no thought of division.' Solidarity is by far the most commonly recognized sentiment associated with community. As Handy (1994, p. 248) puts it, 'We need to belong – to something or someone.' It is this feeling which writers have in mind when they refer to a sense of fraternity, fellowship, togetherness or belonging. Solidarity encompasses all those feelings which draw and hold people together – sympathy, loyalty, gratitude, trust and so on – a river into which many tributaries flow.

Unfortunately, preoccupation with solidarity has led to the neglect of our second key component of community as feeling: a sense of significance. This sentiment is that which MacIver and Page (1961, p. 293) term 'role-feeling', defined by them as: 'The sense of place or station [experienced by group members] so that each person feels he has a role to play, his own function to fulfil in the reciprocal exchanges of the social scene.' Significance too is made up of a complex of related feelings such as a sense of standing, worth or achievement.

Solidarity and significance are, for us, key components of community. They are also feelings which are clearly very important, even if expressed in different terms or given more implicit than explicit recognition, in many of the community studies mentioned in the previous chapter. For example, among the ecologists, Park (1952, p. 181) writes: 'The existence of society presupposes a certain amount of solidarity, consensus and common purpose.' Referring more explicitly to a sense of significance, he adds (pp. 176–7):

> In this social and moral order, the conception which each of us has of himself is limited by the conception which every other individual, in the same limited world of communication, has of himself, and of every other individual. The consequence is – and this is true of any society – every individual finds himself in a struggle for status: a struggle to preserve his personal prestige, his point of view, and his self-respect. He is able to maintain them, however, only to the extent that he can gain for himself the recognition of everyone else whose estimate seems important; that is to say, the estimate of everyone else who is in his set or in his society. From this struggle for status, no philosophy of life has yet discovered a refuge. The individual who is not concerned about his status in some society is a hermit, even when his seclusion is a city crowd. The individual whose conception of himself is not at all determined by the conceptions that other persons have of him is probably insane.

Of those writers more concerned with empirical community studies, Jennings, writing about the factors moulding the old settlement of Barton Hill in Bristol, gives as good an account of the importance of both solidarity and significance as any. She writes (1962, pp. 224–5):

> In the old Barton Hill there emerged a society in which individuals counted [significance] and the social bond was strong [solidarity] and found expression in the wider society. Such a comparison [of the way the old Barton Hill developed in relation to the new estate at 'Mossdene'] offers hope for the future. Yet some new factors seem to demand explicit recognition and purposive action if the old idea of individual significance, social unity [solidarity] and effective democracy [significance/solidarity] are to be given new and appropriate forms of expression. First, the traditional ties which defined localities may be increasingly threatened by the conquest of space and by the fragmentation of interests and bonds [lack of solidarity] resulting partly from new types of economic organisation. Secondly, there is a danger that the individual may come to count for less [lack of significance] if the tendency to large-scale organisation and administration continues. Thirdly, the growth of powerful and specialised and professionalised corporate bodies within the state may tend to make the man in the street less able to play an effective part [lack of significance] in the shaping of society. It may be that another age of discovery demands a rethinking of the aims, machinery and functions of corporate society in relation to the individual and to organised groups.

Among those sociologists taking a more theoretical approach to the concept of community, Tönnies (1955) is particularly concerned with the importance of the folk type of human group where solidarity or Gemeinschaft dominates, but dismissive of more associational forms of collective, termed 'Gesellschaft', in which a sense of significance often remains strong. More perceptive here is Simpson (1937, p. 33) who writes: 'In community men's deepest desires for love, fellowship, understanding, sympathy, solidarity, are realised.' With regard to a sense of significance, Simpson argues (p. 88) that 'what men are now failing to realise is that the individual must be made significant in a new type of community'. 'An individual', he continues (p. 101), 'becomes communally important either negatively, when his actions are restricted in order that certain customs, conventions and laws may remain intact, or positively when his labours are necessary to the further vitality of other men.'

Security

MacIver and Page (1961, p. 293) add a third communal component which they call 'dependency-feeling'. 'This involves physical dependence, since man's material needs are satisfied within it [the community], and a psychological dependence, since community is the greater "home" that sustains him, embodying all that is familiar at least, if not all that is congenial to his life.'

There are, however, certain objections to our including this third possible component of community defined as feeling. If social security, or 'psychological dependence' is considered, its association with a sense of solidarity seems so close that a separate component is uncalled for. As Goldman (1965, p. 67) underlines in his comments on the basic needs of children: 'Emotionally, a child needs to be secure, and the roots of this need lie in the experience of love. A child therefore needs to feel he belongs, first of all, to an intimate family, then to a community which cares for him.' A sense of security of this kind is born out of a sense of solidarity rather than vice versa.

There is, furthermore, a case for arguing that, even if the focus is on physical dependence, a sense of security is not a core component of community as feeling. In some instances (e.g. in a residential home or even school), a physical or material dependence which is enforced can be detrimental to a sense of community. In other situations (e.g. on a dangerous voyage at sea or within the armed forces), lack of physical security can actually strengthen community sentiment.

Nevertheless, *we shall retain a sense of security*, though with a definite emphasis on physical or material well-being, *as a key communal component* for one very good reason. This is that social systems cannot endure physical or material insecurity at too great an intensity or for too long a period without significance and solidarity being weakened. 'A cohesive, organic community is only possible where all have the material means to participate' (Kingdom, 1992, p. 95). This is clearly seen in our own country in relation to the long-term effects of unemployment. It is even more starkly evident in poverty-stricken areas of East Africa or in war-torn Bosnia.

No writer describes the importance of physical security in a more telling way than Michael Ignatieff (1993) when reporting the feelings of ethnic 'minorities' in such places as Yugoslavia, Germany, the Ukraine, and Kurdistan. A key theme throughout his book, *Blood and Belonging*, is that without a land to call their own people feel not only psychologically but physically threatened. Of Kurdistan, for example, Ignatieff writes (1993, p. 161):

> This border region between Turkey and Iraq is where I finally learn the human difference between a people who have their own place, and a people who do not. On one side, hearts and minds are open. On the other, hearts pound with fear. On the one side, they shout 'Allo Mistair' in greeting. On the other, they shrink from foreign contact for fear of trouble. Statelessness is a state of mind, and it is akin to homelessness. This is what a nationalist understands: a people can become completely human, completely themselves, only when they have a place of their own.

But we are learning that it is not just crisis that underlines the importance of the physical as a key component of community as feeling. Increasingly, we are recognizing (Grey, 1993, p. 121) 'that the very possibility for human community is related to the connectedness of human beings with the environment's nurture'. The 'Gaia principle' (Lovelock, 1979), founded on the interconnectedness of human life with the whole 'earth as a self-renewing system, take[s] us on huge leaps back into history and forward into the future' (Handy, 1994, p. 246). A sense of community is rooted not only in our social bonding but in our sense of well-being grounded in the earth and all it provides.

We can, therefore, now expand our communal proposition, embracing more specifically community as feeling, in the following way:

> *The strength of community within any social system is revealed by the degree to which its members experience a sense of security, of significance and of solidarity within it.*

This proposition forms the basis of what, henceforth, we shall define as the *communal task.*

> *The communal task is to create an increasingly strong sense of security, of significance and of solidarity within any social system.*

Those concerned with the development of community need to regard all social systems as having two complementary tasks – a focal task (as we have defined this on p. 29) and a communal task (as defined above). The latter, however, does not simply run 'parallel' to the former. It interweaves with the focal task, as well as with every segment of the social system, in order communally to enrich the whole.

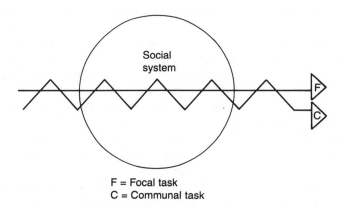

F = Focal task
C = Communal task

Figure 3.1 *The community development process*

The relation between the three 'S's

To have a sense of community is to have a place to stand (security), a part to play (significance) and a world to belong to (solidarity). But how are these core communal components related?

All three are closely linked. No person can experience one such feeling or lack of it, without it affecting the other two. In this respect, community is a seamless robe. Bottery (1990, p. 144), referring to a number of sources, writes: 'There is now quite a body of psychological literature which suggests that the fostering of self-esteem [significance] leads to feelings of altruism [solidarity] towards others.' Boswell (1990, p. 49) writes: 'According to the communitarian perspective, liberty [significance] acutely needs the context of fraternity [solidarity].' He also argues (p. 201) that 'economic health [security] and a community renaissance are inseparable'.

Yet it is not true that the three core components of community are always present to the same degree. For example, some people discover a very strong degree of solidarity within the nuclear family while not finding that it gives them the chance to attain a fully adequate sense of significance. Some people derive a very strong sense of significance from their work while not experiencing a very strong sense of attachment to fellow workers. It is therefore crucial in any study of community that solidarity and significance should be treated as analytically distinct phenomena and not be assumed to vary in direct proportion to one another. Likewise, we have already argued that a weak sense of physical security may not always indicate that significance or solidarity are also weak.

So can or should the three 'S's be placed in any order of priority? We are here sailing very close to the boundary line dividing the feelings segment of the social system from those encompassing values or beliefs. But we would want to argue, not least on psychological as well as sociological grounds, that such a communal order of priority exists.

From a psychological perspective, Maslow (Hilgard *et al.*, 1975, pp. 333–4) has argued that there is a 'hierarchy of needs', with the more physical and material having to be met before the others can be satisfied. At the base of his 'pyramid' he puts physiological needs, such as hunger and thirst, and safety needs, such as the need to feel safe and free from danger (both needs closely linked to our sense of security). Next up the ladder he places 'belongingness' (akin to our sense of solidarity), just below 'esteem needs' (akin to our sense of significance). Cognitive and aesthetic needs follow with 'self-actualisation' at the peak of the pyramid (the last also appearing to have much in common with our concept of significance).

Our view is that Maslow's hierarchy is helpful. But we would contend that a sense of solidarity, rather than significance, should be regarded as the summit of the pyramid. We would argue, this time on more sociological grounds, that the identity (and thus significance) of the individual cannot in the last resort define the nature of community. As a matter of human reality, significance is ultimately dependent on solidarity, identity on belonging to a social system (Shotter, 1993, p. 128). However free the individual may be or wish to be, he or she can only be sustained in that freedom by some form of community within which a sense of solidarity is already experienced (p. 130). 'No man is an Island' (John Donne, *Devotions*, XVIII) is no mere cliché.

The case for placing solidarity rather than significance at the apex of the pyramid is forcefully argued by many feminists, including feminist theologians. Kelly (1992), for example, in *New Directions in Moral Theology* (p. 94) states: 'Reflecting on their experience, women have helped to bring to human consciousness the core insight that the heart of moral agency lies not in individual independence but in mutual interdependence.' Roger Harrison (quoted in Pedler *et al.*, 1991, p. 162), from the quite different perspective of organization and management studies, argues that Maslow's model should have 'survival' at the base with 'security', 'self-expression' and 'community' (we would interpret this as solidarity), in that order, above it.

Figure 3.2 offers a model of our hierarchy of core communal components.

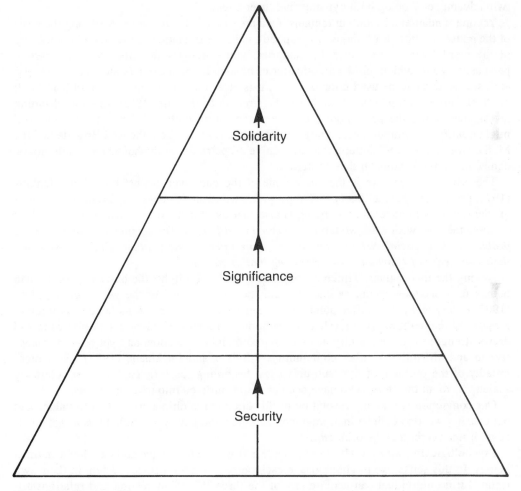

Figure 3.2   *The three 'S's*

THE COMMUNAL DILEMMA

With these reflections on the three 'S's, have we then reached 'the heart of the matter' as far as a definition of community is concerned? In one sense, the answer is 'Yes'. For to define community in terms of such deep feelings offers the concept the status it warrants.

Only when we recognize community as a matrix of such powerful sentiments as security, significance and solidarity do we begin to appreciate why the more perceptive writers regard it as so dynamic a phenomenon in human affairs.

Furthermore, to focus on community as feeling is to keep our feet on the ground. For the concept to be an operational one, applicable to everyday life, a means of change and transformation for all sectors of society, not least for education, we cannot remain for long periods within the values and beliefs segments of the social system. The air there is too rarified for most ordinary mortals. Community defined in terms of the three 'S's thus has the twin advantage of being both dynamic and 'user-friendly'.

Yet one fundamental problem remains if we are to settle for the three 'S's being the heart of the matter. Although Williams (1976, p. 66), in his examination of the changing meaning of the word 'community' over the centuries, quite properly describes it as a 'warmly persuasive word' which 'unlike all other terms of social organisation (state, nation, society, etc.) seems never to be used unfavourably', it is clear that our definition could lead to all kinds of 'unfavourable' outcomes. For if the strength of the three 'S's is the only deciding factor, then while the pre-school play group, the rotary club and Amnesty International might qualify as communities, so might the Davidic sect in Waco, the Red Brigade and the Mafia. Even Hitler's SS, among the most active perpetrators of the holocaust, could not be denied communal status on these criteria.

The issue we face here is the classic one of the part over against the whole. Jenkins (1976, pp. 14–16) puts it clearly: 'That by which we identify ourselves and have our sense of identity, significance and belonging is also that by which we dehumanise others.' This impasse faces us with what we term *the communal dilemma. The communal dilemma is the problem of how social systems can become more open to one another without weakening their own sense of community or destroying that of others.*

Among the theologians, Tillich (1962) perceptively highlights the basic tension human beings face between 'being as oneself' and 'being as a part' of the wider whole. Grey (1993, p. 75) makes a similar point: 'How can I connect with my authentic community group – nation, cultural group, religious tradition – in a way which both contributes to and draws strength from community memory, purpose and celebration, and yet remains receptive to and affirming of other communities?' Berger and Luckmann (1984) speak more broadly of the problem of our 'sub-universes' becoming 'esoteric enclaves "hermetically sealed" ... to all but those who have been properly initiated into their mysteries.'

Our conviction is that any resolution of this dilemma is ultimately related to values and beliefs. But we also believe that pragmatic and practical concerns can help us to acknowledge, if not overcome, the problem.

Psychologically, we need all of the three 'S's if we are to survive and develop as human beings. In this sense, we might envisage each person as a mini social system in their own right. But no individual can acquire any of the three 'S's if interaction and relationships with other persons cease to exist. Our identity as social systems remains crucial, but we must also have access to other social systems if the three 'S's are to be nurtured and strengthened.

From a sociological perspective, we would argue that the same goes for larger social systems. Just as 'no man is an island', so no system which wishes to develop fully as a community can be an island. A maturing sense of security, significance and solidarity depends on the existence of other systems and how each fosters and enriches the others. Grey (1989, p. 32) stresses that each system 'has an integrative tendency, which enables it to function as part of a wider whole, and a self-assertive tendency, which enables it to preserve its individual autonomy. Both tendencies have to be respected for the health of the organism.' Indeed, as our world becomes more of a global village, the ability of systems to strengthen one another communally becomes a matter of mutual survival and not just of growth and development, vital as these latter may be.

It is not surprising, therefore, that in recent times the word 'synergy' has come to the fore. From the Greek 'ergo' meaning 'to work' and 'syn' meaning 'with' or 'together', the concept is also meant to indicate that the whole is greater than the sum of the parts. We regard community as a synergistic phenomenon. For it to reach its maximum potential in respect of each of the three 'S's, emotional energy has to flow between as well as within systems.

Any system which becomes locked into a sector or ghetto may for a while appear the stronger, but its inevitably parasitic nature threatens wider expressions of community and thus, in the long run, its own survival. MacIver (1924, p. 260) puts the matter as follows:

> The service of the large community is to fulfil and not to destroy the smaller. Our life is realised within not one but many communities, circling us round, grade beyond grade. The near community demands intimate loyalties and personal relationships, the concrete traditions and memories of everyday life. But where the near community is all community, its exclusiveness rests on ignorance and narrowness of thought, its emotional strength is accompanied by intellectual weakness. Its member becomes the slave of its traditions, the prisoner of his own affections. Without the widening of gates – nay, without the breaking down of walls – there is no progress. Herein is the service of the wider community, not only a completer 'civilisation' but also the freedom of a broader culture.

The need for social systems to recognize that their communal vitality ultimately rests on the deepening of relationships across boundaries is reflected within many disciplines. Bion (1961), writing about group dynamics, stresses that vision and hope depend to a very great degree on the intensity with which social systems 'pair'. Haughton (1981), writing from a theological vantage point, stresses that an 'exchange of life' lies at the heart of the ability of systems to grow and develop. Capra (1983, pp. 77–8) writes that 'the conception of the universe as an interconnected web of relations is one of the two major themes that recur throughout modern physics. The other theme is the realisation that the cosmic web is intrinsically dynamic.' All these writers are directly or indirectly commenting on the nature and centrality of synergy.

The synergistic nature of community, however, must not obscure two vital issues. First, that the identity of social systems is as important as the links or bonds they may establish with others. Community is not some oceanic sentiment which obliterates boundaries and destroys identities. There can be no sense of community within or across systems if diversity and distinctiveness is undermined or ignored.

The second issue is that tension between social systems as communities is potentially as creative as it is inevitable. Our experience of community would remain incestuous and static if, in spite of growing pains, genuine encounter and exchange between systems did not occur. The 'middle ground' is not a 'no man's land' but the very place where new and dynamic experiences of community can occur, where new possibilities for all systems may emerge.

Hull (1993), commenting on inter-faith relationships, makes this point in a telling way:

> There is a Christianity which says, 'I am holy and you are holy but the ground between us is not holy. If we meet on that ground, if we touch, we shall be contaminated.' There is another

Christianity which says, 'I am not holy; I am on the way; my spirituality and that of the tradition I represent is incomplete. But I have an affinity with you, my Muslim brother, my Jewish friend, my Hindu colleague, if you are prepared to say, "I am holy; I am on the way; the tradition I represent is not complete". Then we will both say, "but the ground where we meet is holy ground because this is the place where we claim our complete humanity".'

The only proviso to add is that where such creative engagement does involve conflict, it must be what Simpson (1937) terms 'communal conflict'. Here the ultimate interests and basic norms which integrate and support the systems remain respected and intact; in contrast to 'non-communal conflict' which undermines the very existence of the systems involved because it means 'conflict between final values, between ultimates' (p. 42). But where social systems do recognize one another's identity and affirm the communal sentiments on which that identity rests, then tension and even conflict can be a powerfully creative component of mutual growth.

VALUES

We believe that defining community as feeling is to regard it as a concept potent yet personal enough to meet head on the challenges of today's world. Underpinning that argument are not just psychological and sociological insights, but ideological principles as well.

MacIver (MacIver and Page, 1961, p. 293) warns us that 'we should avoid confusing we-feeling with altruism'. But unless we address the moral as well as social dimensions of community we shall be in constant danger of selling out to the communal dilemma. We need, therefore, as did Plant (1974, pp. 8–36), to recognize that community is about 'value' as well as 'fact'; that it is as much an 'evaluative' as 'descriptive' word. The really important point is that we recognize and acknowledge when we are emphasizing the one or the other.

All the definitions of community we have considered so far in this chapter and the last have possessed both descriptive and evaluative features. Whatever segment of the social system has been to the fore in our definition, values have not been far below the surface. Values can be environmental, functional (focused on interaction), interpersonal (concerned with relationships), expressive (about feelings) or ideological (related to beliefs). It is particularly important, therefore, that as we now examine 'community as value', we are clear and open about the values we espouse.

The values that we ourselves regard as fundamental to the concept of community are those on which a sense of security, of significance and of solidarity are founded. For us, the three 'S's are sustained by three 'L's: life, liberty and love.

Life

Life as value refers to the right of every human being to physical and material nurture. It means not only protection from violence but the provision of adequate food and water, clothing and shelter. It means the wherewithal to remain healthy and physically fit. It means, too, the individual's right materially to sustain himself or herself and any dependents, without fear or anxiety. Beyond this, the concept of life takes on a more socially qualitative dimension, a *joie de vivre*, which blends into liberty and love, but which still requires physical and material well-being.

Life as a value is being increasingly recognized as bound up with the future of our planet as a whole, as the Gaia principle emphasizes. The security of every person and every social system, even more so in the long term than the short term, is no longer a self-contained responsibility, but an urgent matter of proper global stewardship. In this context, community is about the preservation of all species and not just of the human population as such.

Liberty

Liberty as value is about gaining significance through fulfilment. It rests on our acknowledgement of the uniqueness and dignity of each individual, and on the right of every individual to reach their full potential as human beings through free choice. As Sedgwick (1992, p. 85) puts it: 'Freedom ... is not the power to be able to do this or that. It is the power to decide about oneself and to actualise oneself.' Liberty is the freedom to choose to be as fully oneself as is humanly possible. But liberty is not just a personal affair. As Davis (1994, p. 139) writes: 'The autonomy of the individual conscience is too weak of itself to bring about a fully universalistic moral consciousness.' Liberty, from our perspective, must be a collective phenomenon which frees social systems as well as individuals fully to achieve their corporate potential within the larger scheme of things.

Love

Love as value undergirds a sense of solidarity. But it also nurtures life and liberty. Boswell (1990, p. 36) writes:

> The ability to commune is crucial not just for human survival but also for our growth as persons, indeed our whole personal identity...The deepest form of communion is love ...

Love is about being completely 'at one' with others through a process of caring and sharing. It is the most powerful bonding force known to human beings, and is not to be mistaken for sentimentality. It goes through and beyond sexuality, although this provides a vital bonding component. It embraces, among its other expressions, 'affection, friendship, eros and charity' (Lewis, 1963). That love is a value not confined to religion or romance is indicated by Roger Harrison, the American management consultant, who wrote a monograph now in considerable demand entitled *Organisation Culture and Quality of Service: a strategy for releasing love in the workplace* (1987). Love, as we view it, is the essential glue of enduring human relationships, or as Carpenter (1961, p. 47) puts it: 'Love necessarily begets a community.'

In the same way as solidarity, significance and security form a kind of 'hierarchy' of communal feelings, with solidarity as the peak, so we would argue that love, liberty and life do likewise, with love being the zenith.

Yet, akin to community defined as feeling, and the synergy which makes the whole more than the sum of the parts, one further value is indispensable if we are to avoid the communal dilemma. The three 'L's must be available to and accepted by 'each and all'. It is not enough to seek life, liberty and love just for one's self or one's own social system. The three 'L's are values which can only bear genuine fruit, and indeed survive in the

longer term, if their *inclusivity* is recognized. *For systems to reach their communal poten-*
tial, for real synergy to occur, the three 'L's must embrace the value of inclusivity. This
means that, in principle, none is excluded, otherwise systems become incestuous, destructive of other systems and the wider whole.

All these values, our three 'L's and inclusivity, we sum up in the term the *common good*,
that which takes the well-being of the part as intimately related to the well-being of the
whole, and vice versa. The common good seeks to affirm diversity within unity, the value
and dignity of each person, group, association and society within the precious totality of the
human race. The common good embraces the well-being of both micro and macro forms of
human relationships. It is another way of describing the quest for community.

It goes without saying that this quest is about change. The three 'L's, as inclusive values,
are evident only in part and at times in human affairs. They are not only values but ideals
to be sought after and striven for. Because there is huge resistance to their full expression,
not least because inclusivity is still a radical and revolutionary idea, the search for community as the common good is a daunting as well as exciting task. The journey is and will
remain costly and painful for all of us, but nonetheless utterly essential for the future of
humankind.

So, in the light of the communal dilemma, and the values underlying the necessity of
resolving it if community is to grow and flourish, we need to take our definition of the
communal task just one stage further. We insert the all-important words 'and across' (p. 69)
into our previous definition. This now runs as follows:

> *The communal task is to create an increasingly strong sense of security, of significance and of*
> *solidarity within and across social systems.*

Our final picture of the community development process, embracing the need for a
multi-system approach, is set out in Fig. 3.3.

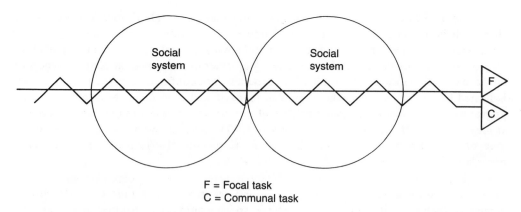

F = Focal task
C = Communal task

Figure 3.3   *The community development process (multi-system)*

By liberating our concept of community from the more restrictive segments of the social
system, not least community as environment or locality, by aligning it closely with
communal feelings, and by recognizing it as fundamentally a multi-system process, we can
now go to work as community developers in a qualitative way across a wide range of

groups, organizations, institutions and societies. Community development, as we see it, must encompass families as well as nations, churches as well as industry and commerce, hospitals as well as government. Not least it is fundamental for the development of schools, if they are to be genuine learning communities, and for 'transforming education' to become a whole life and whole society phenomenon.

BELIEFS

If values are defined as those qualities which a person regards as being of considerable worth and widely applicable, beliefs are those aspects of experience which a person regards as true. Beliefs usually present a more comprehensive picture than values. They provide ways of giving meaning and purpose to human affairs, of enabling us to deal with the complexities of the diverse social systems we encounter daily and of clarifying our relationship to them. Berger and Luckmann (1984, pp. 110–22) speak of beliefs forming 'symbolic universes' which offer us a coherent picture of an often bewildering world.

Irrespective of the precise beliefs which people hold, their importance for community building lies in the immense impetus they can give to the communal task. Simpson (1937, p. 98) wrote: 'Community is an achievement, the highest achievement of man in his relations with other men.' If this is so, as we too would argue, then beliefs are the starter-motor for community development.

Many pages would be required to set out in full the 'symbolic universe' which shapes the understanding of community on which this book is based. I have elsewhere attempted to address this matter in a range of articles and books related to the theme of community making (Clark, 1977; 1984; 1987; 1989, pp. 25–8; 1992). Here it must suffice to say that the beliefs sustaining our three 'S's and three 'L's are Christian. They are shaped by two key Christian images – that of the Trinity on the one hand, and that of the Kingdom of God on the other.

The doctrine of the Trinity seeks to communicate the Christian understanding of 'a divine community' which Christians believe is the source of inspiration and energy for all human community. The doctrine of the Trinity embraces four features central to our beliefs about community. First, it emphasizes that the cosmos is deeply and utterly personal because God its creator is 'a person'. It follows that each human being, created in the image of God, is also a person with the right to life, liberty and love; we are not to be treated as impersonal objects.

Secondly, the very nature of God is communal: three in one, diversity in unity. God as Father, Son and Holy Spirit, as Trinity, represents both the uniqueness and significance for each part, as well as the integrity and solidarity of the whole. The Trinity is thus an image of the synthesis of the one and the many. It portrays a profound depth of relationship (Gunton, 1993) which bonds without destroying identity. So it should be with human community.

Thirdly, the three persons of the Trinity represent and personify our three core values of life, liberty and love; though, at the same time, each person embraces all of these. We can, therefore, seek to learn a great deal about the meaning of life from 'God as creator', about freedom from 'Christ as liberator' and about love from 'the Holy Spirit as unifier' (Clark, 1987; 1989, pp. 25–8).

Finally, the Trinity represents the universal power, pre-eminently 'relational power, the power of connection' (Grey, 1993, p. 99), available to all those seeking to tap the energy of divine community for the building of human community. It is this power which, for Christians, offers the hope that the incestuous nature of much which passes for community can be redeemed, new and open relationships formed and the impasse of the communal dilemma overcome.

The other Christian image or symbol of great importance to us in relation to the beliefs segment of the social system is that of the Kingdom of God (Newbigin, 1980; Arias, 1984; Clark, 1987; Price, 1987). The theme of the Kingdom was central to the teaching of Jesus Christ and portrayed the nature and implications of God's rule 'on earth as in heaven'. The Kingdom was in part already present, yet still to be fully realized in human affairs. For us, the Kingdom gives the fullest meaning to the practical implications of what it is to be a community. Its essential character was 'a world turned upside down' in which the disadvantaged and oppressed were seen as integral members of that 'Kingdom community'. 'The Sermon on the Mount ... (the Beatitudes) ... constitutes the corporate ethics of the Kingdom' (Carpenter, 1961, p. 47).

Thus our definition of community, which relates closely to the values of life, liberty and love, when aligned with the picture of the Kingdom of God, means that the poor (those denied life and a sense of security because of physical and material needs) must have pride of place. Likewise, the marginalized (those denied liberty and a sense of significance) and the alienated (those denied love and a sense of solidarity) must be at the top of the agenda of any genuine process of community building. This is not simply because justice is a hallmark of the Kingdom of God. It is because in that Kingdom all are deprived if some are deprived. Or, as John Donne (*Devotions*, xviii) put it: 'Any man's death diminishes me.'

The Kingdom of God is thus a richly inclusive concept. As the stories told by Jesus Christ show, all are invited to enter it. The priority God gives to the disadvantaged does not mean that the rich and the powerful are excluded; it is just that much harder for them to respond. Thus the Kingdom community is an 'all in' affair. It only becomes exclusive where people choose of their own free will to opt out. The Kingdom community has no final boundaries. It is not only inclusive but ecumenical (from the Greek word *oikumene* meaning 'the whole inhabited earth') and puts an end to any fear that the last word lies with incestuous passions or even cloistered virtues.

The message of the Trinity and the Kingdom of God is that continuous change is inevitable. The Kingdom community is still to come. Its realization is blocked by injustice, oppression and hatred. The beliefs described above do not mean all is well. Rather, they set a communal vision before us and offer resources to address the immense but essential task of making it come true.

For the Christian, these resources, not least of the power to live out on earth the vision of the Kingdom community, can only be accessed 'by grace through faith'. Such power rests on a faith in an ultimate 'Reality' (Davis, 1994, p. 35) who is the source of universal love. Such power is also grace or gift to all, not earned only by a faithful few.

We have here sketched out the basic beliefs on which our own communal values rest. Other value systems and symbolic universes, not least those of the world's great religious traditions, have their own rich contribution to make to community building. Indeed, if we were not to be open to the authenticity and nobility of such traditions, we would be denying the very ecumenicity and universality which we see as lying at the heart of Christianity, not to mention community itself.

For all of us, however, not only values and beliefs but 'faith' is also required if we are to

Table 3.1 *Inner segments of the social system*

	Feeling	Community as: Values	Belief		Faith
			Christian perspective		
Attributes	Security	Life	God as creator	⎫	Grace (gift)
	Significance	Liberty	Christ as liberator	⎬ The Trinity	Conviction
	Solidarity	Love	The Holy Spirit as unifier	⎭	Commitment Works (deeds)
Process	Synergistic	Inclusive	Ecumenical		Universal
Communal outcome	A sense of community	The common good	The Kingdom		'Reality'

build community. It is not just the mental or even social construction of communal values and beliefs which will prevent our world from self-destruction, but the deep conviction that without the rediscovery and renewal of community itself, life on earth has no future. As Drucker (1993, p. 161) succinctly puts it in his review of our civilization on the eve of the next millennium: 'Historically community was fate. In the post-capitalist society and polity, community has to become commitment.'

Chapter 4

Communalizing Education

In our Introduction, we argued that in a world experiencing powerful centrifugal and centripetal forces, there is an urgent need to build new and dynamic forms of community. Chapters 2 and 3 have sought to clarify the often confused and confusing concept of community, focusing particularly on the centrality of beliefs, values and feelings. We have described the communal task, in this context, as the creation and development of social systems which embrace a sense of security, significance and solidarity (the three 'S's), rooted in the values of life, liberty and love (the three 'L's), in as inclusive a form as possible.

Community building, we have argued, is about 'the survival of the species'. Thus it must occur within every sector of society, within business and health, within religion and politics, within leisure and law and order, within the family and within the school. It must also occur across sectors and across societies if we are to have any chance of meeting the challenges of the next millennium.

This means change, both radical and continuing. It will be a painful process but nonetheless a fundamental one. Indeed, for many individuals as well as institutions to raise their awareness from the trivia that has surrounded the concept of community for so long, to the new horizons set out in the last chapter, will require nothing less than a transformation. It will mean the transformation of how community is perceived – as belief and value rather than fact, as quality rather than locality – and the transformation of how it is put into practice.

For our world to experience a new depth of communal living in the years ahead, every sector must play its part. Yet of all those involved, none is more important than education. This is not only because communal openness and breadth depend on education (a concern we return to in Chapter 6), but because a rich and effective education system depends on community. Of all the changes now needed to prepare us for the next millennium, the transformation of education into genuine community education stands at the top of the agenda.

NO EDUCATION WITHOUT COMMUNITY

Education needs community because without it learning becomes a lifeless, impersonal and functional affair. Without community, education loses nourishment, energy and impetus. It is the communalizing of education that transforms it from transmission and training into learning for living. Such a transformation is a far cry from the 'bolt on' approach of many past forms of community education. If we are to bring community as a quality of life to bear on the education system, it is imperative that we transform all educational institutions, not least schools, into learning communities.

Schools only develop as genuine community schools by educating through community. The whole class, the whole staff, the whole school must experience and live out daily what it means to be a learning community. Hands-on experience for all is essential. Only within this holistic and experiential context can the nature of community and its key components become a lived and living experience which is carried over by the young person into the wider adult world. If schools are to educate community makers, then the medium has to become the message.

From the context of special needs education in the USA, the Stainbacks (1992, p. 4) passionately advocate this holistic approach:

> There has been a shift away from how to help only students with disabilities in the mainstream. The focus has been broadened to address the support needs of every member of the school ... to be successful, secure, and welcome in the educational mainstream ... The problem or dilemma is no longer how to mainstream or integrate some students who were previously excluded, but rather how to develop a sense of community and mutual support within the mainstream that fosters success among all members of neighbourhood schools.

Philip Toogood (1984, p. 232), formerly the head of Madeley Court School in Telford, argues that the school 'should be a community within, and related to, community in the wider society'. Keith Evans, formerly Director of Education for Clwyd, outlined one of his top priorities for schools (Evans, 1993, p. 12) as follows:

> *A Sense of Community*: Making it clear that children, young people, parents, governors, professionals and support staff feel that they are all valued members of a caring educational community each with their own contribution to make. Helping young people to understand that they belong to an interdependent world of wider caring communities, including their own families, religious, cultural, sporting, social communities, their own home town/village and the communities of their native land, Europe and a wider world.

Writing in the midst of an ongoing debate about the principles informing education in the UK, Michael Adie, then Bishop of Guildford, presented a similar view (*Times Educational Supplement*, 31 December 1993, p. 9):

> In an over-individualised society, we need to open people's eyes to the fact of interdependence. We are who we are because of parents, teachers, colleagues, critics. The successful and the unsuccessful alike are shaped by one another. A school is a microcosm of society where we can learn and experience community. So the ethos, the attitudes of staff, the valuing of individuals will teach as much as the curriculum ...

In short, therefore, we can learn little about community without a community within which and from which to learn.

But there is much more to the phrase 'no education without community' than this. For one of the fundamental contentions of this book is that for any form of learning to reach its potential (and not just that related to community making *per se*), a communal process is essential. There can be no education (in every sense) without community.

THE THREE 'S's AS INDISPENSABLE FOR LEARNING

In their important study, *Group Work in the Primary Classroom*, Galton and Williamson (1992, p. 131) wrote: 'No analysis of task demand is ... complete which ignores [the] social psychological element.' Our thesis is that the learning process, be that engaged with any 'forms of knowledge' (Hirst and Peters, 1970), any 'areas of experience' (HMI, 1983) or any 'cultural systems' (Lawton, 1983), can only fulfil its possibilities if those social systems engaged in it are communally developed. The stronger the sense of community within learning systems, the more effective will be the teaching not only of the humanities and the arts, but of the sciences too. Or, as Handy and Aitken put it more succinctly (1986, p. 54), 'People who feel good perform well.'

If, then, 'the strength of community within any social system is revealed by the degree to which its members experience a sense of security, of significance and of solidarity within it' (see p. 45), it is to the presence of the three 'S's that we must look for the enhancement of learning through community.

A sense of security

On a visit to one of the South African homelands a few years ago, my wife and I visited a number of schools for primary age black children. One in particular remains a vivid memory. The 'school' was an old Nissen hut, its single room interior so dark that on our entering, it took some while before we could locate the children at all. The room turned out to be packed with an all-age mixed-ability throng being taught by one teacher using a battered blackboard and a tatty piece of chalk, and hopelessly outdated teaching materials. Yet, when the children emerged for break they were not only enthusiastic and cheerful, but immaculately dressed in smart clean uniforms which confounded the dirt and dust all around. They quite clearly gained a real sense of significance from being at school at all.

This kind of situation bears out our contention that the psychological can triumph over the material, that morale is not totally at the mercy of material deprivation. Yet, despite the cheerful pride of these South African pupils, their learning as such was being greatly retarded by the lack of physical and material resources available to the black education system. For learning to take place in any ongoing and developmental way, the basic tools for the task must be available. People must know that they are being resourced in an adequate and sustainable way.

Even more fundamental, of course, are the issues of hunger and poverty. For all their immaculate dress, many black South African school children remain poorly nourished and lacking more than the most primitive forms of hygiene and shelter. And, though on a far different plain, we in the West need to take immensely seriously the effects of high and endemic unemployment. The impact of poverty on a sense of security, which normally enables physical and material well-being to be taken for granted and learning to be unhampered by deprivation, can be deeply destructive.

The learning environment must also be conductive not only by ensuring that pupils have the health and strength necessary to study, and the tools to do the job, but in offering them a place to call their own. Handy and Aitken (1996, p. 29) stress that 'schools are foolish to neglect the importance of territory, for staff or students'. Hargreaves (1982, p. 29) here points to the contrast between teachers who 'own' and are often very possessive about their classrooms, and pupils, at least in secondary schools, who having 'no corporate home' are compelled to wander the corridors carrying their belongings with them. This is a far cry from that 'safe environment' which Ford *et al.* (1992, p. 56) argue is vital to 'enhance the success of all students'.

A sense of significance

A sense of significance is closely related to the physical context of learning. Henry Morris, the founding father of community education, clearly recognized this. He (Rée, 1985, p. 153) set out to establish the village college which would:

> ... express the spirit of the English countryside which it is intended to grace, something of its humaneness and modesty, something of the age-long and permanent dignity of husbandry; a building that will give the countryside a centre of reference arousing the affection and loyalty of the country child and country people, and *conferring significance on their way of life.* (our italics)

A sense of significance, however, is a key factor in learning whatever its origins. Klein (1963, p. 122) writes of groups in general that 'peripheral or lower-status members are less likely to learn', a comment which accords fully with the National Commission on Education's reflection that 'the biggest single problem in secondary schools is low levels of pupil motivation' (Barber, 1993) .

Hargreaves, in *The Challenge for the Comprehensive School* (1982), argues that for 'working-class' children, in particular, there has been a massive destruction of dignity and thus the emergence of a counter-culture hostile to learning. Hargreaves' insistence on the link between a sense of significance, built on dignity, offered from without, and self-esteem, self-confidence and self-fulfilment, experienced within, was amply borne out in my own experience of working within a social education department in a large London comprehensive school in the 1970s (Clark, 1973b; 1975). Pupils previously marginalized and devalued in the mainstream, or transferred to the school because of behavioural problems elsewhere, became keen learners when they were valued as people. Status given to the diverse roles they were encouraged to play, increased motivation through appropriate expectations and rewards and greater self-fulfilment through the completion of approved tasks, all contributing towards a strong sense of significance, made a huge difference to their capacity to learn.

A sense of solidarity

'Employee confidence and self-esteem as part of a team leads to pride in their work and their company' (Macdonald, 1993, p. 55) – a statement coming not from an old-fashioned business studies primer but from the modern world of 'total quality management (TQM)'. As it is with business, so it is with schools as learning communities. Alongside a sense of significance, a sense of solidarity is the basis for increased commitment and energy given to the educational process. The problem is that 'the whole system of schooling at best ignores, at worst actually suppresses the vital network of friendship, allegiance, solidarity among children' (Phillida, 1988, p. 109).

For a sense of solidarity to enhance commitment to learning, it needs to be fostered in a whole range of diverse but complementary contexts. Peer solidarity, solidarity with teachers and the wider school and parent–teacher solidarity all play their part. Where such corporate cultures break down or conflict, as McLaren (1986) describes in his classic study of an inner-city Catholic school in Toronto, a genuine learning ethos is simply destroyed.

Bottery (1990), in his study of values in education, offers 'the furthering of co-operation between children' (p. 30), alongside 'the fostering of the child's self-esteem', as an essential component of moral education. 'Co-operation between pupils', he writes (p. 31) 'can not only lead to generally better than average academic performance, but it has significant beneficial effects on the ways in which pupils see each other, how they get on in class, and how they perceive themselves.' Our only quibble with this comment is its over modest claim for the correlation between a sense of solidarity and educational performance.

Solidarity not only enhances commitment and fosters enthusiasm but releases additional resources for the learning task by facilitating the sharing of knowledge, skills and experience. 'Co-operative classrooms use the motto, "None of us is as smart as all of us",' write the Stainbacks (1992, p. 30) in their investigation of 'inclusive classrooms'. We still have a vast amount of untapped educational resources going to waste because sharing within schools is nominal and narrowly conceived and a world of experience beyond the school gates goes largely unrecognized.

Across social systems

Our communal task, as finally defined (see p. 52), states that the development of a sense of security, significance and solidarity must take place across as well as within social systems if the communal dilemma (strong but separatist groups) is to be avoided.

Our three 'S's can only gain their maximum breadth and depth, and learning reach its full potential, where rigid and restrictive boundaries are done away with. The school as a learning community has to be one which overcomes and crosses such boundaries within and without. Only in this way can education become genuinely synergistic, the whole generating greater energy than the sum of the parts.

Drucker (1993, p. 197) argues that in the world of the future 'knowledges' must become 'knowledge', our specialist but narrow fields of expertise must seek greater complementarity and cohesion. 'Without such understanding the knowledges themselves will become sterile, will indeed cease to be "knowledge"', he writes. This requires the ending of restrictive practices, the breaking down of vested interests (between educational 'disciplines' as much as anywhere else) and the creation of learning communities far more open to one another and the wider world.

The major educational benefits of opening up schools to the resources and experience of other bodies and agencies is slowly but surely being acknowledged. A new relationship between home and school has been developing since the days of Plowden, and a wide range of other partnerships is increasingly well documented (Sayer and Williams, 1989). Links, associations, contracts and compacts between schools and industry, health, arts organizations, environmental agencies and religious bodies, among others, are growing steadily, even if developments remain patchy (see Chapter 9).

Much more difficult to overcome are the deep economic and cultural divisions which still exist between all social systems. Brehony (1992, pp. 217–8) writes:

Putting learning at the centre of education may appear to reduce the problem of education to solely a technical question. But this does not mean that issues of value are thereby eliminated. What the child-centred educationalists have consistently failed to recognise is the social nature of school learning and the fact that the major structural divisions within society of class, race and gender are frequently the seat of obstacles to learning.

Brehony's comments highlight not only the problem facing schools as learning communities, but the fact that school and society are in a symbiotic relationship which often hinders as much as facilitates genuine change.

COMMUNITY EDUCATION: THE TASK OF TRANSFORMATION

'Community education stands for a particular quality of relationships among ... communities of collective interest and need, not only within the education system but also between educational agencies and their publics in the outside world', writes Martin (1987, p. 14).

For our world to be transformed into a place secure and humane enough for us to want to live in, community needs education. Human communities across the globe, through and within their schools in particular, have to learn how to live together in a way which can ensure 'the survival of the species' and a meaningful quality of life to make such survival worth the effort. It is thus a matter of supreme importance that schools learn how to promote community. To do this they have to be communities. Effectively to address this task, the medium has to become the message.

But schools need to become communities for another reason even closer to home. The challenge of the next century requires the transformation of education itself. It demands qualitative learning for all across the whole curriculum. If this is to occur in the way and to the extent now required, learning itself must be communalized. It must be grounded in those feelings, the three 'S's, and rooted in those values, the three 'L's, without which insecurity, lack of confidence and motivation, and possessiveness and competition will undermine the entire enterprise. Schools will have an educational contribution of decreasing importance to offer to our world if learning itself is not communalized. In short, education needs community.

It is because schools have failed to grasp the link between their own transformation and the transformation of the world beyond, that a mere functional competence is so often all that is expected of them or provided by them. Schools are left to fiddle as civilization burns. There is only one way out of this critical impasse: for schools, alongside all other educational institutions, to learn how to become learning communities. Their failure to do this will ultimately spell the doom both of community and of education.

Genuine community education is about the transformation of social systems, within and beyond the education system, into learning communities. Community education, as the few real visionaries have perceived, is not about the dual use of school buildings, getting more parents to become involved in their children's learning, a revamped youth service or new forms of adult education, however important these may be as a means to other ends. Genuine community education, the real thing, is about our learning how to make life, liberty and love available to all in a world that teeters on the brink of destroying all three.

Chapter 5

Guidelines for Community Development

COMMUNALIZING THE LEARNING PROCESS

'Good practice (in schools) should henceforth be treated as problematic, rather than as an uncontentious absolute', comments Alexander (1991) in his report on primary education in Leeds. One such 'uncontentious absolute' expressed by many teachers is that if the message is right 'the medium will take care of itself'. In this chapter, we reverse that order of priorities and, in the conviction that there can be no education without community, lay out a series of 'guidelines' to help to promote the communalization of education.

For all their deep involvement with varied and volatile groups of young people, teachers have paid relatively little attention to the nature of social systems, processes of interaction and the structure of human relationships. Management may at long last be receiving some attention (at least for senior staff) but the equally important area of interpersonal relations remains woefully neglected.

It is true that in the primary school, though much less in the secondary school, small informal groups abound. But as Bennett *et al.* state (1984, p. 220): 'The use of classroom groups in practice has emerged as no more than a convenient seating arrangement rather than a specific site for teaching.' Galton and Williamson (1992, p. 5) describe 'working in groups', as opposed to 'seating in groups', as 'a neglected art', and conclude (p. 170) that primary classroom practice has remained little changed during the 1980s.

The few attempts, not least by community educators, to specify a community development process which will enhance learning have so far not helped a great deal. Some community educators have offered long shopping-lists of 'key features' for the enrichment of education, as for example those outlined by Wallis and Mee (1983) in their checklist of 154 items (pp. 75–81). More often, a 'pick and mix' assortment of communal characteristics is suggested. But these off-the-shelf solutions remain unrelated to any overall theoretical framework for learning (see, for example, the communal indices selected by J. Watts, by Martin and by Watt (Watt, 1989, p. 186), and the 'characteristics of community education' listed by the Association of Metropolitan Authorities and Community Education Development Centre (1991, pp. 18–20). Furthermore, such features, like many others now in vogue, are usually meant for more macro and managerial than micro and group oriented situations.

Our own approach to communalizing education will be to take the model outlined in Chapters 2 and 3 and seek to operationalize its key communal components, the three 'S's (a sense of security, significance and solidarity), for practical use in an educational context. We shall specify a range of 'guidelines' to help to earth our concept of community. We do not claim (or indeed wish) that these guidelines represent the 'hard' features of some so-called 'performance indicators' (UDACE, 1989; CEDC, 1991), but we put them forward, as will be seen, as well authenticated and identifiable communal characteristics. On this basis, we hope that the debate as to how community undergirds and enhances the learning process can at least move forward on an explicit and rational foundation.

Negotiation

> Do not assume that your version of what the change should be is the one that should or could be implemented. On the contrary, assume that one of the main purposes of the process of implementation is to *exchange your reality* of what should be through interaction with others.

In setting out our model for developing community we are seeking, as Fullan (1991, p. 105) here suggests, to 'exchange our reality' with that of the reader. We neither assume we have got it all right, nor got it all wrong. We recognize that if any model for the transformation of education is to work then meanings have to be negotiated.

The need for such a sharing and adjustment of expectations is constantly reiterated in the literature on effective teaching styles. Delamont (1976, p. 25) states that the process of creative interaction in the classroom 'is one of negotiation', even if of an informal kind. Galton and Williamson (1992, p. 144) comment that 'ways of working with groups as well as ways of learning in groups need to be the subject of negotiation between the teacher and the pupils', though they add that in practice little consultation usually takes place (p. 44).

How such negotiation is to be conducted we consider more fully in Chapter 7. Here we simply wish to make it clear that our model and guidelines represent our reality at this point in time, a reality to be shared and negotiated with all concerned in more effective teaching and learning.

Such negotiation is not simply a matter of professional etiquette. It is required by the very nature of our model. The values and sentiments, life, liberty and love (the three 'L's), and the three 'S's, on which that model is based have to be readily espoused, not commanded or accepted out of duty, guilt or fear. To be effective, the nature of their implementation has also to be shared and agreed. Indeed, certain of our guidelines make sharing and agreement explicit, though the negotiation of meaning and delivery is relevant to all of them.

Overview of the model and guidelines

The reader will remember that our model, as outlined so far, is based on the concept of the social system, the segments of which (people, environment, interaction, etc.) together with its focal task, are associated with different approaches to the definition of community. 'The heart of the matter' for us is our three 'S's (located in the feeling segment of the system) founded on the three 'L's (located in the values segment). The communal task we defined as being 'to create an increasingly strong sense of security, significance and solidarity within and across social systems'.

We argue that the guidelines considered below are ways in which the three 'S's can be most effectively operationalized (made real in practice) in order to develop community within and across the social systems concerned. As indicated in Figure 3.3 (see p. 52), the three 'S's (encompassing our communal task) have to be interwoven with the focal task and engage with each segment of the system if community is to be enhanced.

We have opted for the feeling segment of the social system as communally the most significant not only because of the energy it can generate, but because it connects the less observable features of the system (values and beliefs) to the more observable (relationships, interaction, environment and people, as well as the focal task itself). We shall be assuming, therefore, that the three 'S's, as inclusive sentiments, are also the means of operationalizing our three 'L's and, at least implicitly, the beliefs on which they in turn are based.

Our overriding concern is to operationalize the three 'S's in as an effective a way as possible. Unfortunately, the research related to such a task is very limited. The most extensive work in this area has been done by Klein (1956; 1963) and Homans (1951), with others, such as Phillida (1988) and Cohen (1985), exploring the three 'S's from a more clearly psychological or sociological perspective. A wide range of books on group dynamics is also available, although these are often more about skills development than research *per se*. There is a slowly growing literature, often with close links to aspects of our three 'S's, on learning processes and teaching styles, usefully reviewed in such texts as Hargreaves and Hopkins (1991, pp. 109–24) and Galton and Williamson (1992). The guidelines are also based on my own experience within and beyond the classroom in seeking to earth the three 'S's in practice, both educational (Clark, 1975; 1990) and in relation to other sectors of society (Clark, 1969; 1984). However, with regard to the whole of this field, a very great deal more research still needs to be done.

Most guidelines will show all three 'S's to be in evidence, not least because a sense of security, significance and solidarity are intimately related. However, we have indicated by use of S_e, S_i or S_o, in light type (weaker) or heavy type (stronger) which of the three 'S's we believe each guideline delivers most effectively.

Our own definition of community is essentially subjective in nature. It states that the feelings of the members of social systems are all-important. Thus to ascertain the strength of community, it would be simplest to ask each member of the system involved how strongly they experienced the three 'S's and to note the responses. Our guidelines are introduced, however, for two main reasons. First, because it is rarely possible to conduct in-depth interviews with all the members of a system. Furthermore, this would have to be done not only once but continuously in order to keep abreast with how the sense of community within the system was growing or declining. Second, even if we were able to do this, we would have little indication of how to intervene to help change things for the better. It is only when we can pinpoint which aspects of which segments of the social system need attention that action to strengthen a sense of community becomes feasible.

Applying the guidelines

The guidelines provide a means of checking out the communal strength of the social systems involved in the focal task specified. They need to be seen as operating at a 'high' to 'low' level (perhaps rating them on a 0–5 scale) to indicate the extent to which the features characteristic of one or more of our three 'S's is present. All the guidelines need to be scored as they are closely interlinked; to use only a select few, even if these score high, will not necessarily indicate a strong sense of community throughout the system. Generally speaking, however, the guidelines representing segments nearest the 'heart' of the social system (Fig. 2.1, p. 29), such as those relating to relationships, will give a clearer indication of communal strength than those further out, such as environment.

Where and how intervention takes place to develop the communal strength of the system after the guidelines have been rated is a matter to be considered more fully in Chapter 6, on the role of the community educator. However, in the context of such intervention, it might sometimes be helpful to average out the scores within each section (or segment) of the guidelines, and thereby to discover which segments of the social system were scoring high (strong) and which low (weak).

The guidelines can be scored separately for each social system involved in the focal task, and the differences compared. Or, they can be scored in relation to the strength of communal engagement across the focal systems in order to gain greater insight into their overall communal health.

The crucial question remains as to how a 'high' or 'low' rating is to be given to the guidelines. Some of the guidelines are clearly open to more subjective assessment than others. For example, the degree of interaction can be observed and recorded relatively objectively. Other guidelines are less easy to rate in that we use more subjective terms such as 'stimulating', 'conducive' or 'adequate', although we have tried to avoid even more global terms such as 'ethos', 'climate' or 'ownership' which so often slip into lists of indicators used elsewhere. Given more time and more research, we hope that wider agreement about indices to assess the rating of the more subjective guidelines will emerge. However, our present position is as follows.

If at all possible, rating of the guidelines should be undertaken by members of the social systems involved, including those designated as the community developers; and action negotiated on the basis of the findings. Failing this, the community developers (in our case, usually teachers) should themselves undertake the rating exercise, but still negotiate future action with the members of the systems concerned. We would argue that this approach is a valid one, as it is how the participants (and the community developers themselves) construct and experience the strength of community within and across systems that is all important.

Limitations

Any procedure seeking to ascertain the strength of feelings within a social system is dealing with highly volatile material, hard to assess with accuracy. As noted above, a great deal more research needs to be done before the correlation of our three 'S's with the guidelines described below can be more objectively verified. This is a task to which few people, not least community educators, have as yet paid much attention. The means of rating, weighting and summating the guidelines also needs further exploration, although we remain convinced that what matters most is how each system judges its own communal well-being. But despite such limitations, we believe that our model and guidelines are an important first step towards communally assessing and developing social systems and being able to bring the dynamism of community into play for more effective learning.

Beyond the classroom

Our first concern has been to provide a model and guidelines for the development of community, in particular to assist the teacher in the classroom to promote more effective learning. In our description of the guidelines which follow this, context will be to the fore.

However, it is important to realize that although we here begin at the micro or small group level (the class and its sub-groups), we cannot end there. In later chapters, we shall be exploring not only how the classroom and the curriculum can be communalized, but how the school itself can become a learning community. For unless there is communal consistency throughout larger social systems, the communal quality of smaller systems within them will inevitably suffer. But stopping at the level of the school (or other major systems) is still not adequate if community development is to be restored to its proper role in human affairs. If survival is the name of the game, then it is imperative that our guidelines be applied not only to the small, though still complex world of the classroom, nor even to the school as a learning organization, but to other sectors, to society and to international relationships as well.

THE GUIDELINES

Table 5.1 *The communal guidelines*

1.0	**The people (and focal systems)**
1.1	Two or more systems are involved (S_o)
1.2	The systems are clearly identifiable (S_i, S_o)
1.3	The systems have diverse cultural, social or economic features (S_i, S_o)
1.4	The systems include people who are disadvantaged (S_e, S_i, S_o)
2.0	**The focal task**
2.1	The focal task is clear (S_o)
2.2	The focal task is agreed (S_o)
2.3	The focal task is shared (S_o)
2.4	The focal task is stimulating (S_i, S_o)
2.5	The focal task is achievable (S_i, S_o)
2.6	The focal task can be achieved in various ways (S_i, S_o)
3.0	**The environment**
3.1	The meeting places are accessible (S_e, S_i)
3.2	The environment is safe and healthy (S_e, S_i)
3.3	The environment is conducive (S_e, S_i)
Resources	
3.4	Resources are adequate (S_e, S_i)
3.5	Resources are sustainable (S_e, S_i)
3.6	Appropriate time is available (S_i, S_o)
4.0	**Interaction**
4.1	Everyone is involved (S_i, S_o)
4.2	Interaction is collaborative (S_i, S_o)
4.3	Interaction is lively (S_o)
4.4	Interaction is personal (S_i, S_o)
4.5	Interaction is frequent (S_o)
4.6	Interaction is ongoing (S_o)
Communication	
4.7	Communication is public (S_i, S_o)
4.8	Communication is immediate (S_i, S_o)
4.9	Communication is direct (S_i, S_o)
4.10	Communication is informative (S_i, S_o)
4.11	Communication is mutual (S_i, S_o)

5.0   Relationships
5.1   The ground rules are clear (S_e, S_i, S_o)
5.2   The ground rules are agreed (S_e, S_i, S_o)
5.3   The ground rules are shared (S_e, S_i, S_o)
5.4   There are 'equal opportunities' (S_e, S_i, S_o)
5.5   The parts reflect the whole (S_i, S_o)
5.6   Decision making is shared (S_i, S_o)
5.7   Leadership is dispersed (S_i, S_o)
5.8   Accountability is mutually supportive (S_i, S_o)
Symbols and rituals
5.9   Symbols and rituals represent core beliefs and values (S_i, S_o)
5.10 Symbols and rituals are shared (S_i, S_o)
5.11 Symbols and rituals generate energy (S_i, S_o)

A list of all the guidelines is set out in Table 5.1. We shall now look at each guideline in turn in order to indicate the reason it has been chosen and its main characteristics. It should be stressed again that the only reason for the inclusion of any guideline is that it is seen as an essential means of delivering one or more of the feelings associated with the three 'S's, and behind them the values represented by the three 'L's.

1.0   The people (and focal systems)

Our list of guidelines could begin with either the participants or the focal task. It is something of a chicken and egg matter. We choose to begin with the people concerned as without some idea of who is involved the focal task remains a disembodied affair often difficult to identify in any clear way.

However, it is the focal task which brings systems together. Thus intervention should be targeted at those systems for which the focal task is focal. We shall refer to these systems as focal systems:

> Focal systems are those social systems for which the focal task is focal, i.e. necessary for their survival as those particular systems.

Other systems may offer support or resources but not having the focal task as a priority are not our primary concern.

The guidelines listed for the people segment of the social system are closely related to our key concept of inclusivity, as well as to the three 'S's. Inclusivity can of course refer to inclusiveness within systems. With our model, however, it must also relate to inclusiveness across systems.

1.1   Two or more systems are involved (S_o)   The guidelines can be used to assess the communal strength of a single system. In this case, our first guidelines would be omitted and the remainder in this segment recast in the singular.

However, *our paramount concern is to work across systems and not just within them.* Otherwise the danger of exclusivity and the communal dilemma (see pp. 47–50) would loom large. As Boswell puts it (1990, p. 74): 'Associativeness cannot be unilateral, it has to be reciprocal and the work of many hands.' We are concerned about openness to other systems not only because it releases expertise and resources for the achievement of the focal task (the experience of 'synergy' mentioned earlier, p. 49) but because in the long run exclusiveness is communally self-defeating.

'Two or more systems' may be related to the focal task in different ways. As in the case of parental involvement or links with industry or health, the class as a social system might link up with various 'external' bodies. On the other hand, teachers can strengthen a sense of community within their classes by treating them as containing a range of focal systems (boys and girls, different ethnic groups, high and low attainers, etc.) which would benefit from closer engagement. Provided the focal task is common, the community developer can choose with which systems he or she wishes to work, though the greater the number and size of the focal systems the less likely it is that sustainable change will occur.

In the first instance, individuals or small groups acting as representatives of larger focal systems may be involved. Initially, this may meet the requirements of the guideline, though for community development to gather real momentum, more and more members of the system must become actively involved.

1.2   The systems are clearly identifiable (S_i, S_o)   Gestalt psychology reminds us that healthy development will not occur where the 'figure' and its 'ground' are not clearly distinguished. For growth to take place I need to know who I am in relation to others; so it is with social systems and their development as communities.

The emphasis here is not on closure (always destructive in the end) but *identity*. In this context, Morgan (1986, p. 101) wisely reminds us of the importance of 'the principle of minimum critical specification [which] attempts to preserve flexibility by suggesting that, in general, one should specify no more than is absolutely necessary for a particular activity to occur'. Yet social systems are not always easy to identify (for pupils as well as teachers). Interaction and relationships often encompass a range of systems. Thus community developers may need to assist in the clarification of boundaries, though not by artificially creating them.

Social systems may be recognized by employing certain of the guidelines given below, not least those relating to symbols and rituals, to help to clarify where their boundaries lie.

1.3   The systems have diverse cultural, social or economic features (S_i, S_o)   The phrase 'cultural, social or economic features' here refers to such phenomena as ethnicity, religion and lifestyle (cultural); gender, age and class (social); and occupation and wealth (economic). The categories overlap.

This guideline is founded on the importance of difference in community development, in contrast to what Boswell (1990, p. 38) terms 'the narcissism of similarity'. Jungian psychology, in particular, emphasizes the importance of opposites (such as the Yin and the Yang) if significance and solidarity are to be attained. 'Students cannot become a community ... if they believe that they must ignore their own differences and those of their classmates in order to belong', writes Sapon-Shevin (1992, p. 19).

This guideline is about the widening as well as deepening of experience. Here, an important stimulus to opening up new communal vistas is the element of surprise, and a related lateral shift in understanding and attitudes that encounters between different kinds of systems can often bring.

1.4   The systems include people who are disadvantaged (S_e, S_i, S_o)   This guideline goes to the heart of the values on which our three 'S's are based. The three 'L's, the value of inclusivity, and the Christian beliefs upon which for us these rest, require that community embraces the poor, the marginalized and the alienated. This is not simply a matter of altruism. It is because learning in the fullest sense requires the experience and insights of the disadvantaged as much as the advantaged. It is a commonplace observation of those engaged with people who are disadvantaged that, given empathy and openness, as much has been received from the latter as has been given.

In the context of adult education, Westwood (1992, p. 234) argues that 'the ideological construction of homogeneous communities' around the concept of place and space (the neighbourhood) has ignored 'the contradictions and fractures of gender, ethnicity, and age divisions', as well as class. Consequently it has deskilled community developers in utilizing the creative energy resulting from the passions aroused.

Within the school setting, Galton and Williamson (1992, p. 42) argue from their research (substantiated by Bennett and Cass, 1988), that 'groups function best when they are of mixed ability'. But they add that 'such groups must include pupils from the highest ability group within the class'. The Stainbacks (1992) in their extensive work on 'inclusive class-rooms', where those 'having profound disabilities or chronically disruptive behaviour' (p. 5) are treated as an integral part of the social system, state (p. 10) that guiding 'class members to understand and utilise their inherent differences ... is critical to the healthy development of self-confidence, mutual respect, and a sense of community ...'

2.0   The focal task

The focal task of any social system is the task which has to be addressed for that system, as such, to survive (p. 67). In the case of the school and the class, the focus will be on education. Here we pin-point those features of education as a focal task which are closely related to the strengthening of the three 'S's, and thus to the creation of a more effective educational system. In Chapter 6, we look more closely at the nature of education itself.

2.1   The focal task is clear (S_0)   There is an abundance of literature supporting this guideline as being vital for effective learning. Hargreaves and Hopkins (1991) quote Purkey and Smith who advocate 'clear goals ... for students' (p. 111), and Doyle who states that 'successful teachers communicate their work systems clearly to students' (p. 114). Reid *et al.* (1989, p. 10) state: 'Students will learn best ... if they have a clear sense of direction and purpose.' Moon *et al.* (1990) quote Rutter who argues that 'successful schools ... set clear academic goals', and Renihan and Renihan (two Canadians) who argue for 'pre-established standards which are made well known'.

Focal tasks that are left vague and ill-defined – in purpose, content, procedures, outcomes or time-scale – result in diffuse and often conflicting expectations, and the weakening of a sense of solidarity.

2.2   The focal task is agreed (S_0)   This guideline is included largely to re-emphasize the crucial place of negotiation and of the resulting sense of ownership of the task if real learning is to occur. A focal task cannot be imposed without the communal potential of the systems involved being gravely undermined. This is simply because 'the sharing of a commitment is one of the strongest forces in the formation of community' (Macquarrie, 1982, p. 142). Thus, for effective learning to happen the focal task must be negotiated and agreed in a way which fosters the genuine commitment of all. As Vaill (1986, p. 91) puts it, 'Clarity, consensus and commitment' go hand in hand.

2.3   The focal task is shared (S_o)   A key distinction here is between what MacIver calls 'like interests' and 'common interests' (see p. 35). MacIver and Page (1950, p. 32) state that, 'The like is what we have distributively, privately, each to himself. The common is what we have collectively, what we share without dividing up'.

Solidarity is at its strongest where the focal task is centred on common interests, though like interests will play a part not least in the initial stages of the encounter. The more such sharing of interests occurs across systems, the less likely it is that the focal task will fall foul of the communal dilemma.

2.4   The focal task is stimulating (S_i, S_o)   For social systems to have any real interest in, or commitment to, opening themselves up to one another and to the enrichment of learning which will result, the focal task has to be stimulating enough to make the crossing of boundaries worthwhile. 'Stimulating' in this context embodies other terms often used by educationalists such as 'absorbing', 'challenging' or 'exciting'. In general, a stimulating task has three main features:

- First, it is experiential in the sense that 'it starts with the student and builds on his or her strengths' (Stainback and Stainback, 1992, p. 70). In this sense it is very much what Brandes and Ginnis mean by 'student-centred learning' (1986, 1990).
- Second, stimulation is for many pupils about an action-oriented focal task. In much primary school research, Galton and Williamson (1992, p. 60) found 'action talk' gained much more involvement than 'abstract discussion involving ideas'.
- Third, stimulation is enhanced by a focal task which, moving beyond the purely experiential, breaks new ground. As Honey and Mumford (1989) put it, in describing learning styles: 'The opportunities to learn from experience are greatly increased if the normal everyday things which happen to us are supplemented by extra experiences that we create.'

Provided a sense of security is not threatened in a way which undermines community, it is focal tasks that are about discovery and excitement and which embrace an element of risk-taking, which promote genuine communal change.

2.5   The focal task is achievable (S_i, S_o)   'Nothing succeeds like success.' Effective learning is about a strong sense of significance and solidarity based not only on the hope of final accomplishment, but 'little achievements' along the way. Argyris and Schön (1974, p. 100) talk about the need for 'psychological success' within a climate of 'psychological safety'.

This guideline is not about settling for the lowest common denominator. It is not, as Alexander's (1991, p. 15) criticism of primary education in Leeds puts it, about focusing 'on what children cannot do rather than what they can do, and in (rightly) attending to their problems (underplaying or ignoring) their potential'. It is about high but realistic expectations which enhance not undermine morale (NCE, 1993, p. 40).

2.6   The focal task can be achieved in various ways (S_i, S_o)   'A key element in classroom operation is flexibility' (Stainback and Stainback, 1992, p. 11). Flexibility gives the opportunity for participants with different experiences and abilities to find out for themselves, and for the system to which they belong, the most appropriate way of learning. The guideline again emphasizes Morgan's plea for 'minimum critical specification' (1986,

p. 21). The focus here is on the participants being offered a range of appropriate learning paths, the opportunity to choose the most suitable and the means to be supported in pursuing it.

3.0 The environment

The environmental segment of the social system is taken to refer to the natural and built environment on the one hand, and to resources (which include plant, equipment and materials, finance and, not least, people with their experience, expertise and skills) on the other.

3.1 The meeting places are accessible (S_e, S_i) Invariably, there will be a need for some meeting place where those involved can gather. The necessary transport must be available, the location clearly signposted and access unhindered. Pugh, writing about pre-school services, comments (1989, p. 10):

> Where a centre is, whether it is accessible to local families and to those who have to come by public transport, and how welcoming the premises are, are all factors that affect whether parents come to the centre at all and, having arrived, feel inclined to stay.

These relatively obvious features of easy access are frequently ignored. Schools in particular have often been built like fortresses with 'main' entrances tucked away round corners and few signs indicating where access can be gained. Only in recent times is the threatening nature of railings, high walls and long drives being recognized. Within schools, too, the labyrinth of corridors can present a veritable maze to visitors (not least parents) often causing them to feel lost and embarrassed.

3.2 The environment is safe and healthy (S_e, S_i) The environment wherein partici-pants interact needs to be safe, not only in relation to dangers of a natural or technical kind, but from human violence or disruption. The latter feature may until recently have appeared more relevant to a wider world. But in recent times, violence and even murder have occurred within British schools with traumatic consequences. Arson, too, is on the increase. But this guideline also needs operationalizing in the more ordinary context of such things as school playgrounds and gymnasia.

The environment clearly needs to be healthy, with freedom from such hazards as asbestos poisoning, and with healthy school meals on offer. This guideline is about 'well-being' in every respect.

3.3 The environment is conducive (S_e, S_i) This guideline is more 'subjectively' oriented than some of the others, but is meant to avoid even vaguer words such as 'ethos'. It relates to environmental features which strengthen the systems' sense of community as they pursue their focal task. This does not only mean that 'the setting in which children work should be consistent with and supportive of the particular learning tasks they are given' (Alexander, 1991, 8. 37). It emphasizes that the environment should be that which values, affirms and supports them. Shoddy buildings, tatty rooms and dirty sites, imper-sonal and 'clinical' architecture, do not enhance a sense of community.

One of the most abiding legacies of Henry Morris was his insistence that schools should be 'fine and worthy public buildings' (Rée, 1985, p. 153). He believed profoundly in 'the power of architecture to promote humane values' (p. 99) and the necessity of an aesthetically stimulating environment to enhance the education of the whole person. Morris might have been somewhat doctrinaire and romantic in his view of a 'conducive environment', but he was making a vital point in relation to the communalizing of learning which we neglect at our peril.

Resources

3.4   Resources are adequate (S_e, Si)   This guideline concerns the resources needed to achieve the focal task. But the concept of 'adequacy' also has a major impact on self-worth and motivation. Thus resources must be perceived to be adequate by the participants – both in the sense of their being enough of them and in their being fairly distributed. On the other hand, an over-abundance of resources leading to wastage or lax accountability can be communally counter-productive.

The underfunding of many schools over recent decades, in terms of plant, teaching aids and increasingly staffing itself, has not as yet undermined the pursuit of the focal task. But it has made many involved feel frustrated, devalued and deskilled and, of late, increasingly insecure.

3.5   Resources are sustainable (S_e, Si)   Resources can be adequate for a time but then fail to be renewed or replenished. Sometimes social systems are wasteful. More often in recent years, shifts in the wider economic situation or the fluidity of public policy have made the resourcing of education a stop–go affair. The community development process requires that resources are sustainable long enough for enduring change to take place in the sense of community experienced by participants.

3.6   Appropriate time is available (S_i, S_o)   'Time' is an integral aspect of resources in general. It is singled out here for special mention because it is a frequently neglected commodity. Reid *et al.* (1989, p. 32) state that 'the question of time is a vital one for successful small group learning'. Hargreaves and Hopkins (1991, p. 120) quote Fullan's assertion: 'Effective change takes time ... Unrealistic or undefined time-lines fail to recognise that implementation occurs developmentally. Persistence is a critical aspect of successful change.' Alexander (1991, p. 24) in his report on primary education in Leeds writes: 'We commend close attention to the way time is used in the curriculum.' Bottery (1992, p. 138) here stresses the importance of long-term contracts of employment, commonplace in Japan but becoming ever less typical in the West. 'Only by having this commitment to the long term', he writes, 'are trust and subtlety possible in relationships and ... the full commitment of the worker ...achieved.'

The community development aspect of the learning process cannot be rushed. It is often about changing perceptions, values, attitudes and feelings. This takes time. Quite naïvely, it is assumed that community building can be delivered in days or weeks – months and years are more likely. On the other hand, time must be treated as a scarce resource. It is not unlimited. To fail to define 'time-lines', or to waste time, threatens the momentum of change and can be communally destructive. Time has to be 'appropriate', not boundless.

4.0   Interaction and communication

We follow Homans (1951, p. 84) in defining 'interaction' as 'participating together'. Galton and Williamson state (1992, p. 77) that such participation over time brings 'a strong sense of solidarity'. Klein reporting on her meticulous study of groups puts this more formally (1956, p. 106):

> The more interaction, the more positive is the sentiment towards others in the group, and towards those who act frequently in particular.

One fundamental qualification is noted by Klein: that interaction which is felt to be obligatory rarely strengthens a sense of solidarity or significance. She writes (1965a, p. 155): 'Interaction normally varies with liking only if the interaction is freely chosen and can be broken off when desired.' We have not, however, included voluntary interaction as a separate guideline as we take the voluntary principle to apply to all our guidelines and to be part and parcel of the negotiated basis on which the entire community development process rests. Klein also mentions one other qualification to her proposition. This is the need for interaction to provide information. We will return to that particular matter when we look at communication.

For us, interaction embraces all forms of participating together including communication, not least language. Communication is so important, however, that in what follows it forms a separate subsection.

4.1   Everyone is involved (S_i, S_o)   Everyone cannot literally be 'equally' involved, but participants should feel they have a fair slice of the action. Inclusiveness, in this context, should be intra as well as inter-system. It means 'giving everyone a reason to be involved' as Stainback and Stainback describe it (1992, p. 7) in their study of 'inclusive school communities'.

An important question here is what size of social system best facilitates total involvement. On this matter, Toogood's comments (1984, p. 238) might be noted: 'Smallness of scale is more appropriate to a human organisation such as a school. Relationships provided for on a mass scale yield degenerate forms of interaction.' However, Handy and Aitken (1986, p. 67) believe that 'small ... is not always beautiful' and that small groups can all too easily become culturally incestuous, not least where top management is concerned. Our point is that the size must serve involvement and that involvement must not be compromised by size (large or small).

4.2   Interaction is collaborative (S_i, S_o)   The brevity of our comments here do not reflect the importance of this guideline. Collaboration is a fundamental aspect of the community development process. But as other guidelines impinge on and fill out the nature of collaboration, our comments under this heading are of a more general nature.

'Co-operative classrooms use the motto, "None of us is as smart as all of us"', states Sapon-Shevin (1992, p. 31). Such advocacy of collaboration as vital for effective learning is widespread. Galton and Williamson (1992, p. 42) sum up a good deal of American and English research in this field as follows:

> When children sit in groups in a classroom they are likely to achieve more if they are encouraged to co-operate either by working towards a common shared outcome or by making an individual contribution towards a common goal.

Ford (Ford *et al.*, 1992, p. 75) also stresses the communal dimension of collaboration: 'Making the transition from a competitive to a co-operative environment is critical to building a sense of community in the classroom.'

Researchers are agreed that this 'sense of community' is about significance as well as solidarity. Galton and Williamson (1992, p. 16) state: 'Working in this way [collaboratively] also improves individual pupil's self-image in that by working in groups the children come to respect each other's strengths and weaknesses.' The very final sentence of their investigation into 'group work in the primary classroom' (p. 143) touches on both our communal and focal tasks:

> The increase in collaborative group work, with its emphasis on inter-dependency between pupils, offers a practical solution to some ... pressing problems and a sound basis for today's children as they prepare to face adult life in the twenty-first century.

But is competition, and especially conflict, ruled out of court as always destructive of effective learning? To deal with this question we move to our next guideline.

4.3 Interaction is lively (S_o) There is alongside the literature advocating collaboration, a literature commending competition and even conflict as creative phenomena. Competition, by strengthening 'the will to win', is believed to enhance motivation. Conflict, as both Simmel (1955) and Coser (1956) have argued, is seen as a necessary motor of social change. In an educational context, Fullan (1991, p. 105) believes that teachers should 'assume that conflict and disagreement are not only inevitable but fundamental to successful change'.

This is an issue which requires a good deal more research as well as debate because it has implications far wider than the relatively small-scale engagement of systems we are considering here. We make two points. First, as we argued in Chapter 3 (p. 50), there is a world of difference between what Simpson (1937, p. 42) calls 'non-communal conflict', which involves ultimate values, and 'communal conflict', which is about secondary values. The former is likely to be highly destructive; the latter has much greater potential for creative change. Second, as we are concerned about whole systems in which everyone is involved, what does one do about the inevitable losers in a process based on competition or conflict? What happens to their sense of significance and solidarity?

Nonetheless, we still advocate interaction which is 'lively'. Community building is not a passive or sombre affair. It is an energetic and exciting process which opens up new horizons and brings fresh and stimulating experiences. The vitality of interaction, with certain elements of communal competition and conflict involved, could thus be important.

Klein adds one interesting point about lively interaction. She argues (1956, pp. 111; 156) that 'off-task' interaction is more likely to enhance liking and a sense of community than purely task-related engagement. As most researchers (Times Educational Supplement, 15 November 1991) seem to assume that educational achievement must be dominantly task-centred, it may be worth teachers giving some thought to the proposition that communally enhanced effectiveness of the learning process depends on a more appropriate balance between on-task and off-task interaction.

4.4 Interaction is personal (S_i, S_o) For community and thus learning to be enhanced, interaction needs to be of a personal nature. Klein (1956, p. 106) states that interaction produces the most positive sentiments where the personalities and feelings of participants are well known. For this to happen, people need to meet in as real a way as possible. The other person 'becomes real to me in the fullest sense of the word only when I meet him face-to-face', write Berger and Luckmann (1984, p. 44). And Handy (1994, p. 119) writing from a vast experience of management states: 'There is no real substitute for looking someone in the eye while you talk or they talk.'

Three comments need to be made here. First, we are now entering a totally new era in which human beings, including students, can have immediate contact with their fellows across the globe. E-mail and the Internet are only the beginning. Many involved in such transactions have begun to build what some call 'virtual communities' in 'cyberspace'. These are founded on a huge range of interests, from the academic to the bizarre. Does this mean, then, that technology is making our guideline redundant?

We would claim this is not so. Interaction that is literally 'face-to-face' enables exchanges to take place not only far quicker and for far longer, but across a far broader range of non-verbal signals, than technically transmitted messages can ever hope to facilitate. There is also a subtle aspect of personal contact, be it of an intimate or just plain ordinary nature, touched on in the comments of Berger and Luckmann, as well as Handy above, which promotes a knowledge of the other experienced far less intensely via technical media. No wonder, therefore, that even the most ardent 'internetters' need to meet face-to-face from time to time in order to enhance and sustain their interpersonal relationships. As Handy put it in the television series 'Visions of Heaven and Hell' (1995): 'To be a virtual community whom I can only talk to by typing is not the same as people whom I can actually touch and feel and drink with and smile with ... High tec needs high touch to make it human and liveable with.'

Second, personal interaction promotes real if not always intimate relationships. 'It is necessary to love one's mother, but not one's teacher' (Berger and Luckmann, 1984, p. 161). As Cox put it (1965, p. 48) when commenting on the famous categories of Martin Buber, 'I–You' relationships may not be as intimate as 'I–Thou' relationships but they can be very real and very human. What destroys community are 'I–It' relationships which reduce other people to the status of objects.

Third, it is necessary for pupils as they develop to be able to move beyond personal interaction to more formal ways of operating, so that social systems appropriate for sustaining the life of wider society can be created and sustained. Nevertheless, the ability to make this transition smoothly depends to a large extent on the student having internalized the sense of significance and solidarity created by past and continuing interactions of a personal nature within smaller systems such as the family and the peer group.

4.5 Interaction is frequent (S_0) Klein has stressed the importance of frequency as noted in our introductory comments on the nature of interaction (see p. 73). Homans (1951, p. 111) argues similarly: 'Persons who interact frequently with one another tend to like one another.' As we have argued with regards to information technology, where people meet together on only an occasional basis, the communal potential of the systems concerned is limited.

4.6 Interaction is ongoing (S_0) Interaction, even frequent interaction, must continue long enough for a strengthened sense of community to emerge. This is why schools, providing the opportunity for pupils and teachers to remain in contact over a long time span, have great communal potential.

Communication

We define communication, with Klein (1956, p. 121), as 'the transmission of information'. 'Without communication there can be no community', state MacIver and Page (1950, p. 282). Hargreaves and Hopkins (1991, p. 111) quote Purkey and Smith as stating that effective schools are characterized by 'intense interaction and communication'. Such communication, not least through the use of language, is a vital means of enhancing significance and solidarity and thus the effective delivery of the focal task.

4.7 Communication is public (S_i, S_o) Communication, through word, image or sound, needs to span all social systems and reach every participant involved in the community development process. 'No-go' areas must be eliminated. This is not only because 'access to information confers status' (Klein, 1956, p. 36), but because nothing destroys solidarity more than information withheld for ulterior motives.

4.8 Communication is immediate (S_i, S_o) This is a time-related guideline. Messages, however sent, need to be communicated as soon as possible. There should be no delay or procrastination which can cause participants confusion, frustration or a sense of being 'strung along'.

4.9 Communication is direct (S_i, S_o) Communication should be filtered through as few intermediaries as possible. 'The whispering game', where messages pass down the line from person to person, can distort meaning out of all recognition. Directness enhances both the quality of the message and the morale of those involved in the transaction.

4.10 Communication is informative (S_i, S_o) Argyris and Schön (1974, p. 86) state that their 'primary governing variable' to promote effective and satisfying communication is to 'maximise valid information'. Irrelevant information, or too little relevant information, undermines both self-confidence and solidarity. 'Not knowing what is going on' is a major factor in undermining community in whatever shape or form.

Highlighted again by this guideline is the importance of language. Words which participants, not least pupils, can clearly understand need to be normative. The challenge lies not so much in the communication of facts and figures, but in transmitting feelings and ideas. In a world of many tongues, failure to communicate feelings as well as facts is a major cause of the breakdown of community and the ensuing closure of systems to one another.

4.11 Communication is mutual (S_i, S_o) 'Community must not be a one-way process' (Klein, 1956, p. 123). In other words, communication should be about mutuality. All those involved should have the opportunity to exchange relevant information. This is a matter of both 'advocacy' (helping the other person to understand one's position) and 'inquiry' (checking that oneself and the other person share the same view of the content and process of the interaction) (Clark, S., 1994).

Such mutuality can and should operate efficiently 'up and down' the systems involved, as well as across them. This is why the concept of 'networking' has become so popular, as well as important, in recent years. Systems continuously communicating internally and externally in this way exhibit considerable potential for communal growth.

5.0 Relationships

The relationships segment brings us close to the heart of the social system and because of its location provides a very important set of guidelines. One major theme regarding relationships is that of greater 'power-sharing', an issue we shall return to in Chapter 7 when we consider the role of the community educator.

5.1 The ground rules are clear (S_e, S_i, S_o) 'Ground rules' here refer to the basic norms, formal and informal, which steer the life and activities of the systems concerned in achieving their focal task. Ground rules are especially important in relation to the boundaries and thus identity of social systems.

The need for clarity of ground rules is stressed by many writers. For Berger and Luckmann (1984, p. 73), it is their predictability which enables 'me' and 'you' to become 'us'. For Wilson *et al.* (1967, p. 41), 'making the rules, and the point of the rules, as clear as possible to pupils' is one way to foster moral maturity. The research by Galton and Williamson (1992, p. 140) shows that 'for effective learning to take place ... children require that limits are set and clear structures for operating within these limits established'.

Clarity, however, does not mean rigidity. If communal change is to occur, flexibility of roles and relationships remains essential.

5.2 The ground rules are agreed (S_e, S_i, S_o) This guideline again underscores the key role of negotiation in relation to all the indicators of community development listed here. The key concept in this context is 'contract'. Participants must agree to 'the rules of the game' if it is to be played without confusion, continuous argument or manipulation.

5.3 The ground rules are shared (S_e, S_i, S_o) 'Linking and interaction and homogeneity of norms all vary together', states Klein (1956, p. 263). Her research underlines that 'homogeneity' is important for community building and, in this context, that ground rules must be shared by all participants within and across systems if community is to develop. This sharing should encompass a common understanding as well as general acceptance of 'the rules of the game'.

5.4 There are 'equal opportunities' (S_e, S_i, S_o) 'Equal opportunities' is defined here as meaning those procedures and structures which enable participants to enter into and be involved in the community development process on an equal footing. There should be no prior regard given to social distinctions based on such characteristics as class, race, gender, age or disability. 'Equal opportunities' refers not only to issues of access to the learning process, but to the contribution all participants are enabled to make and the esteem in which they are held after access has been achieved.

The more formal aspects of this guideline are now embodied in legislation, but implementation remains patchy in schools as elsewhere and needs to be carefully monitored with regard to each new focal task. For us, equal opportunities is not a static concept. It is a process of continuously 'equalizing opportunities' for all involved.

5.5 The parts reflect the whole (S_i, S_o) For the greater part of the industrial era, the dominant model of working relationships was 'the division of labour'. Emile Durkheim, its great exponent (1933), believed that the principle was not only functionally efficient but communally enriching. 'The ideal of human fraternity', he writes (p. 405), 'can be realised only in proportion to the progress of the division of labour'. He adds (pp. 60–1): 'The most remarkable effect of the division of labour is not that it increases the output of functions divided, but that it renders them solidary.'

In recent years, Durkheim's thesis has been challenged on both functional and communal grounds. Savage (1990, pp. 165–6) argues that in reality a 'division of labour' imposes conformity to established procedures, fragments work, means that 'the worker loses an overview of the entire process' and thus encourages distrust. Morgan (1986, pp. 98–100) contrasts the old-style division of labour (which he calls 'redundancy of parts') with the multiple skills approach (which he calls 'redundancy of functions'). The former he sees as encouraging a 'someone else's problem' attitude, with 'a degree of passivity and neglect ... built into the system'. The latter, where the parts embody the whole, he believes makes involvement 'more holistic and all-absorbing', with the consequent enhancing of a sense of community.

5.6 Decision making is shared (S_i, S_o) On the macro level, this guideline is closely related to what is now known as the principle of 'subsidiarity'; that those most affected by decisions made should be most involved in making them. Handy (1990, p. 100) summarizes this in the dictum: 'To steal people's decisions is wrong.' We would argue with Bottery (1992, p. 64) 'that participation in decision making should not only occur at an institutionally smaller level (than national and local government), but should also be begun as early as possible. Schools fit the bill perfectly.'

Community development requires that the maximum number of people involved with the focal task have the opportunity to express their views, hear those of others and be active participants in the decision-making process within and across the social systems concerned. This not only enhances a sense of solidarity but of significance. 'Shared decision making ... improve[s] pupils' self-esteem and increase[s] pupil motivation' (Galton and Williamson, 1991, p. 42).

5.7 Leadership is dispersed (S_i, S_o) We define 'leaders', with Brown (1988, p. 88) as 'those who have attributes which can help the group achieve particular task goals, or are those whose personalities are well matched to particular situations'. Thus, 'leadership is a function of all group members and of the task' (Klein, 1956, p. 23).

This guideline seeks to increase so-called 'leadership density' (Beare *et al.*, 1989, p. 126), the degree to which leadership roles are shared and the degree leadership is broadly exercised. This does not imply that all forms of hierarchical leadership are inappropriate. It means that, as far as the focal task permits, power and influence within and across social systems should be exercised by those, at whatever organizational level, with relevant knowledge, experience or expertise. It also means that the ability of every participant to play some leadership role is recognized and affirmed.

5.8 Accountability is mutually supportive (Si, So) 'Self-expression', states Klein (1963, p. 53) 'and the sympathetic response of others give the individual an assurance of his own worth.' Many writers stress the communal importance of accountability providing the emphasis is on affirmation and reward (for achievement rather than 'winning'), not on inspection and sanctions. Moon *et al.* (1990) quote Rutter, Mortimore and the Canadians Renihan and Renihan as all upholding the ample use of rewards, praise and appreciation. In this context, 'the need for immediate feedback followed by further discussion with the teachers appears critical' (Galton and Williamson, 1991, p. 43). It is a process which should embrace not only facts but the mutual exchange of feelings (pp. 139; 192).

Accountability should also operate among pupils themselves. For those mature enough, there is no reason why this should not also involve supportive feedback to teachers on their performance. For all, collectively organized learning and appraisal can foster significance and solidarity (Stainback and Stainback, 1992, p. 10), with pupils sharing and accepting responsibility for the learning process.

Symbols and rituals

Our definition of a symbol is 'a simplified "re-presentation", in publicly acknowledged form, of a culturally distinctive idea, belief, relationship, action or object'. We define a ritual as a 'form of symbolic action related to a repetitive order of gestures and postures' (McLaren, 1986, p. 129). He adds that 'rituals are to symbols as a metal container is to a radioactive isotope'.

Symbols and rituals embrace a vast area of human experience, verbal, aural and visual. The most fundamental, but often ignored, is language itself. Religion, arts and the media provide the sectors within which symbols and rituals are particularly prominent.

Symbols and rituals are much more than a subcategory of relationships. They often form the glue that binds each segment (and all segments) together. Thus we can talk of symbolic people, who often form role models or significant others (the people segment) and symbolic places (the environment segment). Symbols and rituals combine to make up symbolic events (Clark, 1973a, pp. 399–400) (our interaction segment) and symbolic relationships (often, like marriage, enshrined in law) (our relationship segment). Thus symbols and rituals can span the entire social system.

Symbols and rituals play a key role in the community development process. Cohen (1985) has written an entire book on this topic, *The Symbolic Construction of Community*, in which he stresses the essential role of symbols and rituals in offering people a powerful sense of significance and solidarity. As schools in particular appear to be 'ritually saturated institutions' (McLaren, 1986, p. 24), symbols and rituals become critical aspects of community education.

But symbols and rituals can block, as well as further, the communal developments we seek. It is a problem characteristic of 'the communal dilemma' (see pp. 47–50). Their very ability to express culture can freeze culture (Klein, 1956, p. 124). Thus Alfred Whitehead's cautionary words, quoted by McLaren (1986, p. xvi), need to be heeded:

> Those societies which cannot combine reverence to their symbols with freedom of revision, must ultimately decay either from anarchy, or from the slow atrophy of a life stifled by useless shadows.

5.9 Symbols and rituals represent core beliefs and values (S_i, S_o) Symbols and rituals can range from the trivial and relative (such as commercial slogans and trade marks) to the profound and comprehensive. Berger and Luckmann describe the latter as 'symbolic universes' (1984, p. 113). A symbolic universe is 'the matrix of all socially objectively and subjectively real meanings', and it provides 'an all-embracing frame of reference' for 'all sectors of the institutional order' (p. 114). Religion, philosophy, art and science make the major contribution to this frame of reference. At its heart lie people's core beliefs and values. 'Such symbolisation is conducive to feelings of security and belonging' (p. 117). Likewise, 'identity is ultimately legitimated by placing it within the context of a symbolic universe' (p. 118).

5.10   Symbols and rituals are shared (S_i, S_o)   'Culture is a construction that remains a consistent and meaningful reality through the overarching organisation of rituals and symbol systems' (McLaren, 1986, p. 5). For a rich culture and strong sense of community to develop, therefore, symbols and rituals need to be shared and owned by all members of the systems involved.

There is an inevitable tension between symbols and rituals which characterize particular systems and those which span a number of systems. It is here that the malleability yet durability of symbols and rituals, about which Cohen (1985) has a good deal to say, becomes extremely important.

5.11   Symbols and rituals generate energy (S_i, S_o)   Communally important symbols and rituals are about private and public passion. They encompass and express feelings which not only maintain but transform social systems. 'Without feeling', writes Abbs (1989, p. 198), there is 'no creative act, only sterile imitation'. Our concern is with the fostering of the energy to change things, not least schools.

But 'rituals and symbols can become sick, just as organs can' (McLaren, 1986, p. 230). They can 'help dismember group cohesiveness or promote creative unity' (p. 237). A careful distinction needs to be made between symbols and rituals which fulfil the latter function, those which act as safety valves for potentially destructive passions, and those which are 'corruptive and tear apart' (p. 219).

CONCLUSION

The communal guidelines presented above are offered as a basis for further development and refinement. They have been hammered out over many years of teaching and testing, and as a result of an ongoing search for relevant research. That the latter is still so sketchy is merely a commentary on the long neglect of the dynamic process of community development, not least in an educational context.

Certain of these guidelines will in time be adapted or replaced. In any case their application always necessitates negotiation and agreement. What matters most is not the inerrancy of this or that guideline, but its importance as a tool to help to build learning communities and to begin to transform the educational process. For there can be no genuine education without community.

But there is another side to the coin. If we wish to transform education into a process which can prepare the young (and old) to engage in 'learning for living' to meet the challenges of the next century, then the nature and role of education itself must come under scrutiny. Just as community must liberate education, education in turn has to liberate community from the local and the parochial, from the tribe and from the nation, in order to offer us a vision of one world. In Chapter 6 we turn to the role that education has to play in this process of communal liberation, focusing first on the curriculum.

Chapter 6

Education for Community

Our contention is that there can be no genuine education without a genuine community engaged in the learning process. This is why the learning community is our primary concern.

We have argued that the learning community is the foundation for all our futures. On the one hand, it makes the medium the message. In a world where the rediscovery of a sense of community within and especially across groups, associations and nations is so critical an issue, learning about community through living it, and not just studying it, is the only way to prepare ourselves for the immense challenges ahead. On the other hand, the learning community is essential if education itself is to come alive and enable people to reach their full potential. Deprive learners of this communal context and education becomes a turgid and sluggish affair. Only as schools become more fully learning communities can education be transformed, as well as itself become a means of transformation.

There is, however, the other side of the coin to which we have already drawn attention. Just as there can be no education without community, so there can be no community without education. If community itself is to be transformed, if it is to avoid being hijacked by the clique, the sect, the tribe or larger incestuous groupings, then it must become an experience of openness, of growth and development, not of closure and defensiveness. The impasse of the communal dilemma must be overcome if the centripetal and centrifugal forces at work in our world are to be handled creatively. Awakening to this reality, preparing for this commitment and attaining the skills and wisdom for this undertaking is a profoundly educational matter. From the classroom to the nation, from the school to the multi-national company, community and education must go hand in hand (Clark, 1992).

WHAT IS 'EDUCATION'

But what is this 'education', without which there can be no community? Just as we needed to clarify the concept of 'community' in order to give it meaning and relevance for today's world, so too we have to rescue the concept of 'education' from death by a thousand (mis)uses.

The debate over the meaning of 'education', and thus the meaning of 'curriculum development', has raged fast and furious ever since Plato's *The Republic*. The focus has shifted to and fro between 'forms of knowledge' (Hirst and Peters, 1970), 'areas of experience' (HMI, 1983; 1985), skills and competences (Burke, 1989), teaching styles, and methods of delivery (Nicholls and Nicholls, 1978). As Meighan (1986) has pointed out, there is a veritable 'network of ideologies' (p. 183) and range of foci for curriculum development approaches.

Our approach to a deeper understanding of what education is all about will be by means of an exploration of the nature of 'pedagogy', often defined as 'the science of teaching' (*The Concise Oxford Dictionary*, 1982, p. 281). We use the term here in a broad sense to encompass the whole process of learning, but seek to clarify the latter through the use of five pedagogic models (Table 6.1).

Table 6.1   *Pedagogic models*

	INDOCTRINATION	NURTURE	INSTRUCTION	TRAINING	EDUCATION
	◄─────────────── TOWARDS EDUCATION ───────────────►				
KEY CONCEPT	Closure				Openness
TASK	Conditioning	Socialization	Imparting knowledge	Imparting skills	Learning to learn
FOCUS	'The cause' or 'The system'	Culture	Subject	Technique	Life and the person
MORALITY	Immoral (imposes values)	◄─── Non-moral ───► / ◄─── (accepts values) ───►			Moral (questions values)
RATION-ALITY	Irrational (ignores or distorts evidence)	◄─── Non-rational ───► / ◄─── (accepts evidence) ───►			Rational (questions evidence)
MEANS OF LEARNING	Imprinting	Assimilation	Memorizing ◄─── Understanding ───► Mastery		Discovery and commitment
CHOICE	Determined by the teacher	Determined by the tradition	Determined by the syllabus		Negotiated with the learner
LEADER-SHIP	Autocratic – imposes (avoids assent)	Paternal/ maternal – guards and guides (fosters assent)	◄─── Directive ───► / Informs and explains ┆ Demonstrates and practices / ◄─── (assumes assent) ───►		Democratic – fosters partnership (seeks assent)

Like all models these have the strengths and limitations of 'ideal types', and frequently overlap or merge into one another. Nonetheless, distinguishing pedagogic types in this way can give a clearer picture as to which has most to offer the process of community development.

Table 6.1 builds on the work of Hull (1975, pp. 52–75) who approaches pedagogic styles from the perspective of religious education. (The main terminological difference is that what he calls 'specific education' we call simply 'education'.)

Education, as we define it, is:

> *The process of learning to learn.*
> *The educational task is to further that process.*

Education is a lifelong endeavour concerned with the ongoing exploration of new knowledge, skills, insights and attitudes and their implications for daily life. In its openness to 'truth', to people in relationships and to the future, education is a profoundly ethical undertaking.

Education cannot in any way encompass or condone indoctrination, our first model in Table 6.1. Indoctrination is a completely closed form of communication wherein 'learning' is a matter of the assimilation of prescribed material without question or reflection. Nurture, instruction and training are educational, but only in so far as they are seen as springboards for a more mature process of questioning and growth.

Education's core value is openness.

Openness is a concept intimately related to that of inclusivity, which is an essential component of our definition of community (see p. 52) and the values and beliefs on which the latter is based (see pp. 50–55). Thus while retaining its own distinctive purpose and identity, education is admirably placed to foster a deeper and broader understanding of community as a quality of life vital for the well-being of future generations. Converging on similar values, community presents a picture of living together (the three 'Ss); education presents the means of painting that picture (learning to learn).

Some educationalists go further, believing the purpose of education to be explicitly associated with building community. For example, in the forepiece to *The Challenge for the Comprehensive School* (1982), Hargreaves quotes Read as follows:

> The general purpose of education is to foster the growth of what is individual in each human being, at the same time harmonising the individuality thus educed with the organic unity of the social group to which the individual belongs ...
> (Herbert Read, *Education through Art*, 1943)

Derek Morrell, an Assistant Under-Secretary of State at the Home Office in the early 1970s, and architect of the so-called 'community development projects' of that era, speaks in similar vein (in Keeble, 1981, p. 44):

> This is the purpose of education: to foster the growth of loving persons, who are aware both of their own individuality and of their membership one of another; who accept one another, and who, understanding their own interdependent nature, choose to use their experience creatively in co-operation with one another.

It is, therefore, more than reasonable for us to assume that the operationalization of education will produce guidelines of immediate relevance to the development of community.

MODELS AND GUIDELINES

We can gain a clearer picture of the values and principles upon which education as such is based by comparing it with the other four models set out in Table 6.1. At the same time we will seek to identify a number of educational guidelines which characterize this learning process (see Table 6.2).

The task of education is learning to learn

As Hull puts it (1975, p. 65), education 'has no purpose other than to make further learning possible'. In this sense, 'education cannot be finished because man is immortal – there is not enough time'. This task is supported and furthered by a number of related principles and, for us, related guidelines (see Table 6.2, p. 90).

1.0   Focus

The concern of education is life as a whole, its nature, purpose and meaning, and the person in that context. The development of the student as learner is paramount, though the student seen not as an isolated individual but in relationship with others. Education is about apprehending, comprehending and responding to the whole of experience. It is cognitive, normative and expressive (Davis, 1994, pp. 49–51).

Education, as we describe it here, does not become weighed down with long arguments about a 'balanced' or a 'whole' curriculum, where the debate is essentially about content. In genuine education, the integration of learning lies primarily with the learner, not with the subject matter or even the teacher. As Hull (1975, p. 58) puts it: 'The authority of education is ... intrinsic to the person, the authority of other forms of communication (nurture, instruction and training) is extrinsic to the person.'

From this aspect of education we derive two closely related guidelines:

1.1   Learning is life-focused.

1.2   Learning is person-centred.

2.0   Morality

Education has a moral quality in that it seeks to discern new values rather than simply adopt or accept uncritically those which already exist. Thus ethical concerns 'although not normally absent from ... other means of communicating (except indoctrination), are integral to the concept of education' (Hull, 1975, p. 58). 'Moral' in this context embraces fundamental questions of values and beliefs and not just 'appropriate behaviour'. Education sees the learning process as a moral endeavour not a functional option.

Our guideline here is:

2.1   Learning questions values.

3.0   Rationality

Of all the pedagogic models, education is the only one which is intrinsically rational. Whereas the other models ignore or simply accept evidence, education is about analyzing and questioning it in order to find a reasonable foundation on which to build. This means 'openness to the truth and to the future through enquiry' (Hull, 1975, p. 57). But it also fosters the personal ownership of the outcome of questioning and debate. In short, as Davis (1994, p. 109) puts it: 'Rationality consists in openness to development.' It is an essential ingredient in producing what Schön calls 'the reflective practitioner'.

Our guideline here is:

3.1   Learning questions evidence.

4.0   The means of learning

The means of learning appropriate to education can best be described as a process of discovery. The technical term for this is 'double-loop learning' which 'depends on being able to take a "double look" at the situation by questioning the relevance of operational norms' (Morgan, 1986, p. 88). Morgan pin-points four key features of double-loop learning. First is 'an openness and reflectivity that accepts error and uncertainty as an inevitable feature of life in complex and changing environments' (p. 91). Handy (1990, p. 54) refers to this characteristic as 'a negative capability', or 'the capacity to live with mistakes and failures without being down-hearted or dismayed'.

Second, double-loop learning adapts 'an approach to the analysis and solution of complex problems that recognises the importance of exploring different viewpoints' (Morgan, 1986, p. 91). Handy (1990, p. 52) calls this feature 're-forming': 'The ability to see things, problems, situations or people in other ways, to look at them sideways or upside-down; to put them in another perspective or another context; to think of them as opportunities not problems, as hiccups rather than disasters.'

Morgan's (p. 92) third feature of double-loop learning is an approach which does not 'impose goals, objectives and targets' but is open to a range of possible outcomes. His fourth feature (p. 95) is 'the need to make interventions and create organisational structures and processes that help implement [these] principles'. This last feature is a more managerial one to which we return in the next two chapters.

Hawkins (1991, pp. 172–87) adds an important rider to our understanding of double-loop learning. He sees even the latter as inhibiting real discovery because it is so often bounded by an implicit philosophy, at best, of effectiveness in a competitive world and, at worst, of survival. Hawkins argues that genuine discovery and growth rest on the potentiality for 'treble-loop learning' wherein the issue is not that of effectiveness (or survival) but of how best to serve the evolutionary needs of the planet.

Hawkins views treble-loop learning as encompassing a readiness to come to terms with mortality, for only if there is an end to continuity can re-creation and renewal take place. He sees such learning as a spiritual process, rooted not in operative or strategic skills but in wisdom, or what he calls 'integrative awareness'. Treble-loop learning is not about a death-wish or escape into mysticism (though an element of the intuitive may well be there). It is about the ability to break free from the subtle confines of even double-loop thinking, often circumscribed by a 'survivor mentality', and see the world as a whole in order to find one's part and purpose in it.

The other major aspect of the means of learning is that it requires commitment. Education is not simply about discovering what is new, interesting or challenging; it is about a commitment to pursue the journey of discovery wherever it leads. Education is no quick fix or easy option. It is the continuing pursuit of learning often over difficult terrain where the path is uncertain and the destination unclear. This requires that the learner is dedicated as much to the excitement of learning as to what is learnt.

Our examination of the means of learning yields two important guidelines:

4.1   Learning is a process of discovery.

4.2   Learning involves commitment.

5.0   Choice

In education, the students' role is not determined by the teacher, the tradition or the curriculum *per se*, but by themselves. This is often referred to as 'autonomous learning', the opportunity for the student to be in charge of the learning process and to make choices appropriate to the educational journey in hand. But we must here be careful that the teacher's contribution is valued and fully utilized. Choice does not mean a wayward freedom which ignores valid evidence or informed guidance. It means learners being encouraged and able to take personal responsibility for their own learning after making use of all the skills and resources offered to them.

Our guideline here is:

5.1   Learners take responsibility for their own learning.

6.0   Leadership

The teacher's role in education complements that of the students. It is essentially democratic in nature and involves the teacher working in partnership with them. The teacher is primarily concerned with seeking the students' assent to the process of learning. The teacher is more an enabler than instructor or trainer, sharing expertise and fostering the students' ability to learn.

The teacher has a particular responsibility for connecting the student to resources for learning. As we shall see more clearly in Chapter 7, the teacher's role as networker here comes to the fore. The teacher's task is to foster what Dorman (1994, p. 18) calls 'dialogical connectedness' and Davis (1994, p. 26), borrowing from Habermas, terms 'communicative action', the ability to enter into open-ended debate with others in pursuit of knowledge, understanding and wisdom.

Our guideline under this heading is:

6.1   Learning is a partnership between all those involved.

CURRICULUM CONTENT

Our educational guidelines have so far focused primarily on principles and process. But what of curriculum content? Does this have no part to play in education for community?

We have stressed the limitations of nurture, instruction and training as adequate educational models in their own right simply because they often occur within a closed learning environment. But where they are regarded as a preparation for education proper, where the knowledge and skills they seek to impart are seen as a preparation for a deeper learning experience, then their content becomes an integral aspect of education itself. In the case of community education, it is knowledge (instruction) and skills (training) with particular relevance to the nature and development of community that can most obviously help further community education.

Are there, then, available any examples of such 'communally friendly' content? It would here be possible to explore a range of informal learning approaches, such as those associated with nurture, but our main concern remains with the school, not least its more formal curriculum.

The National Curriculum

The communalizing role of education is recognized (if only implicitly) in the Education Reform Act (1988, p. 1) which aimed to set up a National Curriculum which:

> ... promotes the spiritual, moral, cultural, mental and physical development of pupils at the school and of society; and prepares such pupils for the opportunities, responsibilities and experiences of adult life.

The two words 'of society' emphasize the role of education as both comprehensive and qualitative, at least in theory far removed from a narrow vocationalism or functionalism.

In practice, the National Curriculum probably came closest to the formal implementation of a communal brief through the recommendation of cross-curricular 'themes', one of which was *Education for Citizenship* (NCC, 1990d). Section 3 of this document states explicitly (p. 3) that:

> Pupils should develop knowledge and understanding of the following.
> *The nature of community:*
>
> - the variety of communities to which people simultaneously belong – family, school, local, national, European and world-wide;
> - how communities combine stability and change;
> - how communities are organised and the importance of rules and laws;

● how communities reconcile the needs of individuals with those of society.

One problem with this contribution to education for community is the ambiguity of the concept of 'citizenship'. As in the report of the Speaker's Commission (HMSO, 1990) preceding the publication of materials, nobody seems quite sure whether citizenship is primarily about knowledge, experience or skills. Though the National Curriculum Council's *Curriculum Guidance Notes* 8 (NCC, 1990d, p. 1) stress 'essential information' and 'opportunities ... to participate in all aspects of school life', Home Office material recently introduced into primary schools appears to be much more focused on making 'moral' decisions (Home Office, 1994). The citizenship portfolio is thus not so much communally friendly as communally confusing.

Three other cross-curricular themes of the National Curriculum which are closely related to citizenship are:

● Education for Economic and Industrial Understanding (NCC, 1990a),
● Health Education (NCC, 1990b) and
● Environmental Education (NCC, 1990c).

All these thematic documents lay down, at least as a statement of intent, that education in England should be closely connected with important aspects of what we have defined as community development. Economics, health and the preservation of the environment are major factors in the creation of a stronger sense of security. 'The role of the individual within different types of community' (NCC, 1990d, p. 4) is a major concern within education for citizenship, and converges on that aspect of our communal task concerned with creating a stronger sense of significance. Education for citizenship is also based on the affirmation that 'all citizens can and must be equal' (p. 6) reflecting our concern for a greater sense of solidarity, as well as on 'the interdependence of individuals, groups and communities' (p. 6), reflecting closely our concern for inclusivity.

The problem with all this, however, is that intentions have outrun implementation. Cross-curricular themes are now very much on the back-burner in many schools and in others have disappeared out of sight as foundation subjects have increasingly dominated the scene.

Other approaches

A more sophisticated approach to giving the content of the curriculum a communal dimension, as well as employing similar systems terminology to our own, is that put forward by Lawton (1983; 1989). Lawton sees the curriculum as being linked to nine 'cultural subsystems' (1989, p. 21) which are essential to the sustainability of societies in general: socio-political, economic, communication, nationality, technology, morality, belief, aesthetic and motivation.

This model is far clearer and much more comprehensive than that related to citizenship. It envisages the curriculum as plugging into a range of (cultural) subsystems not unrelated to the segments of our own social system. Lawton's economic and technology subsystems might correspond to our environment and resources segment; his socio-political and motivational subsystem might link with our relationships segment; and his morality and belief subsystems are akin to our values and beliefs segment. On the other hand, although Lawton takes society as a definer of curriculum very seriously, his categories are sometimes hard to differentiate (for example, between the morality, belief and motivation subsystems). It is thus a little difficult to know how an actual curriculum would emerge from these broad and overlapping aspects of societal life.

A practitioner who has approached curriculum development employing communally user-friendly material of a more pragmatic kind is Hewlett (1986), then Principal of Quorn Rawlins Community College, Leicestershire. He coined the phrase 'regions of application' (e.g. the domestic sphere, the world of work, leisure, etc.). These are recognizable sectors, even if rather broad and unwieldy. But when he adds (pp. 58–9) regions such as 'personal/social relationships in various informal and formal contexts' and one called just 'self', the picture becomes confused. Nevertheless, Lawton and Hewlett at least hold out the possibility that a curriculum focused on communally friendly content might at some stage in the future offer a credible alternative to a National Curriculum at present dominated by traditional subjects and 'disciplines'.

Another approach is that which takes the life and work of the local 'community' surrounding the school as the core material for curriculum development. This was the emphasis of a number of the community development projects set up by the DES and SSRC in 1968, especially that focused on Liverpool 8 under the leadership of Eric Midwinter. Since then 'the community as a curriculum resource' has resurfaced on numerous occasions, boosted by the Schools Curriculum Award scheme set up in 1982, and more recently advocated under the title of 'core-plus education' by Townsend (1994). The value of this approach to the curriculum is that it expands the walls of the classroom to embrace a range and diversity of social systems within a world generally felt to be 'real' and meaningful for the students concerned. The problem (to which we will return in later chapters) is that this remains a local and often circumscribed world which prevents education from liberating community to be the dynamic and potentially universal concept needed at this point in history. As Entwistle (1978, p. 90) puts it: 'In the modern world, the notion of a social environment which is bounded, for anyone, by the immediate physical environment, is woefully inadequate as a curriculum focus.'

Curriculum content often contains social skills. Where it does, the learning process can come close to bringing our communal guidelines and the content of the curriculum into a symbiotic relationship. Aspects of moral education, such as the work of the Farmington Trust, not least through the endeavours of John Wilson and his colleagues (1967), the Humanities Curriculum Project (SC/NHP, 1970) and the work of Peter McPhail (1972), exemplify this position. The life skills part of personal and social education (DES, 1989) also relates closely to the community development process, although actual teaching, as with other aspects of this field, tends to be more cognitive (especially through discussion methods) than experiential (Clark, 1976). However, the social skills concerned are rarely targeted at community building as such and thus serve complementary not identical ends. In particular, they concentrate primarily on the personal development of the individual rather than on the main focus of the communal task, social systems and their interrelationship.

7.0   Curriculum content – guidelines

Knowledge and skills, in the form of curriculum content, should not be excluded from any set of educational guidelines which can further the development of community. We thus add two final guidelines to our list:

7.1   Knowledge acquired furthers an understanding of community.

7.2   Skills learnt help in the development of community.

However, it must be emphasized that it is the principles and process of education, rather than particular knowledge acquired or skills imparted, that remain paramount in education for community in its deepest and broadest sense.

Our educational guidelines are set out in Table 6.2.

Table 6.2   *Educational guidelines*

1.0	**Focus**
1.1	Learning is life-focused
1.2	Learning is person-centred
2.0	**Morality**
2.1	Learning questions values
3.0	**Rationality**
3.1	Learning questions evidence
4.0	**Means of learning**
4.1	Learning is a process of discovery
4.2	Learning involves commitment
5.0	**Choice**
5.1	Learners take responsibility for their own learning
6.0	**Leadership**
6.1	Learning is a partnership between all those involved
7.0	**Content**
7.1	Knowledge acquired furthers an understanding of community
7.2	Skills learnt help in the development of community

'COMMUNITY EDUCATION'

It is important to retain a clear distinction between the concept of community and that of education. The former is primarily defined by that segment of the social system we designated as feeling, and manifest particularly through a sense of security, significance and solidarity. The latter we have defined in this chapter as the process of learning to learn.

Nonetheless, the affinity between community's core value of inclusivity and education's of openness means that the two concepts are built on very similar foundations. It will come as no surprise, therefore, that our communal and our educational guidelines are in many respects complementary and at times overlap. The application of educational guidelines would follow the same procedures as those for applying the communal guidelines (see pp. 64–5). Their implementation must be preceded by negotiation (see p. 63) and agreement about their suitability. The limitations (see p. 65) which we have noted apply to our communal guidelines are also relevant to our educational guidelines.

The affinity of community and education means that we can now bring the two concepts together in a way that helps us to move towards our own definition of *community education*. This is as follows:

Community education is the creation of an increasingly strong sense of security, of significance and of solidarity within and across systems through the learning process.

The phrase 'through the learning process' now becomes all important. It refers here and hereafter to what we have defined above as 'education'. In this context, the learning process becomes both the medium and the message. It furthers the creation of community both through what is learnt and how it is learnt.

Community education can also be defined in a more succinct form, provided it is recognized that the concepts used carry the full meaning of the definition previously given. We can thus say that:

Community education is the process of creating learning communities.

And that:

The task of community education is to create learning communities.

Alternatively we can begin with the learning community itself defined as follows:

A learning community is a social system engaged in the process of community education.

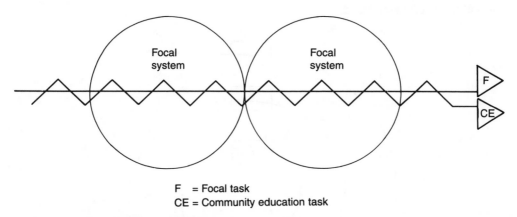

F = Focal task
CE = Community education task

Figure 6.1   *The community education process.*

THE SPIRAL OF TRANSFORMATION

Community education reaches its zenith when the two concepts, community and education, bringing with them all the riches we have described, join forces in pursuit of a common focal task. Community education is a dynamic synthesis of two immensely powerful concepts, but ones which depend on each other for their fulfilment and consummation. Community transforms education; education transforms community. It is, as depicted in Fig. 6.2, a spiral of mutual transformation. It is a process which offers not just the opportunity to enhance education a little, or community a small amount, but one through which we have a chance of redeeming the destructive potential of the centrifugal and centripetal forces now impinging on our world.

CURRICULUM DEVELOPMENT

'The curriculum or bust'

One fundamental weakness of the community education movement, as described in Chapter 1, was its inability to engage with the world of education in any radical and effective way. It is true that the school, as a provider of plant and resources, and to some extent its management, remained reasonably prominent, but the curriculum as a whole was virtually ignored.

Yet the curriculum is the heart of the learning process. This is why the Education Reform Act (1988) got it right when it made the centre-piece of its legislation the introduction of a 'national curriculum'. Begin to legislate for what must be cultivated in 'the secret garden' of the curriculum and one's power to shape the future is immensely strengthened. It is 'the curriculum or bust' (Clark, 1989, pp. 39–40) as far as all true educators, as well as community educators, are concerned. It is no use community educators becoming frenziedly involved in 'extra-mural' activities, championing 'lifelong education' or promoting such roles as 'home–school liaison teachers' or 'outreach workers' if, in the process, the curriculum is left unreformed.

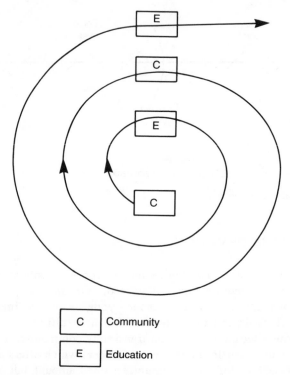

Figure 6.2   *The spiral of transformation*

But what is 'the curriculum'? Much ink has been spilled around concepts of 'manifest' or 'hidden', 'actual' or 'intended', 'formal' or 'informal', 'core' or 'supportive' and so forth (Kelly, 1989, pp. 10–15). We have no hesitation in claiming that our communal and educational guidelines can apply to every form of curriculum. But it would be foolish to ignore the fact that, for most schools and most legislators, the curriculum and curriculum development are about what might be called 'the organized learning process'. It would seem, then, that if we wish to bring the principles of community education to bear effectively on the life and work of schools, the organized learning process cannot be ignored.

The challenge for community education, therefore, is to find an alternative to current approaches to curriculum development so that learning can be enhanced and the urgent communal needs of our world realistically addressed. We are more than aware with Skilbeck, in words written as far back as 1985 (p. 26), that: 'The tendentious and ill-considered back-to-basics movement has gained ground partly because we have offered no powerful alternative curriculum theory.'

Our quest is thus for an 'alternative curriculum theory'. Or, to put it in rather different words, our search is for 'a community curriculum'.

Bottery's four 'codes'

Bottery (1990, pp. 6–16) has suggested that current practice in schools, related particularly closely to the formal curriculum and its development, reveals 'four codes of education'. These governing codes he terms 'cultural transmission', 'child centred', 'social reconstruction' and the 'GNP code'.

We have adopted his title 'curriculum codes', but set out their main features in a rather different format in Table 6.3. We have also added a fifth code, 'the synergistic code', the term 'synergy' (see p. 49) summing up the key features of a community curriculum.

Bottery's four codes rely heavily on the work of a number of other writers. His cultural transmission code is akin to what Skilbeck (1976) and Lawton (1983; 1989) call 'classical humanism'. Bottery's child-centred code is normally called the 'progressive' model of education. Skilbeck (1976; 1984; 1985) and Lawton (1983; 1989) also write at length about reconstructionism. What Bottery calls the GNP code, and we term the 'technological', code is (at least in this explicit form) a more recent development gaining prominence with the increased stress on vocational training and 'the competing revolution' (Burke, 1989).

Bottery's codes are useful in that they seek to bring together a range of features which have influenced and shaped, often at a profound level, curriculum development. In particular, they are open about the beliefs and values upon which all educational processes rest and thereby facilitate rational debate about what has hitherto been very much 'a secret garden'.

The fifth code, the synergistic code which we have added, brings together our concepts of community and education and thus sets out those features which we believe should characterize community education.

The synergistic code

We outline the main features of the synergistic code in Table 6.3. We only include in the table those characteristics of the other codes which are of relevance to the synergistic code.

Table 6.3 *Curriculum codes*

TITLE	TRADITIONAL Classical humanism (Skilbeck, Lawton) Cultural trans-mission (Bottery)	PROGRESSIVE (Skilbeck, Lawton) Child-centred (Bottery)	RECONSTRUCTIONIST (Skilbeck, Lawton) Social reconstruction (Bottery)	TECHNOLOGICAL GNP (Gross National Product) (Bottery)	SYNERGISTIC (Clark) Community curriculum
BASIC CON-STRUCT	Culture	The person	Society	The market	**Community**
TASK	Preservation of the culture and socialization of individual	The personal growth and fulfilment of the individual	Changing society for 'the better'	Wealth creation	The creation of learning communities
PARTICI-PANTS	The whole society	Individuals	Interest groups and pressure groups	Economic units (producers, consumers, etc.)	Social systems as partners in learning
CURRICU-LUM CONTENT	Traditional and classical	Aesthetic and sensual	Social and political	Scientific and technical	The human sciences Communal skills
BELIEFS – LOCUS OF AUTHORITY	The tradition	Personal experience	Political, religious or secular ideologies	The scientific method and economic theory	Political, religious or secular ideologies

Table 6.3 *(continued)*

TITLE	TRADITIONAL Classical humanism (Skilbeck, Lawton) Cultural transmission (Bottery)	PROGRESSIVE (Skilbeck, Lawton) Child-centred (Bottery)	RECONSTRUCTIONIST (Skilbeck, Lawton) Social reconstruction (Bottery)	TECHNOLOGICAL GNP (Gross National Product) (Bottery)	SYNERGISTIC (Clark) Community curriculum
VALUES	Obedience/duty Respect 'Manliness' Loyalty	Autonomy Spontaneity Enthusiasm Creativity	Vision Critical awareness Commitment	Self-sufficiency Enterprise Efficiency Competence	Life, liberty, love= inclusivity and openness = the common good
FEELING	Solidarity (national/cultural)	Significance (personal)	Solidarity (class, race, gender, party)	Significance Security (individual)	Solidarity Significance Security (social systems)
ATTITUDE TO CULTURE	Approve	Detached	Critical	Accepted	Openness/ inclusivity
NATURE OF CHANGE	Maturation	Development	Revolution	Production	Transformation
PEDA-GOGIC MODEL	Instruction	Nurture	Education	Training	**Education**
ROLE OF STATE	Guardian of the tradition	To live and let live	Upholder of social justice	Protector of rights and property	Works for subsidiarity

The code is entitled 'synergistic' (see pp. 47–50) because at its heart lies a common quest for a richer experience of community by two or more social systems working together in partnership. The outcome of this corporate quest will be greater than the sum of the parts (Willie and Hodgson, 1991, pp. 164–6).

Basic construct

The synergistic code's basic construct is 'community', as defined in Chapter 3. The social systems concerned are not engaged in a superficial undertaking to enhance their own well-being, but in a deeply demanding process which is ultimately about the creation and sustainability of one world.

Task

The task for this code is the creation of learning communities. It requires a synthesis of our communal and educational tasks. It involves learning to create a stronger sense of community within and across social systems. The guidelines for this task are set out in Chapter 5.

Participants

The participants are social systems as partners in learning. These systems may be very small, but the emphasis is on the collective not persons as such. The systems are partners in learning, engaged in a shared endeavour at the heart of which lies the search for new forms and expressions of what it means to be a community.

Curriculum content

The curriculum content for this code has two main features. On the one hand, it is about those communal skills which enable students to understand and acquire the abilities needed to translate the concept of community from ideal to reality. On the other, it embraces those aspects of the human sciences which provide knowledge and insights into the nature of society and culture, how the latter maintain themselves and how they change.

Beliefs – locus of authority

The beliefs which give authority to this code are those which promote the common good.

Values

The code's values, as defined in Chapter 3, can be described as life, liberty and love, but exercised in an inclusive not exclusive manner. The three 'L's are for each and all.

Communal inclusivity is reflected in and enhanced by education's commitment to openness.

Feelings

The feelings which empower and energize this code are a sense of security, significance and solidarity. The other codes distort the meaning of community by focusing predominantly on one or other of the three 'S's. Although we see solidarity as the most important, the synergistic code encompasses all three. Feeling is especially prominent in this code. Community is a passionate concept and community education is a passionate affair.

Attitude to culture

The synergistic code's relation to culture is also one of openness and inclusivity. The code encourages social systems to value their cultural identity, but regards an openness to engage with, learn from and assimilate aspects of other cultures as a vital characteristic of a community curriculum.

Nature of change

The nature of change most conspicuous within this code is transformation. Revolution (characteristic of the reconstructionist code) is concerned first with destruction and only after that with (possible) transformation, although the old often reappears with depressing regularity. The synergistic code is primarily about recreation not annihilation. It is concerned far more with the coming of a new order than with the deliberate destruction of the old.

Pedagogic model

The pedagogic model which stresses the synergistic code is that which we have defined as education (see Table 6.1). *All aspects of this model should be seen as integral to the synergistic code and fundamental to its effective operationalization.*

Role of the state

Finally, the role of the state in this code can best be described as espousing the principle of 'subsidiarity', that which 'allows as much liberty as possible and as much association as necessary' (Stamp, 1992). Stamp, however, adds the qualification that 'subsidiarity carries with it an obligation to solidarity' with other social systems.

BEYOND THE CURRICULUM

Community education begins with the curriculum. It is there that the education of the hearts and minds of students is explicitly focused. If the curriculum is ignored or neglected, community education may as well pack its bags and settle for the modest advances it has so far achieved. Some other formula will have to be devised to transform schools into genuine learning communities.

Yet even if community education grasps the nettle of the community curriculum, it is only a beginning. What starts with the curriculum cannot end there. The community curriculum may be the initial focus of community education. But the community curriculum, the synergistic code, requires a learning community, such as a community school, to foster, develop and sustain it. The community school, in turn, requires other agencies and organizations to work alongside it as related learning communities if the synergistic code is to reach its full potential. And beyond these systems lies the need for the communal local authority and communal state to ensure that medium and message support and energize one another. The concept of the learning community refers not only to the class or the school but to what each sector and every society must become if that global community of communities which we urgently require is to become a reality.

We consider this wider scenario in Chapters 9 and 10. First, we look more closely at some of the skills required by the community educator, not least within the school context, in order to put the synergistic code into operation.

Chapter 7

The Community Educator*

'A NEW WAY OF WORKING'

The community educator is an agent of social change because all involved in education are change agents. 'Theories of learning [are] also ... theories of changing' (Handy, 1990, p. 44). But community educators are more than educators; they are *community* educators. They are about the radical transformation of the education system itself so that all schools become learning communities, and in that process give impetus to the communal transformation of both society and world.

All 'teaching requires intervention' (Toogood, 1984, p. 243). The authority of the teacher to intervene lies in the need to socialize all children into a culture where they can find identity and meaning, to offer them the opportunity for personal fulfilment and to equip them to meet the needs of the society of which they are a part. But for community educators, authority to intervene lies deeper. It rests on an ultimate responsibility for the survival of humankind on the one hand, and for enhancing the global quality of life on the other. Whether this responsibility is exercised on a small or large stage does not detract from its profound significance.

Because the role of the community educator is about the transformation of pupil, school, society and ultimately world, it requires very careful delineation, considerable skill and continuous development. It is the nature of this role that forms the substance of this and parts of the subsequent two chapters.

We define the task of the *community educator* as follows:

To create an increasingly strong sense of security, significance and solidarity within and across social systems through the learning process.

or more succinctly:

To create learning communities.

The community educator seeks to weave the community education process into the focal

---

*In this and subsequent chapters, the terms 'education' and 'learning process' refer to the pedagogic model outlined in Chapter 6 and set out in Table 6.1. The terms 'community education' and 'community educator' henceforth also embrace 'education' and 'the learning process' as defined in Chapter 6.

task. In schools, he may himself be directly involved in teaching subjects from maths to English, history to PE. Our concern here, however, is not so much with content or even the particular teaching methods traditionally associated with such subjects, but with how the community education process can be integrated into the focal task (in this case the teaching of the subject concerned). The teacher as community educator will seek to achieve the focal task through the medium of the communal and educational guidelines outlined in Chapters 5 and 6.

The community educator is always an educator. This apparently tautological statement needs to be made because history has seen the role of the community educator diverted into a host of other functions and responsibilities. The list of titles often used illustrates the point. Not only have the terms 'community teacher' and 'community tutor' been used, but 'community director', 'community education service officer', 'community education development officer', 'home–school liaison teacher', 'home link teacher', 'community organizer' and so forth. In these various contexts, the community educator's role has taken on aspects of supply teaching, adult education (especially teaching English as a second language), promoting a diversity of links between schools and parents, as well as counselling and pastoral work, youth work, organizing social and leisure events, and site (or room) management. It is not in question that some of these responsibilities can be the vehicle of community education proper. But this can only happen when the learning process and the community curriculum underpin the focal task concerned. Community education has in the past lost its way and been deemed at best optional for – and at worst irrelevant to – education, simply because it has taken on a host of diversionary tasks.

If community education had moved to the centre of the educational stage, instead of into the wings, a very different scenario would now be before us. For every teacher should be a community educator. As Ford *et al.* (1992, p. 60) state: 'Building a sense of community is not an "add-on" to what busy teachers are expected to do. Teachers do create a classroom environment – it is a matter of how consciously they build in the positive features that result in "community".' The synergistic code is of fundamental importance for all teachers and all schools. Education cannot be transformed and become transforming without it.

The teacher as community educator must be engaged in what the Birmingham Community Curriculum Project termed 'a new way of working' (Clark, 1990, pp. 77–8). Handy and Aitken (1986, p. 125) describe this as a role change 'to more that of agent than expert, to counsellor and facilitator, manager of learning situations, co-ordinator of projects, team leader or network resource', although we would want to ensure that education itself was at the heart of all these functions. What is clear is that this new way of working requires not less but a great deal more insight, skill and experience than is currently evident within the education system, and that teachers will need to extend considerably the professional boundaries of their present narrowly conceived role.

All teachers should be community educators. But community education must not be confined to the classroom. Community education depends on schools as a whole becoming learning communities, and on staff with a particular brief to help them do so. The quality of schools as learning communities depends on the head and the caretaker, the deputy head and the school secretary, as much as the teachers. It also depends on some staff being assigned the synergistic responsibility of linking the school to the wider world, be that of parents or business, of health workers or the police, of environmental agencies or religious bodies.

If all teachers should be community educators, so too should all learners. This is of necessity a developmental matter, older children being able to articulate and own the role in a more mature way. But community education is not just for the professionals. 'It is crucial', write Stainback and Stainback (1992, p. 12), 'that the classroom teacher serves as a role model for the students by welcoming every child and including every child in social interactions and classroom activities.' Community education is a skill that each learner, as well as teacher, must come to appreciate, own and themselves practise if our world is to meet the formidable challenges of the coming century.

PREPARING TO INTERVENE

Connecting and resource systems

A major 'weakness of research on collaborative grouping is that it offers very little guidance to teachers about their role in the process' write Galton and Williamson (1992. p. 44) in their review *Group Work in the Primary Classroom*. It is little wonder, therefore, that the role of the community educator is even more poorly documented. What follows is an initial attempt to outline the key features of this role.

The community educator is essentially 'a boundary manager' (Morgan, 1986, pp. 169–70). It is a role attracting increasing attention across many sectors. Willie and Hodgson (1991, p. 7) in describing the world of business speak of 'people-linkers', and Boswell (1990, p. 130), in the context of 'sectional organisations, public opinion and government', talks about 'para-intermediaries'. In relation to community education, the role is one of resourcing and linking social systems in a way which strengthens the sense of community within and across them. In this context, the community educator can be regarded as a *connecting system*, with special responsibility for making the synergistic code a reality (Fig. 7.1).

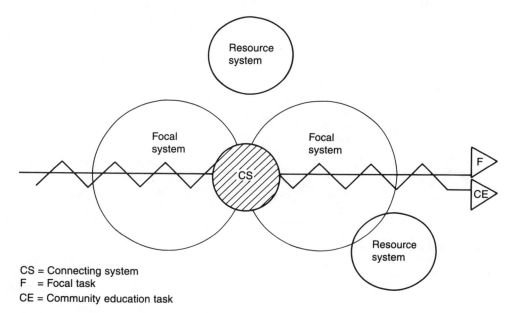

CS = Connecting system
F = Focal task
CE = Community education task

Figure 7.1   *The various systems*

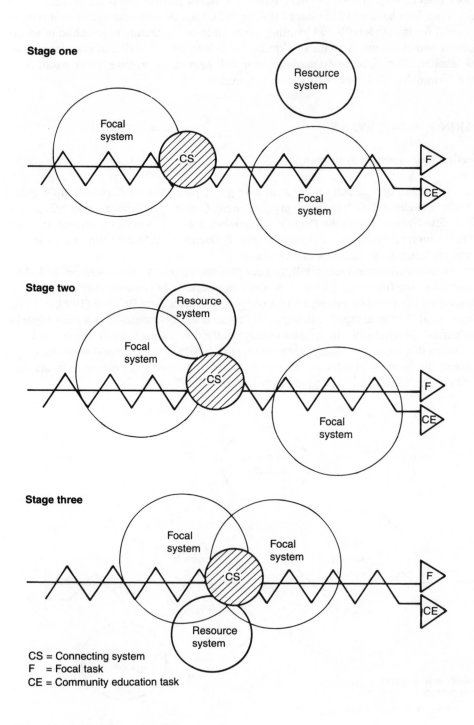

Figure 7.2 *A possible community education programme*

One other system, which we call a *resource system* (Fig. 7.1) needs to be added to our model at this point. Resource systems are social systems which offer assistance or support to focal systems, but which we do not operate with the focal task as their major concern. If the latter dwindles in importance or is not achieved, this has relatively little impact on a resource system as such. The changing relationship of the social systems involved in a possible community education programme are depicted in Fig. 7.2.

Focal systems and the focal task

The community educator, in his role as integrator of the community education and the focal tasks, has at his disposal the guidelines set out in Chapters 5 and 6. But first he must be quite clear which are the focal systems and what is the focal task with which he is primarily concerned. This is something of a chicken and egg problem. Sometimes the focal systems are the prior concern. For example, a secondary teacher wishes to twin her class of white suburban children with a multi-ethnic class in an inner city school (two focal systems) so decides on a joint writing project (focal task) to facilitate this. Sometimes the focal task is to the fore. For example, a primary head teacher wishes to raise the awareness of children to environmental issues (focal task) so sets up a morning during which every class (focal systems) shares in a green campus project. At other times, it is hard to know which is the prior concern, the focal systems or the focal task, as both are so interdependent. Nonetheless, it remains essential that the community educator is clear about which are the focal systems and what is the focal task for which he is responsible, or confusion will reign when any attempt is made to apply the guidelines.

Teachers often argue that they cannot link social systems simply because they have only one system to deal with (such as a particular class scheduled for a particular time of day). This could be true. But there is often a failure to recognize that it is frequently neither necessary nor helpful for the teacher to 'construct' his class as a single system. There are always many 'subsystems' within it which focus on gender, race, ability, seating prefer-ences or simply personal affinity. It is as important that these subsystems discover how to become learning communities, across as well as within normative boundaries, as it is that the whole class opens up to other systems.

The task of transforming such subsystems into learning communities is a vital contribu-tion to the task of developing larger learning communities within the education system, and indeed beyond. It also shows that teachers can operate as fully fledged community educators with groups of any size involved in any aspect of the learning process.

From guidelines to gateways

Once the focal systems and focal task have been clearly identified, the communal and educational guidelines can be used to offer both an indication of the strength of the three 'S's present within and/or across the systems involved, and of the quality of the learning process. The guidelines thus become gateways to intervention and action for change.

The time chosen for such an assessment depends on the use to which it is to be put. It is sometimes helpful to go back in time and apply the guidelines to a past situation so that any future attempt to develop an educational approach can be built on sounder foundations. Or an assessment of an ongoing exercise or project might be useful to discover where a hand on the tiller could assist the community education process. It is important, however, that the community educator is clear about the time at which such an assessment is made and realizes this will apply to that time alone, social systems always being in a state of flux.

The guidelines are primarily gateways for intervention. They are meant to reveal where systems are communally and/or educationally weakest and thus where intervention is most likely to improve matters. More research is needed. But for the moment they offer the best means we have of clarifying where and how to intervene most effectively to create and sustain learning communities.

'Symbolic universes'

To educate for an increasingly strong sense of security, significance and solidarity within and across social systems is a difficult undertaking. It means so 'reconstructing' the connections between systems that a deeper and broader experience of community, a 'reconstructed' experience, emerges.

The process is an ongoing and developmental one, in that a reconstructed 'subjective' experience of community (feeling, values and beliefs) will in turn impact upon and help to reshape the more 'objective' segments of the social system (relationships, interaction, the environment, people and the focal task). Likewise, we can assume that changes in the more 'subjective' segments of the system will bring about changes in the more 'objective' segments. Does this process give us any clue as to where community educators can make their most effective interventions in order to create learning communities? In short, are certain communal guidelines more important than others in helping to effect communal change?

Berger and Luckmann (1984), two leading exponents of the power of experience and perception to 'construct' and 'reconstruct social reality', and thus social systems, have brought to the fore the importance of what they term 'symbolic universes' (such as political or religious cultures) which give overall meaning and direction to human affairs (see pp. 79–80). Symbolic universes are themselves gradually 'constructed' from the moment of our conception onwards. This process (adapting Berger and Luckmann) is depicted in Fig. 7.3. Individuals as they develop participate in these stages in an ever fuller way gradually 'constructing' their symbolic universes *en route*. From this figure, it will be seen that change within the whole social system will occur (in theory at least) whenever change takes place in any segment of it.

The work of Berger and Luckmann is particularly important for the community educator for two reasons. First, they show how vital a role symbolic universes play in helping us 'construct' or 'reconstruct' the nature of our social systems. In the context of community education, this underlines the importance of our three 'S's, as well as those values and beliefs underpinning them, not least inclusivity and openness, in bringing about communal change. Second, the authors offer a 'best buy' checklist for catalysing communal change. They indicate that for community development to be a genuinely educational affair, change must eventually occur in the symbolic universe or universes which shape and guide the life of the systems concerned. Thus community educators must have the influencing of values and beliefs, in a way which make them increasingly supportive of the communal task, as a major concern.

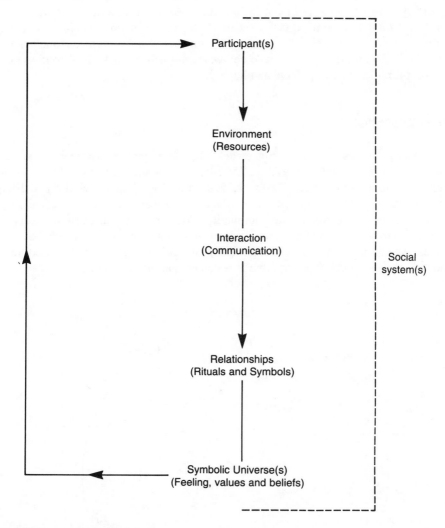

Figure 7.3   *Reconstructing social systems*

But here there is a problem. For values and beliefs are, of all features of the social system, most resistant to change. Thus the 'reconstruction of reality' as a communal phenomenon will usually have to begin within more malleable segments of the social system, such as the environment or interaction. On the other hand, never to take risks is to plan for failure. No social system is going to opt for inclusivity and openness if community educators always play safe. All change is disturbing; communal change is especially disturbing because, in time, it must involve our symbolic universes. Thus, to go through gateways – which offer some hope of the reconstruction of values and beliefs as well as feeling – is essential for genuine community education.

Other concerns will guide the nature of intervention chosen, from a system's internal 'readiness' to the many external constraints. All systems are part of much wider networks of systems. Though here we have concentrated on focal systems, resource systems and connecting systems, these do not exist in splendid isolation from a range of other systems which are uninvolved in the focal task as such but can have a major influence on its attainment. In this sense, every situation and every intervention is unique. Nonetheless our guidelines, along with other points made below, should help to make intervention rational and purposeful rather than impulsive and haphazard.

THE INTERVENTION CYCLE

There are many models which attempt to describe the educational process as such. For example, Kolb (1984), Lawton (1973, p. 15; 1983, p. 16) and Handy (1990, p. 46) focus more on a learning cycle; Tyler (Skilbeck, 1984, pp. 40–5), and Nicholls and Nicholls (1978) focus more on a teaching cycle. Our concern, however, is also a communal one, and is related primarily to the role of the community educator. Thus our cycle of intervention (Fig. 7.4) seeks to combine features directly relevant to both our communal and educational tasks. The cycle may relate to how a community curriculum is set up and carried through, or to how an already existing programme is reshaped and redeveloped.

Figure 7.4   *The intervention cycle: the ten 'A's.*

All our communal and educational guidelines (and gateways) are potentially relevant to each stage of the intervention cycle (Fig. 7.4). *The overall purpose of the cycle is to enhance the three 'S's within and across social systems through the learning process.* At each stage of the cycle, one or more of the guidelines may have particular relevance for intervention. But it remains essential to keep all guidelines in mind throughout the whole cycle.

Intervention can be said to begin with making approaches and works clockwise round the circle, although with an ongoing curriculum the community educator can intervene at any stage. It should be noted that facilitating action and working for attainment are here placed relatively late in the cycle. This is because proper preparation for action is as important as action itself. In Fig. 7.4, the objectives of intervention are portrayed as discrete. In practice, some, such as enhancing authority, continue throughout most of the cycle and will need to be returned to at appropriate times. Likewise undertaking appraisal may well begin early in some cycles.

Making approaches

The community educator's approach to potential participants in the community education process is a vital first stage. Initial intervention may be guided by either the nature of the focal task (with social systems 'recruited' accordingly), or by the social systems it is intended to involve (with the focal task defined appropriately). The decision about where to commence the cycle will depend on a range of factors, including how important it is to connect certain systems, the flexibility of the focal task, the availability of resource systems and so on.

Whatever factors determine who is to be involved, the first contacts with participants must be made with care and sensitivity. This requires that the community educator finds out as much as possible about the focal systems which are to engage with each other. This may well mean some form of preliminary audit, touching on the segments of the social system to which the guidelines will later be applied. Thus, to help ascertain the systems' communal strength, the community educator would want to discover data about:

- the participants (number, age, sex, ethnic origins, etc.);
- the nature of the focal task;
- the environment;
- their activities (particularly related to the focal task);
- their relationships (including their rituals and symbols);
- their values and beliefs.

The approach stage of the intervention cycle should be both gradual and 'reflective'. It is about building up the community educator's credibility and trustworthiness with those involved. Thus it is concerned a great deal more with listening and learning than offering opinions and making judgements. At the same time, the community educator is seeking to clarify the focal task to be addressed and the focal (and resource) systems which will be involved.

Forming alliances

This task is at the very heart of the community education process: educating for community across as well as within social systems (see, in particular, our communal guidelines relating to people, and educational guidelines relating to leadership). The forming and development of alliances or partnerships will ideally have their origins in the approach stage and continue through to the appraisal stage.

The community educator's task is to enable focal systems to engage around two tasks. The focal task will usually be the manifest task for, unless this is clear and agreed, little work can be done together. Strong alliances depend on the identification of a shared focal task that can command commitment and energy. At the same time, the community education task must be interwoven with the focal task to help to transform social systems into learning communities. An important aspect of the community educator's skill is in the choice of systems which might engage in developing effective alliances as focal (or resource) systems. This is where the quality of any preliminary audit will come to the fore, as well as the community educator's ability to espouse 'the art of the possible'.

Giving affirmation

A key responsibility of the community educator is to affirm the human worth of all those who may be engaged in the community education process. Handy (1990, p. 184) calls this offering 'unconditioned positive regard' for the individual, and Harrison (1987) speaks of it as 'releasing love in the workplace'. It is a matter closely associated with person-centred learning. Community educators need to take the experiences, skills, and values of those with whom they are involved, whatever their gender, age, educational background, class culture, as seriously as they take their own. Unless this occurs, genuine community education, which as Alter and Hage argue (1993, p. 16f) is all about building 'a culture of trust', will not even begin.

Affirmation does not mean sentimental or vague gestures of goodwill. It means a practical and positive attitude towards the value and human potential of each person or system, and the ability to communicate this without condescension or paternalism (or maternalism). In particular, as our communal guidelines relating to people stress, affirmation must be given to those undervalued by society, the physically weak, the unemployed, the poor and the socially marginalized.

Affirmation of this kind is an art which has to be learnt and practised. It is founded on an empathy with others which is not picked up from textbooks (this one included!). It arises out of a genuine concern for others based on the communal values of life, liberty and love in pursuit of the common good. It is essential for any learning process at whose heart is life and the person.

Enhancing authority

This stage of the community education process is often described as 'empowerment'. However, there is often considerable confusion as to what sort of 'power' empowerment is referring.

Our view is that authority frequently encompasses power but is not dependent on it. Power comes from those impersonal and 'external' means of influence which an individual possesses – wealth, status, information, etc. Authority has two sources:

● it comes from an individual's view of his or her own human worth; and

● it is ascribed to an individual in so far as his or her human worth is affirmed by others.

Thus the person who is an able organizer, competent cricketer, teller of funny stories, caring friend or good mother may have little power but considerable authority.

The task of the community educator is to help to strengthen the authority of all individuals and systems in ways which encourage them to take increasing responsibility for their own lives and for their contribution to the welfare of others. Such authority is closely related to our pedagogic model's categories of choice and leadership. It is enhanced by many of our communal guidelines concerned with relationships. Enhancing authority involves weaning participants away from self-centredness and over-dependence on others (including the community educator) in order that they themselves can help facilitate a more dynamic experience of community for those involved in the learning process (the shift from A to B in Fig. 7.5). In some cases, this task may involve the community educator encouraging people to assume power as well as (but hopefully not in place of) authority.

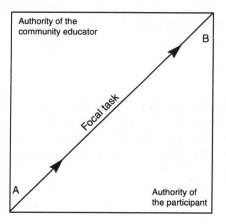

Figure 7.5 *Enhancing authority*

Negotiating agreement

If giving affirmation is about 'a culture of trust', negotiating agreement is about 'a culture of consent' (Handy, 1990, p. 128f). As Bottery (1990, p. 124) puts it: 'The development of education ... is dependent upon the interaction and negotiated agreement between teacher and pupil.'

We have already stressed the vital importance of negotiation and agreement in presenting and implementing the community education process, especially with respect to our guidelines. Negotiation has to be undertaken with all parties concerned (including all pupils if of an age to make this possible). Agreement may take diverse forms. Some kind of formal or informal 'contract' (Meighan, 1988, pp. 45–8) is often involved. What is essential is that such a contract is public, clear and open to renegotiation.

Exploring alternatives

The community educator's art is to be imaginative and enterprising in pursuit of the most effective means of communal and educational change. Our range of guidelines are intended to assist the process. They are meant to alert the community educator to potential entry points for effective intervention. They also offer a wide choice of gateways through which he or she can go to address the communal task. Exploring alternatives is also a key aspect of the learning process, with morality encouraging the questioning of values, rationality the questioning of evidence, and the whole being a journey of discovery.

Effective community education will depend not only on the community educator examining alternatives as fully as possible, but having the 'flair' to grasp which has most chance of opening the way to communal and educational development in the particular circumstances encountered.

Imaginative alternatives need to be sought not only at this stage but throughout the intervention cycle, not least in relation to the access and action stages below. Novelty and surprise can often jolt systems out of a rut and enable participants to glimpse wider horizons so important for stimulating excitement and fostering motivation. 'Discontinuity', writes Handy (1990, p. 44), 'is a great learning experience.'

Providing access

Here, access refers to the community educator's role of ensuring that adequate resources are available to the focal systems in their pursuit of the focal as well as community education task. The community educator, defined by Stainback and Stainback (1992, p. 15) as a 'resource locator', will be concerned to widen access to resources such as:

- relevant information
- plant and equipment
- transport
- useful skills and expertise
- training
- financial support.

This stage will involve the community educator in:

- identifying the resources required
- locating where they can be provided, and
- furthering their use in a way which fosters community education.

At this stage of the intervention cycle, resource systems come to the fore. The community educator's skill is to be able to locate and enlist the help of those resource systems which have a real contribution to make to the focal systems involved.

This stage of the cycle relates closely to our communal guidelines concerned with the environment and resources, and to aspects of the content and leadership categories of the learning process.

Facilitating action

That seven stages of the cycle should have been outlined before we come to action may seem to unbalance the whole intervention process. In fact, preparation and planning for community education are so vital that effective action will largely depend on them. Action focuses on systems working in partnership to accomplish the focal task. Here, that task comes very much to the fore, underpinned by a synthesis of our communal and educational guidelines.

All our communal guidelines and every aspect of our pedagogic model may be relevant to the action stage of the intervention cycle.

Working for attainment

The community educator is concerned not only with action but the successful attainment of the focal, the educational and the communal tasks. Focal tasks should be realistic as well as challenging. What may be termed 'a philosophy of little leaps' is called for; a series of clearly delineated and short-term focal tasks can, in the long run, often achieve more than a single grandiose plan or programme.

Undertaking appraisal

There are many theories of educational assessment (Meighan, 1988, pp. 8–9, 43–4; Kelly, 1982, pp. 148–73). Our concern, however, is with the effectiveness of the community education process. Such an appraisal focuses on four main questions:

1. Have the communal and educational guidelines been effectively applied?
2. Has effective application of the guidelines resulted in:
   - a stronger sense of security, significance and/or solidarity within and across systems (the communal task), and
   - a learning process which has become more educational (the educational task)?
3. Has the focal task been (more effectively) achieved?
4. Have learning communities been created and/or developed?

Question 1 relates to whether or not the communal and educational guidelines have been effectively implemented. Judgement on this could be by an external assessor, but is likely to be more accurate if both the participants and community educator are fully involved. If the response is negative, all concerned need to explore how things can be improved next time around. As the guidelines cover a wide field, additional expertise and resources may need to be sought from a diversity of sources, with the resource systems being the first port of call.

If the answer to Question 2 is positive, then the accuracy of the correlation between the communal guidelines and the three 'S's discussed in Chapter 5, and the educational guidelines and the educational task discussed in Chapter 6, is strengthened. If not, then the linkage will need to be examined further and the guideline(s) possibly adapted or changed.

In response to Question 3, if a more effective focal task performance (in comparison with previous performances) has been achieved, then our claim that community education enhances task attainment will be enhanced.

If performance has not improved then we must go back to the drawing board. We will need to research more fully the extent to which our three 'S's (and their communal guidelines) and our educational model (and its educational guidelines) do or do not lead to a more effective focal task performance.

For Question 4, if the appraisal of Questions 1, 2 and 3 is positive then learning communities will have been created and/or developed.

ATTRIBUTES AND SKILLS OF THE COMMUNITY EDUCATOR

The community educator is a person of many parts. Below we outline the more important attributes and skills needed. We do little more than list these for two reasons: first, space only allows a profile of what is in reality a multi-faceted role; and second, an extensive literature already exists in terms of many of the 'tools for the job'. Our concern in this chapter has been to clarify 'the job' rather than to offer a detailed description of the tools, and the skills needed to use them effectively.

Personal attributes

At the risk of simplistic generalization, the following qualities of a more personal kind can be very important for those seeking to fulfil the role of a community educator.

- *Wisdom*–the ability to discern and articulate the fundamental connectedness and interrelatedness of the universe.
- *Vision*–a conviction that the growth of learning communities is an essential requirement for the survival and well-being of humankind.
- *Enthusiasm*–excitement and energy flowing from this vision and the desire to communicate it.
- *Love*–the ability to exemplify love as a core value at the heart of community education, and in particular, the capacity to care for human beings as persons, each of unique worth and irreplaceable.
- *Empathy*–the capacity to see life from others' perspective and feel as others feel.
- *Imagination*–an openness to lateral or 'double loop' (and 'treble loop') thinking, and to the radical alternatives for action deriving from this.
- *Courage*–a readiness to enter into situations of hostility and conflict in order to overcome barriers to cross-system engagement, and to establish new and creative connections.
- *Determination*–the patience and perseverance to press on when no doors seem to be opening, or others shut.

Knowledge and insight

Knowledge permeates personal attributes and operational skills. But it can be particularly helpful if the community educator has knowledge and insight relating to three key aspects of his or her role.

Construct theory

- How individuals and social systems 'construct' and 'reconstruct' what for them is 'real', and thus becomes an integral part of their experience.
- How such 'constructs' shape their attitudes and behaviour (Bannister and Fransella, 1986; Berger and Luckmann, 1984).

Symbols and rituals

- The key function of symbols and rituals in promoting (or preventing) the development of community (Berger and Luckmann, 1984; Cohen, 1985).

Social change

- The basic theories and operational approaches to social change, in particular the nature of conflict and conflict resolution.

Operational skills

Below we list, again in brief, some key operational skills required by the community educator. The list is by no means definitive.

- *Pedagogic*–the ability to teach well in terms of both the content and methodology of the particular subject or skill concerned, but above all the ability to practise as an educator as defined in Chapter 6.
- *Participant observation*–the ability to observe with both empathy and objectivity while remaining actively involved in the community education process.
- *Auditing*–the ability to gather, store and retrieve valid, relevant and adequate data to accomplish the focal, communal and educational tasks.
- *Communication*–this is a core skill: the ability to communicate with people in a direct, open and non-manipulative manner, and to enable them to do likewise. (The work of Argyris and Schön (1974) and of Schön (1983; 1988) is especially important here.)
- *Negotiation*–the skills required to engage in genuine and purposeful dialogue with a variety of individuals and social systems, including skills of mediation and conflict resolution.
- *Group work*–the skills to develop small social systems as learning communities. Particularly important here are knowledge and skills in relation to the main stages of group development (Benson, 1987).
- *Networking*–the ability to create and sustain a web of links between individuals and across social systems. This will be a major area of skill development for community educators in the future and, consequently, we return to networking and alliance building in Chapter 9.
- *Management*–the ability to guide, oversee and resource programmes of community

education in a variety of sometimes complex situations. We look at this matter on a school-wide scale in Chapter 8.

'A NEW KIND OF PROFESSIONAL'

If community education is 'a new way of working', the community educator is 'a new kind of professional'. The community educator works on the boundaries between systems, small and large, seeking to create and develop learning communities. As such, he or she requires a 'multiplex nationality'. The community educator must be a competent and experienced educator, simply because one of his or her concerns is to ensure that the focal task as such (embracing anything from National Curriculum maths to cross-curricular health education) is effectively addressed. But the community educator also needs the skills of the community educator to ensure that into the performance of the focal task are woven our communal and educational guidelines.

The role of the community educator as 'boundary manager' is a demanding one. The skills required cannot simply be acquired as and when time allows. They need to be clearly identified and preparation for their use built into the training of all teachers. This will mean a thorough review of approaches to and training for work in the classroom (so far as education remains focused therein), as well as new courses to equip this new kind of professional.

The role of the community educator beyond the classroom is an even more challenging one. It is clear that at the level of year, department or school management, where the full range of attributes and skills listed above will be in considerable demand, no single individual can be equipped to deliver the 'ideal type' role on which this chapter has been based. The response to this situation – indeed, the proper response in accord with the principles of community education – is the team approach.

This accords with the fact that community education is a collective undertaking. Connecting up systems should be the task of teams with a range of skills and abilities. In this chapter, we have explored the role of the community educator largely in the singular. In practice, however, it is a role requiring a wide range of skills which needs to be the responsibility of trained teams with a diversity of experience and expertise.

The next two chapters examine the phenomenon of the whole school as a learning community, and the role of community educator in that broader context.

Chapter 8

The School as a Learning Community

THE MICRO AND THE MACRO

Within

'Organisations are nothing if they are not communities of people', writes Handy (1994, p. 152). We would add that organizations are nothing unless they are learning communities, the culture of which is determined by the nature of the curriculum code which they espouse. From our perspective, it is operating on the foundation of the synergistic code (as defined in Chapter 6) which makes the learning community what it is.

Learning communities are at the heart of a learning society. And learning societies are what we now need to equip ourselves to face the demands of the century on the horizon. The changing and challenging nature of the new era into which all of us are now being plunged will require nothing less than what the world of business and commerce, so often at the sharp end of what is going on, terms 'continuous transformation' (Willie and Hodgson, 1991, p. 168); the transformation of our multitudinous and often waning social systems into learning communities, and in furtherance of that goal, the transformation of education itself. As Pedler *et al.* (1991, p. 2) put it: 'The key word is "transformation" – a radical change in the form and character of what is already there.'

Of all those institutions which need to play a lead role in such transformation, the school is pivotal. Its influence on the up and coming generation, despite all the qualifications about the conditioning power of the home and neighbourhood, and its ubiquitous nature, give it a critical part to play in 'the survival of the species'. The school has two key functions in this context. First, it should be a role model for the learning community. If it fails here what hope is there for all those other institutions whose focal task is not an educational one? Second, it must be a catalyst for change. 'Transforming education' means not only the transformation of education itself, but an education system which can transform other systems into learning communities.

So far, much of our attention has been focused on small-scale systems and the role of the community educator in relation to them. This has been a necessary exploration as the class, or its equivalent, is itself a model of and catalyst for the learning community. As Handy and

Aitken (1986, p. 14) put it: 'Each class is but a mini-society within the larger society of the whole school.' If the class fails to embrace the synergistic code and to develop as a mini learning community, there is no hope of the school itself becoming a macro learning community.

The school as an entity, therefore, needs to affirm and nurture its mini learning communities. The parts are precious for the whole. Pedler *et al.* (1991, p. 114) put the same point from the perspective of a necessary diversity: 'The whole cannot be enhanced without first splitting; division is needed before greater synthesis and synergy can be brought about; learning begins in difference.'

A first priority for school management, therefore, is to give explicit attention to fostering these diverse mini communities which go to enrich the whole. This task relates first and foremost to the school class. But much more attention needs to be given to the effect of class size on its communal, and hence, educational development, on adult (the teacher plus other adults working in the class)–pupil relationship, and the quality of the links between mini communities of pupils within the class itself. A second priority is for management to ensure that these mini communities connect up in a way that brings about a 'greater synthesis and synergy'. As Handy (1984, p. 29) observes: 'The potential danger for schools lies in the privacy of the classroom'. If either curriculum or class remain a 'secret garden', then the potential of the part is lost to the whole.

A major issue in this context is how large and complex a school can become before synergy becomes synthetic. This is more of a problem for secondary than primary schools, but the latter cannot ignore the issue. One possible way forward is the creation of mini-schools, as Handy (1990, p. 39) suggests, based on age or specialisms, or as Toogood (1984, p. 246) conceives them, all age small schools forming 'a federation of learning communities'.

'The small school' as such is not an uncommon phenomenon, many being described in the 'Penguin Specials' of the late 1960s and early 1970s and, more recently, by Toogood (1991). But, it is creating 'a city of villages' (Handy 1984, p. 40), and an appropriate balance between the authority of the centre, and the autonomy yet dovetailing of the component parts, which is the real challenge.

Highly pertinent to the development of the whole school as a learning community is how disadvantaged systems, which often cross the mini communities of learning on which we have so far focused, can be treated both justly and with integrity. Davies (1994, pp. 41–6) calls this the search for 'equity' – not just 'equal opportunities' but 'equalising rights'. It is an issue, as she notes (p. 43), which 'has widened from a primary concern with race and gender to include such possible areas for disadvantage as disability, sexuality, mature students, and re-entrants to teaching'. Thus the search for 'greater synthesis and synergy' is not simply about feeling, a stronger sense of security, significance and solidarity within and across systems – though it is certainly that – but a search for inclusivity, and the values of life, liberty and love which sustain it.

Without

There is more to the school as a learning community than pupils, teachers and ancillary staff. There are governors and parents. If in business, as Willie and Hodgson argue (1991, p. 168), 'the learning culture [should] also [be] extended to all stake holders', how much more important is it for schools to do likewise. And beyond these groupings lie other 'resource systems' of diverse kinds – industries, libraries, health education services, youth organizations, religious bodies, parks and leisure associations to name but a few, all of which have a part to play in that learning culture, that synergistic code, if the school is to reach its full potential as a learning community. To the nature and form of these partnerships we shall return in Chapter 9.

The 'spirituality' of interrelatedness

The school which becomes a genuine learning community is a social system embracing a wide diversity of other learning communities within and without. But, as Beare *et al.* (1989, p. 193) put it: 'It is the pattern rather than the individual pieces which reveals the picture.' Pedler *et al.* (1991, pp. 6–17) speak about 'learning companies' developing from a pioneer, through a differentiated, then an integrated, to what they term a 'spiritual' phase. This resonates with what we have called in Chapter 3, 'community as spirit'.

Schools which discover the spiritual dimension of being a learning community are aware not only of the dynamic interrelatedness of their own reality but of all reality. They recognize not only their own role as models and catalysts in helping to transform other systems into learning communities, but their indebtedness to those learning communities which are in turn helping to transform schools. The consequence should be that schools become suffused not with pride and pomposity but with humility and awe at their pivotal role within and on behalf of humankind.

MODELS OF MANAGEMENT

Each learning community is unique. The school is no exception. Its 'integrative awareness' (Hawkins, 1991, p. 184) may enable it to gain inspiration as part of the wider world, but each school lives and constructs its own bit of reality. Each has its own special context and culture, otherwise its contribution to the whole would be of relatively minimal significance.

Nevertheless, all schools should share a common educational task which we have defined as 'learning to learn'. Thus it is an asset that a literature has emerged, now very large, on the management of schools as organizations. This literature offers many helpful insights, not least to head teachers, about how to put principles into practice. Our question, however, is which of the many management models now on offer is of most use to schools envisioned as learning communities?

The language of management

'Educational management is not a discipline, but a collection of languages, a collection of different ways of seeing ... Before managing schools in particular directions, one has to manage meaning' (Davies, 1994, p. 5). Thus in looking for insights from the field of management which are congruent with the school as a learning community, it is important to try to clarify the values and beliefs on which they are based. Indeed, management theories which appear the most 'neutral' are often those most vulnerable to manipulation by hidden ideological agendas.

One way to ascertain the nature of core values and beliefs underpinning such theories is through focusing on what Beare *et al.* (1989, p. 64) call 'governing metaphors'. The list below offers a few examples:

School as:	Student as:	Teacher as:
Family	Child	Parent
Nest	Brood	Mother hen
Body	Member	Member
Prison	Prisoner	Warder
Church	Laity	Priest
Welfare state	Client	Social worker
Army	Troops	Officer
Battle ground	Combatant	Combatant
Sport	Competitor	Official
Factory	Worker	Manager
Market	Customer	Salesperson
Society	Citizen	Politician
Journey	Traveller	Guide

That most schools are governed by mixed metaphors and are often the scene of 'a series of competing (management) discourses' (Davies, 1994, p. 4) is not surprising. What is surprising is how often such governing metaphors are taken for granted and yet how powerful they can be in shaping the culture of the school concerned. Leaving aside the fact that the concept of community must become an influential governing metaphor in its own right, most interesting for us are those metaphors, such as 'body', 'society' or 'journey', which also throw light on the school as a learning community, and those models of management having some affinity with these metaphors.

'Community education'

> Community education is not a department or a subdivision or a subject within the education service. It is a philosophy and a spirit which imbues all else. It is not the special job of a few, nor an extra task on an educator's already overcrowded job description. It is the task of education itself.
> (CCC, 1990, p. 5)

The problem is that this exciting description of 'the Cambridgeshire vision', with which we are in full accord, has only earthed itself in the past practice of community education (see Chapter 1) in a pragmatic and piecemeal way. Thus the concept of the school as a learning community, and any possible models of its management, have been largely bypassed in both the practice and literature of community education.

The core problem has been originally a semantic and then *de facto* separation of the school and 'the community'. Traditional approaches to community education have produced some interesting models of partnership between schools and the local neighbourhood, to which we return in Chapter 9. But the idea of the school as a learning community as such has received scant attention.

The community school has traditionally opened its doors to a mass of would-be learners of pre- or post-school age, at both secondary and primary levels, from Morris' village colleges onwards. But with the exception of a relatively small number of adults joining secondary school classes, these incomers have simply formed part of a parallel adult education programme meeting in separate buildings or at separate times from school pupils. There is little indication that our synergistic curriculum code and the guidelines linked to it are any more operative in such learning programmes than they are in most schools.

Community education has come nearer to shaping the school as a learning community in its growing focus on the neighbourhood as a learning resource. The Educational Priority Area Project in the early 1970s, not least in Liverpool at that time and later, stressed this approach. But it is only in relatively recent years, in such places as Northamptonshire (CS, 1988), Waltham Forest (Brett *et al.*, 1989) and Birmingham (Clark and Burgess, 1990; CEDC, 1992a; CEDC, 1992b), that this concern has been pursued with any sustained commitment. And even here community education, as traditionally defined, has been matched in energy and overtaken in practice by many schools not formally designated as community schools, as the Schools Curriculum Awards (launched in 1982) for 'community involved' schools amply demonstrate.

Community education's energetic pragmatism has likewise failed to produce any innovative models of management for the school as a learning community. Only Poster (1982) and, in a more recent book, Townsend (1994), have seriously addressed this subject. And they too seem preoccupied with the community as neighbourhood rather than the community of the school. This locality bound perspective has led to most traditional models of management for community education being largely concerned with how community councils, community associations or user committees (made up of those using school premises) can best relate to governing bodies, and whether the head should or can be the chief executive of school and 'community centre'.

How management communalizes the school has hitherto not been an issue for community educators, with one or two notable exceptions. And these have been in relation to particular schools not to management theory in general. One classic exception is Countesthorpe (Watts, 1977; 1980; Chessum, 1989) which set out from its opening in 1970 to operate as a thoroughgoing learning community in relation to both its internal and external structures. Its school 'Moot', in particular, was an innovative and courageous attempt to translate communal principles into managerial practice and, although it eventually foundered for both internal and external reasons, many important lessons about democratic management had been learned. But Countesthorpe, like the Sutton Centres (Fletcher, 1984) and Madeley Courts (Toogood, 1984) of this world, were swallows that did not foreshadow a summer, and no body of theory embracing the management of so-called community schools has lasted the course.

School effectiveness

The concept of 'school effectiveness' is now a well established and international one (Moon *et al.*, 1990; Townsend, 1994, pp. 1–26). As with all relatively young educational movements, it has a diversity of facets. Predominant is the attempt to distinguish those factors within the life and work of schools which produce clear outcomes. Research over the past two decades to discover measurable indicators of 'success' has been detailed and painstaking, and written up with care and thoroughness.

The school effectiveness literature has a contribution to make to our understanding of the school as a learning community in three main areas.

● First, it offers schools a stronger sense of significance in that it is now recognized that what goes on within their walls shapes the life of the pupil in important and lasting ways, however powerful the influences of home and neighbourhood remain. Thus schools have a major role to play in both the life-opportunities open to pupils and the nature of a future society.

● Second, the school-effectiveness literature offers some practical clues as to how schools can indeed become more effective. The indicators they produce have been reasonably well tested for reliability and are useful pointers for senior management to employ. Thus they need to be carefully borne in mind when our own guidelines are used to see if they can offer further practical insights as to how to earth our three 'S's in the ongoing life of schools.

● Third, the importance of 'effective leadership' (DES, 1977, p. 36) has come through again and again. In particular, the role of the head teacher has been pin-pointed as crucial to positive educational outcomes.

There is, however, a general feeling that the school effectiveness movement has plateaued. In the context of our search for insights from a management perspective which can inform the life of the school as a learning community, there are likewise reservations about this movement. At the heart of these is the simple but vital question: 'What is "effectiveness"?' As Townsend (1994, p. 5) puts it: 'The definition of what an effective school is becomes critical to any other questions that might be asked.' Davies (1994, pp. 27–39) argues that the question is impossible to address as it stands because the answer must be politically and/or culturally conditioned. Hence 'the selection of the outcomes by which to compare schools is not a neutral activity' (p. 31). Handy (1984, p. 21) sums up the problem in his usual lucid way:

> It may not be the fault of schools that they are the repositories of society's hopes and fears, whims and fancies, but it compounds the problems of management, it turns the practical into the political, the objective decision into the personal opinion, the committee into a debating chamber and the organisation into a microcosm of society.

The school effectiveness movement fails to audit this deeper dimension of feeling, values and beliefs which are so crucial to the life of all social systems.

School effectiveness also experiences some confusion in the ordering and prioritizing of its indicators. Lists of factors associated with good educational practice abound but discussion of the framework within which they are set, not only ideologically but organizationally, is frequently neglected. In this sense, school effectiveness is hardly a model, let alone a theory of management (Rosenholtz, 1989, p. 1).

Just as important, from the perspective of the learning community, school effectiveness fails to throw much light on the connections between indicators, the correlation of the variables themselves. It is here, as Townsend comments (1994, p. 30) 'that the heart of the matter lies'. Thus 'the school effectiveness criteria lack the comprehensiveness required for a practical whole-school strategy' (Hargreaves and Hopkins, 1991, p. 16).

All in all, therefore, school effectiveness has much to offer us, not least in providing further insights into and in helping to test out the reliability of our suggested guidelines. But the lack of a clear overall perspective in principle, purpose and practice considerably weakens its contribution to our understanding of the school and its management as a learning community.

Total Quality Management (TQM)

TQM has its origins in an unexpected marriage between the ideas of an American management consultant, Edward Deming, and the determination of Japanese industrialists to achieve commercial success in a highly competitive post-war world. The offspring was the so-called 'total quality' movement which in more recent years has swept through the business sector of the entire Western world. Even though its origins are within the business sector and not the education system, has this movement anything to offer to our understanding of the school as a learning community?

A number of TQM's features underscore our synergistic curriculum code. The first is TQMs insistence that the 'quality' sought after must be a feature of the whole system, involving change not only in techniques and organization but in the entire culture of systems. Such cultural transformation, as Drummond (1992, p. 129) states, is of a profound nature, not 'change within the system' but 'change which changes the system'.

A second important feature of TQM, from the point of view of both community and education, is its focus on the potential of people and on the importance of healthy personal relationships. 'Building a quality culture', writes Drummond (1992, p. 130), 'is about developing resourceful human beings to enable them to manage.' West-Burnham (1992, p. 8) adds: 'Above everything else it [TQM] is about the quality of personal relationships.' And quality, like community education, should engage people at the feeling as well as functional level. Even if Tony Henri (quoted in Sallis, 1993, p. 125) goes somewhat over the top when he speaks of quality as being 'about living, loving, passion, fighting, cherishing, nurturing, struggling, crying, laughing', nevertheless words like 'joy', 'delight' and 'excitement', commonplace in TQM, have a real contribution to make to community education.

A further useful aspect of TQM is its ability, like our communal guidelines on people, to distinguish between what it terms the 'internal' and 'external customer'. Both are important, yet neither suffice in themselves. No organization can hope to delight its external customers if it does not enable its internal customers to delight one another. This feature of TQM also underlines the primacy of collaboration and team work (West-Burnham, 1992, pp. 119–35; Sallis, 1993, pp. 91–8).

The last characteristic of TQM which dovetails with our concept of the learning community is the central place given to education as the motor of organizational change. Great emphasis is put on Deming's advocacy of a vigorous programme of 'education and self-improvement' (Sallis, 1993, p. 49), and much attention given to such concepts as 'feedback', 'second-order change' (our double-loop learning) and 'transformation'. And all this refers not only to the internal education of staff but external 'customer education' too (Drummond, 1992, pp. 49–51).

Yet for all its important features, energy and popularity TQM as applied to the world of education presents us with some major problems.

First and foremost is the ambiguous meaning of 'quality'. Pfeffer and Coote (1991, p. 31) call it a 'slippery concept'. Lawton (1994, p. 3) in discussing a number of educational ideologies finds that 'quality has a slightly different meaning for each'. The basic question is 'Quality *for what*?'; which the associated TQM slogan 'fitness *for task*' only echoes in a slightly more functional way. 'For what' is such an important issue, yet potentially so open, that it can confuse the whole meaning of TQM's key concept. To leave 'quality' as such an open-ended term presents a major threat to the claim that TQM is a dynamically transforming agent. 'The slogan of "improving quality" is essentially static', writes Sayer (1989a, p. 144). It simply leads people to try to do a bit better those things that they are already doing.

TQM originates in a business context dominated by market forces of a competitive nature. There, 'quality' is actually pursued to further economic success. Thus, as Townsend (1994, p. 28) points out, the relationship 'between the notion of quality and the notion of equality', a major issue for community education, is at best ambiguous. Although Drummond (1992, p. 144) states, in an assertion we would welcome, that this 'new industrial revolution' will enable 'organisations to develop as communities serving the greater community', TQM exists in a sector where if some 'win' others must 'lose'.

'It is a curious paradox', writes Kingdom (1992, p. 63), 'that while free-market theorists expect firms to behave competitively, they do not advocate such behaviour within the firm.' Because TQM in general accepts a market philosophy, two fundamental questions must be raised by community educators. If collaboration is so important internally, why does TQM not espouse it more explicitly externally? And if TQM condones external competition, how can it create a conducive culture for community-building across systems?

Another problem is that 'the quality organisation exists for its customers; it has no other purpose than providing products and services which satisfy customer needs' (West-Burnham, 1992, p. 28). If in schools the child is the customer, then at what age is he able to articulate his needs – at five, at eleven, at sixteen? And are we talking here about 'needs' or 'wants', two very different things? But is the child the customer? What of parents, local residents who use school premises for various activities, and of wider society? Are they not customers too? And if so, what are they paying for – top grades in tests or examinations, the preparation of mature citizens, good school facilities or the production of economically efficient 'units'?

The label 'customer' turns the community education process into an essentially impersonal transaction with knowledge as a commodity, some thing to be bought and sold. It ceases to be a journey of discovery shared by all involved. And, fundamentally antithetical to the concept of the learning community, that contract is seen as a transaction focused on the school and the individual, as 'customer'. It is not one established between diverse social systems committed to a learning partnership for, about and through community.

The final problem with TQM is its incoherence. For a model of management sporting the word 'total', it is extraordinarily bitty. For example, Deming's fourteen points (Sallis, 1993, pp. 48–9) are constantly quoted and re-quoted, yet are set in no coherent theoretical framework of any kind. TQM seems to consist of a range of unrelated slogans, albeit in themselves quite insightful, jostling for pride of place beneath the total quality (another slogan) banner. The slogans have the great asset of being easy to remember, but how they are supposed to interrelate is often hard to discern.

TQM has a number of significant features which reinforce and resonate with the concept of the school as a learning community. Its slogans, for all their cliché-like nature, have been for some 'inspirational' as well as 'instrumental' (Drummond, 1992, p. 17), and it has certainly placed people and their potential, whether as consumers or workers, high on the agenda. But TQM is in practice being shaped as much, if not more, by market forces as its own ideals. Its potential contribution to our understanding of the school as a learning community has an inherent ambiguity about it and must thus be treated with considerable caution.

The learning organization

In recent years, yet another management model has come to the fore entitled 'the learning organization'. A number of notable authors have developed the theme: Argyris and Schön (1978); Morgan (1986, pp. 77–109); Garratt, (1994); Handy (1990, pp. 44–63; 179–87); Senge (1990); Willie and Hodgson (1991, pp. 163–77) and Pedler *et al.* (1991). The concept itself is very similar to that of the learning community which we have advocated, so does it throw more light on the latter?

The model of the learning organization has been developed largely in relation to the business sector. Its ideas often overlap with those of TQM. One strength is its focus on a particular phenomenon (i.e. the learning organization), rather than a diffuse concept like 'effectiveness' or 'quality'. From our point of view, its major contribution is in the attention it gives to the learning process.

This contribution is twofold. First, the theorists writing about the learning organization have brought to the fore a dynamic understanding of learning which many of those writing about school-based education have long since forgotten or never fully recognized. We have already drawn on a range of these ideas in previous chapters – negotiated learning processes, learning to learn, double-loop learning, and that all can learn from each. Pedler *et al.* (1991, pp. 38 and 23) sum up the learning organization in two key concepts closely related to our own: 'the transforming company' and 'a learning climate'.

A related feature of the learning organization which we have not explicitly drawn on is Handy's (1990, p. 46) so-called 'wheel of learning' (mentioned in somewhat different terms by numerous other writers, many not specifically associated with learning organization theory), which sees genuine learning as moving through the cycle of 'question–theory–test–-reflection–question ...'. All of these features, however, are incorporated in our pedagogic model of education (see pp. 82–90) or in our guidelines related to the focal task (see pp. 69–70).

A second major contribution from learning organization theory is that it shows quite clearly that genuine learning is as vital to the business and commercial sectors as it is to the education system. This is a real breakthrough. It endorses one of the key themes of this book that the school as a learning community, though having a pivotal role to play in communalizing education and education for community, is only modelling what needs to be happening in every sector and throughout society if our world is to mature as well as survive. And in that modelling and catalytic task, like all learning organizations, the school itself needs to learn from as well as contribute to the learning of others.

Nevertheless, learning organization theory does not quite deliver the goods. On the one hand, it provides no clear framework of organizational theory and management. Charles Handy has his own range of models, some specifically related to the school as an organization (Handy, 1984; Handy and Aitken, 1986), and Pedler *et al.* (1991, pp. 18–33, 52–3) present a list of eleven 'dimensions or features' of a learning company. But there are few seminal models or profiles on offer. If there is convergence, it is greater around the concept of learning than around that of appropriate organizational structures.

As with TQM, learning organization theory and learning organization practice do not always demonstrate a very convincing consistency. The question of 'Learning *for what*?' is again glossed over. The theorists may argue for collaboration over competition, may champion 'inter-company learning' (Pedler *et al.*, 1991, pp. 22–3), and may talk of being 'a good company' (p. 148) with even a 'spiritual' ethos (pp. 12; 17), but how all this squares with often cut-throat market forces which by definition mean that some win and some lose, is by no means clear. Holly and Southworth (1989, pp. 1–23) persuasively apply learning organization ideas to 'the learning school', but how community can be built across as well as within such systems in a competitive world is an issue never discussed. What is, in reality, a political agenda remains unaddressed.

Nevertheless, the learning organization theorists have produced some very important insights into the management of community education, and our description of the school as a learning community is indebted to their ideas, if not so clearly as yet to the practice deriving from it.

LEADERSHIP

'A school is not an engineering model; it is a city-state with citizens, with passions and factions, dreams and fears' (Handy and Aitken, 1986, p. 100). If it can become a vital, open learning community what a message it has to offer to a wider world of 'passions and factions, dreams and fears'!

The kind of leadership required to transform schools into genuine learning communities is, above all, that which can enable the numerous mini-communities which make it up (notably school classes, but also many other pupil-related and staff-related social systems) to engage together in the co-creation of a new kind of organization. The task is to create a macro learning community out of mini learning communities. It is a hugely difficult but vitally important task not only for the future of education but for the future of civilization. It is an indispensable task not only for the enhancement of the economic and social, but of the spiritual quality of human life.

It is no wonder, therefore, that ultimately all management models concerned with education stress the crucial role of the head teacher in the formation of the school as a learning community. This role is often defined in terms of 'leadership' rather than 'management', Handy (1984, p. 23) even suggesting schools should shun the latter term and replace it with a concept such as 'administration'. Others believe that the term 'head' is now also outmoded.

Beare *et al.* (1989, p. 106) see leadership being about 'transformation', management about 'transaction'. There will obviously be much overlap, but the point that leadership is essentially about vision and change, management about effectiveness and efficiency, is a helpful one. Nevertheless, we wish to retain the term 'boundary manager' (used in Chapter 7) to describe the main function of the role of the community educator. For us, it is a term which is very much about leadership, even though entailing certain integral administrative responsibilities.

Because all teachers working in a school founded upon a synergistic curriculum code will in one way or another be operating as community educators, the head must be the role model for all staff. As the educational aspects of the synergistic code focus on learning to learn, the head becomes what Holly and Southworth (1989, p. 18) call 'the leading learner'.

He or she should be the epitome of our pedagogic model of education. As key community educator, he or she will be committed to education as a moral endeavour, to a person and life-centred approach to learning, to questioning and discovery, to fostering the learner's choice and to democratic forms of leadership.

Managing a system of systems

One of the head's greatest challenges as a role model for community education is strengthening a sense of community across as well as within systems. From the head's perspective, the school as a learning community is constructed out of a host of mini social systems overlapping and interlocking, diagrammatically depicted in Fig. 8.1.

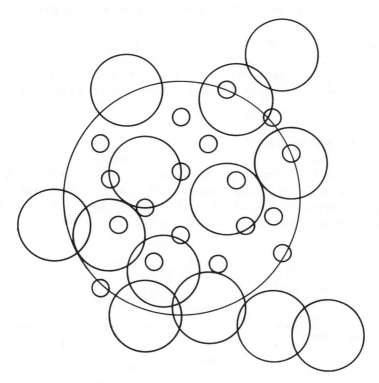

Small circles – classes and groups
Medium circles – departments or years
   (inner)
Medium circles – governors, parents, sponsors, etc.
   (outer)
Largest circle – teaching and ancillary staff

Figure 8.1   *The school as a system of systems*

The head's communal task is to foster a sense of security, significance and solidarity across these systems in order that the whole attains a strong sense of community. The head's main work, with regard to the internal life of the school, will be done on the boundaries between mini social systems. In this task he or she will normally have access to the services of other boundary workers (deputies, year and subject heads, senior teachers, curriculum co-ordinators, etc.), often with a more specific focal task to perform. The strength of the total school as a learning community will very much depend on these personnel working together as a team, and in the process forming a connecting system (and a learning community) in their own right.

For the head and this team seeking to create a genuine learning community out of the complexity of the school as a system of systems, the communal dilemma (see pp. 47–50) looms large. This is the problem of how social systems can become and remain open to broadening their experience of community without weakening it. The boundary manager knows that all systems regard their autonomy, be it territorial, economic, political or cultural, as precious. Thus how to foster a greater degree of inclusivity while enabling systems to sustain their own communality is one of the greatest challenges for the head as an internal and external boundary manager.

The actual skills needed to address this kind of challenge appear in many books about the management of change. Here we offer only two extended comments: one about the various forms of engagement possible between those social systems making up a school; the other on key aspects of managing change in the context of the school as a learning community.

Engagement between social systems

It may be helpful, in reflecting on the school as a community of communities, to draw on insights gained from the study of multi-ethnic societies. Figure 8.2 drawn from this source (Clark, 1982, p. 80) and adapted for the school as 'a mini city-state', sets out a number of ways in which systems which engage with one another can respond to the communal dilemma.

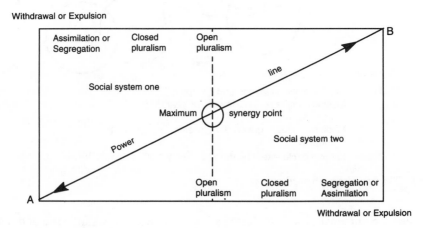

Figure 8.2 *Forms of engagement between social systems*

Where the ability to influence each other is out of balance, at the A or B ends of the power line, there is a strong possibility that one system will be isolated, assimilated (absorbed into the stronger system) or withdraw (or be forced to withdraw) from the engagement. Where power is more evenly distributed, towards the middle of the power line, closed pluralism (with contact tolerated but not encouraged) and open pluralism (where cross-cutting ties are fostered by all systems) are more likely to be in evidence.

It is open pluralism which enables the synergy required to transform the school into a genuine learning community to be most easily generated. This may in turn lead to a fresh synthesis whereby the systems merge to form new systems and new communities. But this is a far cry from assimilation where the stronger system simply swamps the weaker, negating its culture and identity in the process.

Figure 8.2 depicts the possible relationship between systems in 'ideal type' terms. In reality, the school, embracing 'citizens, with passions and factions, dreams and fears', is a dynamic and volatile entity where the relationships between systems will be in constant flux. But the head, as a community educator and boundary manager, must be constantly seeking to foster open pluralism and engagement at the centre of the power line.

Managing change

In promoting both the educational and communal tasks at the heart of a learning community, the school head is first and foremost a manager of change. We shall deal in the next chapter with the head's role in relation to the wider world. Here we stress again that this role is a key one in enabling the school to develop into a learning community of learning communities.

In this very demanding task, a number of management functions stand out as of particular significance. Of all the requirements, few are more important than promoting a 'shared vision' (Senge, 1990, pp. 205–32). Beare *et al.* (1989, p. 117) quote the definition of vision offered by Bennis and Nanus as follows:

> A mental image of a possible and desirable future state of the organisation ... as vague as a dream or as precise as a goal or mission statement ... a view of a realistic, credible, attractive future for the organisation, a condition that is better in some important ways than what now exists.

Vision is not a conglomeration of bright ideas. Nor does it come without a great deal of hard debate with one's supporters and opponents, as well as mental wrestling often in isolation. Visions have the stamp of the visionary writ deep into their substance. They are initially minority viewpoints – shared visions follow on. Thus visions as such begin and often stay for a long time on the margins of social systems. This book is seeking to present a vision of transforming and transformed education rooted in the school as a learning community. We are not asking for heads and other educators to 'buy into' or impose this vision without question or adaptation. That would deny the very nature of community and the synergistic model. But we are arguing for the validity, indeed necessity, of our vision as an affective, cognitive, moral and spiritual driving force in the shaping of human affairs if we are to survive as well as enjoy a quality of life worthy of the twenty-first century. Others will have different visions. What matters is that all are given a genuine hearing.

From visions flow what has been called 'the management of meanings' (Davies, 1994, p.

5). This is not a *laissez-faire* juggling act with values, but the creation of inclusivity, of a shared vision, around a diversity of convictions, expectations, hopes and fears which can enable the school to develop as a dynamic learning community in an openly pluralistic way. It is the head's task to manage the meanings of all those to whom he or she is accountable – pupils, teachers, governors, ancillary staff, parents and others – so that this shared vision can develop and give impetus and energy to the life and work of the school.

The management of meanings and a shared vision are best related to actual practice through what Drummond (1992, pp. 48 and 134) calls 'loose tolerances, tightly enforced'. Such loose tolerances allow the autonomy and diversity of mini-communities within the school, possessing their own characteristic meanings, to thrive. At the same time, the framing and setting of limits gives the whole school an identity and coherence which allows it to operate as a recognizable and definitive social system. This is important not least for its relationship with other social systems and effective partnership building in the wider world.

The overall boundary management function of the head is made a good deal easier if he or she is able effectively to handle symbols and rituals (to which three of our communal guidelines in Chapter 5 specifically refer). Ceremonies, rites, displays, cultural heroes, logos, emblems and so forth are a potent means of enhancing both a sense of community within, and the distinctiveness of the school without (Beare *et al.*, 1989, pp. 172–200; Cohen, 1985).

The head will need to induct all staff into the nature of community education and of boundary management, with middle management having a particularly strategic role (Handy, 1984, p. 37). The head's skills as a team builder and group worker will be extremely important, issues dealt with at length in most management text books, not least those concerned with TQM.

In dealing with the management of change in the context of the many mini-communities which make up the school, two complementary responsibilities are vital. First that the head enables staff 'to feel secure enough to take risks' (Holly and Southworth, 1989, p. 21). In the synectics branch of management (Nolan, 1987, pp. 67–9), trainees are required to rate their solution to problems on a threefold scale: feasibility, appeal and novelty. It is the third of those features which is regarded as crucial to personal and social change. Risking novelty requires the head to foster what Handy (1990, pp. 54–6 and 183–4) calls 'negative capability', the potential for an organization to make mistakes as an integral aspect of its existence as a learning community.

A responsibility of the head complementary to fostering negative capability is the skill in steering competition and conflict into a 'win–win' situation. Davies (1994) rightly reminds us that schools are, like most social systems, a focus of 'micro politics' and resistant to change. Creating a learning community will almost inevitably bring the head up against those systems which neither want to learn nor develop as communities, convinced that change may threaten their very existence. We are here into the field of 'conflict resolution' and the skills required to implement it. Indeed management theory (West-Burnham, 1992, p. 109) is increasingly insisting that much more attention must be given to concepts such as negotiation and mediation, if social systems are to become and remain learning organizations.

The final word, however, must again be that all organizations and all schools are unique. Management text books have only limited value in helping heads to transform their schools into learning communities. The art of the community educator, and of boundary management, has to be mastered on the job, in a particular place, with particular people and at a particular time. No two situations are identical. But this is all the more reason why schools need one another, as well as the wider world, if they are to achieve the task of learning about and learning through the process of community building.

Chapter 9

Partnerships and Networks

This book is written out of a conviction – portrayed in vivid and often violent form on our television screens and in our newspapers daily – that our world has to find a new understanding and experience of community if it is to survive. We are caught between the push and pull of centrifugal and centripetal forces which could annihilate human civilization for good. But we are also offered the possibility of creating one world, rich in diversity yet united in pursuit of the common good, which promises a fullness of life of a kind and on a scale never known by humankind before.

Communal salvation, however, is no easy option. Its attainment is a complex and demanding undertaking. At its heart lies our ability to learn from one another. To retreat into our lagers will spell doom for those inside as well as out. But to open our minds and hearts to new insights and new experiences, risky and hard as this seems, affords real hope for the future.

An awareness of this situation is slowly beginning to dawn. We are gradually moving beyond learning being seen as the key only to individual advancement pursued through monolithic institutions. We are beginning to grasp the fact that all agencies, organizations and institutions have to become learners if we are to shape up to the immense challenges of the next millennium. Thus emerging concepts such as 'the learning company', 'the learning organization', and 'the learning society' no longer seem quite so Utopian or misplaced.

But a learning society cannot come into being unless we are prepared to share our experience, expertise and resources. The quality of community we need demands it; the nature of learning in our post-modern world necessitates it. The institutionalization of education over past centuries, so vital to the original development of expertise and professionalism, has to give way to an exchange and pooling of knowledge and understanding which democratizes learning to an extent never known before. We are painfully realizing that 'the survival of the species' requires that all our institutions become 'partners in learning'.

But what is 'partnership'? Pugh (Wolfendale, 1989, pp. 1–19), writing about parental involvement in schools, describes that link as characterized by non-participation, support, participation, partnership, or control. The penultimate category, partnership, involves parents (p. 6) 'in a working relationship that is characterized by a shared sense of purpose, mutual respect and willingness to negotiate'. Pugh's is in fact one of the few attempts actually to define partnership found in current educational literature.

Our own definition follows from the discussion that has preceded this chapter. In Chapter 7, we used the term 'alliances' instead of 'partnership', simply to fit in with the alliteration of the ten 'A's of intervention. For us, the terms are synonymous.

For us, partnership is essentially a communal concept. We define partnership as follows:

A sense of community created across social systems.

The value of partnership as a concept is that it highlights one of the main aspects of community development, that of community building across systems. As such, it emphasizes that strengthening a sense of security, significance and solidarity within systems alone is inadequate and can eventually lead us up the cul-de-sac of the communal dilemma. What matters, as Sayer and Williams put it (1989, p. 167) is 'development ... through inter-linking sentient groups, with shared enthusiasm and the will and capacity to share skills'. Partnership, as a communal concept, is rooted in what some call 'a collaborative relation-ship [of] trust' (Steffy and Lindle, 1994, p. 21) and others 'a culture of love' (Harrison, 1987). As a communal concept, partnership is operationalized through the kind of guide-lines outlined in Chapter 5, not least those relating to the people segment of the social systems involved.

Because community is characterized by diversity and the inclusion of the disadvantaged, partnership has to be more than like-liking-like. It has to seek out creative relationships with those who belong to different cultures and possess different life-styles. It also has to embrace those who, for whatever reason, are disabled or marginalized by society. Partnership has little to do with courting favours from the influential and wealthy (a habit often going under the euphemism of 'sponsorship').

Partnerships are strongest when they are established and maintained *through the learning process*. This means that the engagement will take on many aspects of the synergistic code. If this happens then the social systems involved will develop as learning communities. Thus *building partnerships involves a process of community education engaged in across learning systems*. This is never a one-way affair where one system instructs and the other learns; all involved must be concerned that their system, as well as others, develop educationally as well as communally.

SCHOOLS NEED OTHERS AND OTHERS NEED SCHOOLS

In the new era into which we are entering, schools need partners. We are hopefully past what Handy and Aitken (1986, p. 119) call 'moated self-sufficiency'; that 'no school is a traffic island' (Sayer and Williams, 1989, p. 142) is a sentiment with which most teachers would now agree. But we have hardly begun raising the awareness of schools to what being genuine partners in learning is all about. 'The school's learning – the basis of (its) devel-opment work', write Holly and Southworth (1989, p. 22), 'arises from a partnership of resolve, involving partners from both inside and outside the school.'

First and foremost for all schools come the demands of a National Curriculum. But it is in fact the cross-curricular 'dimensions' (personal and social development, equal opportu-nities, and education for life in a multi-cultural society) and 'themes' (economic and industrial understanding, careers education and guidance, environmental education, health education, and citizenship), rather than the core and foundation subjects, which are the real pointers to the future. (That such dimensions and themes currently seem to be losing their grip on curriculum time is but a commentary on our current myopia.) However, to address these dimensions and themes in any effective manner schools need to forge partnerships with a wide range of systems representing a diversity of cultures, sectors and concerns.

There are many other reasons why schools require partners. These range from a better image to economic resources, from the need for new management skills to improved communication channels. Writers stress the changing nature and role of 'knowledge' (Drucker, 1993) and, no less frequently, the climate of market-forces in which we now live, as bringing increasing pressure on schools to end their isolation. 'Increasingly', writes Drucker (p. 190), 'the competition will be between schools and "non-schools", with different kinds of institutions entering the field, each offering a different approach to schooling.' If society produces rivals, schools will need friends.

But whether or not this competitive scenario is here to stay, a growing range of organizations throughout society will need schools, above all as prototypes and models of learning communities, just as much as schools will need them; and this for a number of cogent reasons. In the first place, schools as learning communities of both a specialized and universal kind, are essential to further the education of the next generation. They are needed not only to provide the basic skills of literacy and numeracy, but to teach what Sacks (Hargreaves, 1994, p. 37) calls 'the first and public language of citizenship', a language often made most explicit in the cross-curricular dimensions and themes to which we have already referred.

Second, schools are still able to provide much of the expertise and many of the resources required to educate the young effectively and creatively. That they need to do this in partnership with others we shall continue to argue. But there remains within schools a trained profession, as well equipped as any at this juncture in time, to nurture, instruct, train and educate up and coming 'citizens for a new age'.

Third, and of paramount concern from our point of view, schools are able to provide the young with a 'base community' which offers them a social system within which they can learn how to learn for, about and especially through community. This base community is important, not least for those disadvantaged who need to be the focus of continuing personal affirmation. But the school as a community is a vital model for all pupils if they are to be educated in a way which will enable societies to live creatively together throughout the next century.

In the fourth place, the school has a potentially pivotal role within any partnership of learning communities – that of experiment and innovation. The school exists not only to socialize the young but to educate them. As we have seen, education embraces a zest for questioning, for discovery, for 'double-loop' learning and for change. The school must provide a model of learning from which other learning communities draw inspiration and stimulation. It is this innovatory role which should place schools at the heart of every learning partnership and not on the periphery.

But what about a potential 'rival' to the school in relation to certain functions mentioned above: the home as a learning community? We are not referring here to the case where home and school assume the role of partners in learning (to be discussed more fully below), but that of 'education otherwise', where home-based education becomes the norm (Meighan and Toogood, 1992, pp. 80–91). There is a strong case to be made out for a home-centred approach to the education of the young, and many children have clearly benefited from it. Our main concerns, however, are the virtual impossibility of home-based education becoming universal and 'comprehensive', the danger of neglecting the child for whom the home has failed as a community, and the difficulties faced as children need to move from an experience of primary to secondary forms of social relationships. Our own preference would thus be for what Meighan (1988) himself terms 'flexi-schooling', where there is the opportunity for much more give and take between the roles and responsibilities of both home and school.

THE LEGACY OF COMMUNITY EDUCATION

The historical contribution of community education, in the traditional sense, to the issue of partnership, has been as much by way of awareness raising as effective and sustainable practice (with the one major exception of parental involvement in primary schools). Five models of partnership have been evident within community education over this century, notable aspects of which have already been touched on. Here they are summarized.

Dual or multi-use of building

This can hardly be called a model of 'partnership' at all. The opening of premises for the use of a clientele other than pupils has more often than not resulted in what has been called a 'hokey-cokey approach' (Clark, 1989, p. 35): users coming into the school building, shaking themselves about in pursuit of a wide diversity of vocational or leisure interests, and going out again. The dual/multi-use of schools has offered valuable facilities to the youth service and for further and adult education, as well as providing facilities for social and welfare services. Dual/multi-use has often given rise to community association and user committees, but it has rarely created a learning partnership as such between the school and its users. Yet this has consistently remained the most common form of 'partnership', above all at secondary school level, promoted by community education. Indeed, so synonymous have dual/multi-use and traditional community education become that it is the only definition recognized in the Education Reform Act (1988, Part I, Section 47) which states categorically: 'A school is a community school if ... activities other than school activities ("non-school activities") are carried on on the school premises.'

The adult education and youth services

Overlapping with the dual/multi-use model of 'partnership' has been the reification of community education in the form of a combined youth and adult education service throughout Scotland, and not infrequently in England and Wales, this then being called 'the community education service'. This development is simply a relabelling of existing services for the sake of administrative convenience (and cost cutting). The community education service's main contribution to our understanding of education is its insistence that education should be lifelong, but as this implicitly excludes the school as well as learning communities in other sectors, little is thereby added to the meaning of partnership.

Inter-agency co-operation

In certain local authorities, community education has been seen predominantly in terms of inter-agency co-operation, often given practical expression through some form of neighbourhood council; Derbyshire and, to a lesser extent, Dudley have followed this model. Most often involved with schools have again been the adult education and the youth services. More informally, schools have sometimes been the location for lunches or forums involving a wide cross-section of agencies and groups, statutory and voluntary, involved in the neighbourhood.

Parental involvement in schools

This has been the one major sustainable innovation in partnership which community education past has helped to put on the map. As described in Chapter 1, the urban origins of parental involvement go back to Plowden and the EPA schemes of that era (though Leicestershire was developing links with parents well before that) with community primary schools in many places being instrumental in developing links in innovative ways, as for example with the Birmingham Experiment in Community Education in the 1970s (BCC, 1986). One of the major contributions of this kind of partnership has been its support of disadvantaged families in areas of considerable urban deprivation. More will be said about current aspects of this model later in this chapter.

The neighbourhood as a curriculum resource

This model of partnership has been a late starter in traditional community education terms. We touched on it in Chapter 8 (pp. 118–19) indicating a number of relatively recent initiatives which have taken the neighbourhood as a curriculum resource seriously. Even so, the neighbourhood has frequently been seen as a resource in fairly static terms (environmental studies, urban trails, visits here and there, etc.). Where local adults have been involved this has been seen more as teachers' aids than fellow learners.

The overall problem with most of these models of partnership is that they have failed the 'quality' test with regards both to community and education. Community has been equated mainly with the local neighbourhood. There has been minimal recognition of the latter as an aggregation of many communities (including the school itself), very diverse and not infrequently in conflict with one another. Thus the task of building a new quality of community across systems (i.e., of building new partnership) has never been explicitly addressed.

These models also diminish the meaning of education. It is true that parental involvement in schools has figured prominently. But that initiative apart, and leaving aside the tentative excursion into enhancing the curriculum from neighbourhood resources, traditional community education had equated education largely with adult education and the youth service. Even here, it has added little to these services' own understanding of education other than giving them a more comprehensive title and emphasizing that learning should be lifelong.

Overall, therefore, community education's historical weakness in offering any qualitative definition of either community or education has meant that its understanding of the nature of partnership and, in particular, its potential for transforming learning communities into a learning society, has been very limited.

PARTNERS IN LEARNING

Community education's past failures to liberate itself from captivity to anachronistic constructs has meant that the public education system in England has eventually stolen its clothes. The pioneers of community education may have sown the seeds of the school without walls. But it has been those who have never heard the name of Henry Morris and who rarely use the term community education, who have broken the mould. The more enlightened have grasped that the day of the school as a self-sufficient learning system is drawing to a close, and that the future of education lies in ever widening and deepening learning alliances of learning communities.

Such partnerships, albeit evolving relatively recently, have steadily proliferated across the whole education system and beyond. Schools have linked up with parents; with further education and higher education; with the youth service; with sectors such as industry and commerce, health, the environment, the arts, law and order, and the social services; with the media; and, associations of longer standing, with the churches and other religious bodies. We shall here comment on only three of these partnerships, those that schools have established with the churches, with parents, and with the world of industry and commerce. These represent one long-standing, and two more recently developed spheres of co-operation.

Our main concerns will be the extent to which the focal systems involved in these partnerships are engaged in a common educational task, and the extent to which the partnerships are communal ones. Overall, we shall be exploring ways in which such partnerships further the principles and practice set out in our synergistic code (Chapter 6).

The churches

In theory (and theology) the churches ought to be at one with the most enlightened schools in epitomizing what it is to be an open learning community (Clark, 1992). Unfortunately history has proved otherwise. The churches, both in the form of local congregations and, later, the church school, have played an enormously important part in preparing the way for a learning society. But their denominational ties and traditions now find them in something of a quandary.

Christian involvement in education is currently manifest in three forms: the institutional church's own educational programmes for children and adults; the church school; and the daily assembly and RE lessons obligatory in all schools. The nature of school–church partnerships is thus a complex one.

Church schools, dominantly Anglican and Roman Catholic and of aided or controlled type, attended by some 25 per cent of children within the total school population of England, are classically victims of the communal dilemma. As denominationally selective institutions, albeit in an increasingly tenuous way, they continue to struggle with the problem of how to broaden their communal boundaries (for financial reasons as well as altruistic motives) without loss of identity (Lankshear, 1992). Their essentially exclusive principles can bring them up against those of our communal guidelines which refer to the need for the systems within a partnership to be culturally diverse, and to include those who are disadvantaged. The overall picture remains complex, however, with some church schools seeking a more elitist character (for example by moving to grant-maintained status), while others remain deeply committed to serving very deprived populations. The one challenge they all share is a steady decline in the number of overtly committed Christian families.

Church schools find it most natural to build learning partnerships with local churches, though only of their own denomination. The educational partnership focuses largely on nurture and instruction, and the communal links on symbolic people (priest or minister), symbolic place (church buildings and artefacts) or symbolic events (festivals, ceremonies). These symbolic links are reasonably strong, Roman Catholic schools in particular very much manifesting the ethos of their tradition.

All church schools maintain links with their denominational cultures through daily school assemblies for worship. Here they are not yet facing the problems of conscience experienced by their non-Christian counterparts in making such gatherings 'wholly or mainly of a broadly Christian "character"' (as recent government legislation insists). But the declining Christian commitment of those families sending their children to church schools could eventually present problems in this respect. Church schools also sustain a link with their denominations through RE lessons and, in certain traditions, through formal instruction of a doctrinal and liturgical kind. However, most of this is a far cry from building dynamic partnerships which foster a sense of community across systems (school and church), as witnessed by the tiny minority of children who go on to become active church members.

Indeed, the links which church schools have with their local congregations as such are generally very weak. This is because congregations gather for worship on a non-school day (Sunday), and because most adult worshippers have little knowledge of or even interest in what goes on in their local church school. Even more of a barrier to developing the quality of partnership we are concerned about here is the fact that very few congregations themselves manifest the features of a learning community. Some congregations are communally strong in a more exclusive sense, although many Christians now only attend Sunday worship. But inclusive partnerships, with non-Christian agencies and even other churches, remain fragile. Even more significant, very few congregations embrace what we have defined as the educational model of learning. As Hull (1985, p. 69) puts it: 'Ideological closure is a necessary feature of ideological commitment.' The communal dilemma surfaces again.

For non-church schools, the partnership with local churches is much more tenuous. Such schools also have symbolic links with clergy, church buildings and religious events, but these are normally manifest only within school assemblies or RE lessons. The debate continues to rage as to whether school assemblies verge on indoctrination, not least as a result of the government's continuing insistence on their frequency and Christian content. RE itself, still compulsory though not a foundation subject, fosters only a passing interest in what the church stands for, in part because it rarely resonates with the culture of the wider world and in part because of its increasingly multi-faith dimension. RE often remains essentially instructional in nature, though numerous schools do give it a more educational character, exploring ethical and philosophical questions.

As a whole, therefore, non-church schools do not regard the churches as significant partners in learning, not least because the latter are locked into the communal dilemma already indicated.

Parents

If there is one context in which partnership has blossomed in the past few decades it is in the relationship of the school with the home. The Head Start programme which took off in the United States in the 1960s, and the Plowden Report (1967) and Educational Priority Area action research projects (Halsey, 1972) in England about the same time, are regarded as the triggers for this charging scene. In this process, community education played a prominent role, not least in places such as Leicestershire, Coventry, Liverpool, Birmingham and the Inner London Education Authority (see Chapter 1). By the early 1990s, Bastiani (1991, p. 81) could write that 'the tangible benefits of mutual co-operation and support have now been established beyond reasonable doubt'.

Two questions concern us here: What was the strength of the communal links established between the school and the home? What was the quality of the learning partnership involved?

In communal terms, 'the home' is often an ill-defined focal system. In gender terms, fathers have frequently been peripheral and (as with some ethnic minorities) only appear on the scene as their wives' chaperons, to lend an ear at parents' evenings, to offer occasional practical assistance or here and there to serve as governors. Women have predominated not only in the role of parent but as teachers of their own children, as well as learners and helpers. In social class terms, the nature of parent–school links has shifted from a dominant concern with working-class families in deprived areas (compensatory education and positive discrimination) to middle-class families across the board (collaboration and partnership). With respect to ethnic minorities, the inner cities have been the main focus with the emphasis being on parenting skills and the learning of English as a second language.

With 'the home' as a focal system taking so many diverse forms, communal links with the school have understandably varied in form and quality. In broad terms, six types of 'partnership' can be discerned.

- First, parents have engaged with the school as a place to bring their pre-school-age child and, in the process, socialize with one another.
- Second, parents have engaged with primary schools to enhance their own learning – of English, parenting skills, knowledge of health matters or (occasionally) to gain qualifications of an access type, such as those offered by the national accreditation of parental learning scheme launched by the Royal Society of Arts in 1993. At secondary level, parental learning focuses much more on such things as curriculum workshops and careers information.
- A third form of partnership has been where parents have entered into some kind of home–school 'contract' to support and 'coach' their own children at home in co-operation with the school (Wolfendale, 1992, pp. 112–14), recent moves being taken to make this a more formal agreement. Again, largely at primary school level, this support has encompassed literacy and numeracy skills in particular.

- Fourth, parents have become increasingly involved as classroom assistants (paid or voluntary), often on a rota basis, working alongside teachers.
- More general assistance to schools in the form of social events and fund-raising have characterized a fifth form of partnership at both primary and secondary levels, often given organizational expression through some form of parent–teacher association.
- Sixth, the Education Act (1986) put in place legislative procedures to ensure that representatives of parents sat on all governing bodies.

There is no doubt that these various forms of partnership have been given a powerful boost by government policy over recent years. The Education Acts (1986, 1988) raised the profile of parent governors in both primary and secondary schools. The Education Act (1988) put the issue of parental choice (of school for their child and of possible grant-maintained status for that school) high on the agenda. Alongside these, *The Parent's Charter*, published in 1991 and revised in 1994, laid great stress on parental rights, above all to information about their child's school and its academic performance. There was a rather less prominent end section (1994, pp. 25–6) on 'Partnership in Education' which began with the somewhat ambiguous words: 'The Parent's Charter will help you get the best education for your child. You can do this most successfully as an active partner with the school and its teachers.' Once again, therefore, the 'partnership' profile is a complex one but a few general points can be made.

At the primary school level, mothers dominate the scene. At times they form a strong community in their own right, especially when their children are very young and where schools provide a special room or meeting place for their use. At the same time, Westwood (1992, p. 236) warns us against assuming 'a cosy conception of family' which ignores 'power relations or abuses' within and between families. A small minority of parents enter into home-based learning schemes or assist in classrooms. Generally, the partnership with teachers as such is with particular members of staff and of a functional rather than communal nature. Parental learning itself is often informal and of a genuinely educational kind, though once parents seek specific knowledge or skills learning usually takes place on the basis of a more instructional or training model.

The attitude of primary school teachers to parents is becoming more open but is still a professionally cautious one. Knowledge of parents can remain 'rooted in hearsay and stereotypical thinking' (Bastiani, 1991, p. 81). There is little evidence of any realization among teachers that they themselves might have a good deal to learn *from* parents. Differences in educational and cultural expectations between teachers and parents can still lead to 'tension, contradiction and conflict' (p. 83). Greater parental control of the learning process (as opposed to sharing in it) is a major issue yet to be addressed. Nevertheless, a new recognition of the real and potential value of partnership has emerged on both sides over past years.

At secondary level, the scene is very different. Partnership in a communal sense between parents and teachers remains weak, apart from the few places where parent–teacher associations (or their equivalents) are vigorous or parents have reason to play an active role in school politics. What Williams (Sayer and Williams, 1989, p. 153) calls 'remote sensing' still characterizes the parent–school relationship in the secondary school context.

Overall, therefore, parents and schools as partners in learning is now a clearly recognizable phenomenon, especially among mothers at the primary level. Significant advances have occurred in that partnership both communally and educationally, but a fundamental breakthrough – not least in terms of gender, class and post-primary schooling – has still to occur.

Industry and commerce

If the greater involvement of parents with schools over the past few decades has been impressive, that of industry and commerce with schools has been equally striking. From the launch of the Technical and Vocational Education Initiative (TVEI) by the Department of Employment in 1982 to the present day, a host of government schemes and projects has engulfed both business and schools. Our concern here, however, is not with the minutiae of these ventures but with the quality of the learning partnership established.

The school–business partnership has been promoted in four main ways: the so-called 'work-related curriculum' (Wellington, 1993), 'compacts', exchanges of pupils and personnel (often overlapping the first two categories), and sponsorship. In all cases, partnership of an ongoing nature has mainly involved secondary schools, especially pupils over 14, but many primary schools are increasingly coming into the frame and have now set up short-term projects in this field.

Work-related curriculum

The work-related curriculum has focused largely on TVEI and its extension in 1987; aspects of the Certificate of Prevocational Education (CPVE) launched by the Department for Education and Science (DES) in 1982; on the growing number of National Vocational Qualifications (NVQs) promoted by the National Council for Vocational Qualifications (NCVQ) set up in 1986; and aspects of the National Curriculum encompassed within the Education Reform Act (1988). The nature of the schools–industry partnership in the curriculum context is twofold. Less directly, it relates to curriculum content; more directly to the range of work study, work observation and work experience undertaken by pupils under the guidance of teachers and/or industrial 'supervisors'.

Some believe that 'the Technical and Vocational Education Initiative ... was the most significant attempt at educational change undertaken by the Thatcher government prior to the Education Reform Act' (Finegold, 1993, p. 54). From our point of view, its significance lay not so much in those features which naturally reflected the technological curriculum code, but in its affinity with a good deal of the synergistic code and educational pedagogy (Chapter 6). TVEI was nationally financed but locally delivered and thus diversity of interpretation became the name of the game. For example, in Birmingham (Clark, 1990, pp. 93–9) the TVEI 'principles' included 'equal opportunities' and 'community partnership', its 'action and processes' included 'student-centred learning and formative assessment' and its 'outcomes' specified 'records of achievement'. As Wellington states (1993, p. 255), its aim was the 'restoration of faith, morale and belief in schooling'. CPVE, in conjunction with the Business and Technical Education Council's (BTEC) Foundation Programmes, likewise embraced many synergistic features such as 'experiential learning' and 'pupil/teacher negotiation' (Clark, 1990, p. 89).

Unfortunately, these educationally qualitative developments have been considerably weakened by the appearance of an all-consuming and test dominated National Curriculum.

Only in technology is a business-oriented subject content compulsory. The cross-curricular themes of 'economic and industrial understanding' and 'careers education and guidance' suffer from marginalization in a crowded timetable, and then only seek to inform pupils about the business world, rather than enable them to learn through it (Jamieson, 1993, p. 211).

The work-related curriculum has also had its own internal problems. It often remains focused on low skills and 'the less able' pupils. It thus meets our criterion of involving the disadvantaged but becomes stuck there. Indeed, there is evidence that employers still prefer pupils with more traditional qualifications, and that vocational education could prove too narrow a training in an era where flexibility is so vital (Wellington, 1993, pp. 79–97). Nor has the work-related curriculum's success in enabling pupils to make an easier transition from school to work yet been proven.

Nevertheless, the work-related curriculum has sown the seeds of a synergistic (as well as technological) approach to curriculum development and communally opened up the school–industry partnership. The communal dimension of this partnership has been enhanced by such things as schools setting up industry fairs (Morgan and Williams, 1990), and industry days. In particular, work experience programmes for older pupils (even if these are not always part of a larger work-related curriculum) is now commonplace within many secondary schools' programmes.

Compacts

A second form of school–business partnership has focused on so-called 'compacts'. These originated in the USA but were initiated in the East End of London in 1986, two years later dramatically expanding across the country. The scheme was basically a contract between specific pupils and specific employers whereby the former's good performance on such things as attendance, course work, punctuality, personal and presentation skills and work experience ensured them initial entry into the firm concerned. Compacts were more about training than education and the partnership was dominantly a functional one. Thus, as 'the job guarantee' has become impossible to sustain 'the programme's aims have become vastly more modest' (Wellington, 1993, p. 30).

Exchanges

There have been a wide variety of exchanges of pupils and personnel between school and industry, some of which have already been mentioned. Alongside pupils' work-experience have gone 'teachers into industry schemes', those sponsored by the Department of Employment getting near to providing placements for ten per cent of teachers per year. At the same time, business has linked up directly with schools through industrial tutors or (in a more limited way) Trades Union personnel, enabling personal and sustained contact with teachers and pupils. But it must be added that business as a whole has not shown itself all that interested or willing to discover very much at first hand about schools and schooling today.

Sponsorship

Industry has become involved with schools, most conspicuously in the City Technology Colleges (CTCs), through a wide diversity of forms of sponsorship ranging from the relatively small scale (provision of transport and materials) to the large scale (maintaining industry rooms or resource centres on school premises).

The explosion of such school–industry links over the past decade has been astonishing. The impetus originally came from the need for British society to have a more skilled workforce in a highly competitive world, as well as from rising youth unemployment. But it also embraces a genuine desire for a new partnership summed up in the title of the white paper announcing the TVEI extension, 'Working Together: Education and Training' (Jones, 1989, p. 69). At the same time, this title exposes the problem of partnership building across philosophically diverse systems. Is the partnership about 'education' or 'training', an issue still 'unarticulated and undisclosed' (Carr, 1993, p. 224). Despite the educationally enlightened nature of TVEI and work experience in general, the two partners have as yet failed to draw very much closer in relation to this fundamental issue.

It is true that schools have taken into their system many aspects of the contract culture and the language of the market-place. But they pursue their original ways (now assisted by a strongly traditional National Curriculum) with amazing tenacity. At the same time, employers, while promoting school–industry links, still appear to give high priority to academic qualifications and the personal qualities of the old English 'gentleman'. Indeed, Watts (1993, p. 48) has persuasively argued that they do not actually relish taking on young employees who appear too entrepreneurial.

School and industry as partners in learning have done a good deal more than say 'Hello'. But it would seem that both still remain in their cultural enclaves, and both need transformation into genuine learning communities. It may be that new approaches to management (Chapter 8) will move industry and commerce further in this direction and in its turn, as with TVEI, this will impact on schools. Or dare one hope that schools might begin to develop along the lines indicated in this book and take even industry with them? At this point in time, however, the partnership seems to be facing the question: 'What do you say after you've said "Hello"?' A new vision of what being partners in learning is really about is urgently needed.

NETWORKS

For partnerships to come into being, be maintained and to foster the growth of learning communities, there must be the means by which connections of a less intimate, demanding and continuous kind can be made. Schools need partners in learning. But they also need a wide range of resource systems (see p.103) which, though not engaged in the same focal task, can still offer a multiplicity of ideas and resources. Such resource systems may for ever remain just that, but they may in time become fully fledged partners. On the other hand, certain partners may disengage from a school's focal task but remain as valuable resource systems. Likewise, learning communities other than schools may need the latter not as partners but as resource systems.

The means by which resource systems can be brought into the picture, and partnerships made and unmade, is now very much a part of everyday life. In common parlance, it is called *networking*. A decade ago Handy and Aitken (1986, p. 123) forecast that '"network" ... will be the emerging word in education'. And so, as in other sectors, it is slowly proving to be. We would not go quite as far as Ferguson (1982, p. 231) in claiming that networks are 'a tool for the next step in human evolution', but even Handy and Aitken (1986, p. 124) describe them as 'a new art form, a new culture' and Alter and Hage (1993, p. 12) 'a stunning evolutionary change in institutional forms of governance'.

Networks have emerged for a complex diversity of reasons. First and foremost must be the technological revolution in systems of communication. The typewriter and telephone laid the foundations on which the computer and the telex have built a means of information exchange which has annihilated distance and time. Such information networks, local or global, have stimulated and been stimulated by other developments of an economic or social nature. Alter and Hage (1993, p. 23–4) pin-point such things as constraints on resources, product differentiation and diversification, strategic alliances, and an innovatory culture, as well as the need for functional information, as factors encouraging systems to network. Add to all this, the global phenomenon of increasingly literate societies and the desire for people to want to know more about their world as fast as possible, and the importance of networks and networking is clear.

'Networks' are not easy to define. 'If the academic literature is complex, the popular literature on networking is vague and vacuous', write Alter and Hage (p. 46). They themselves attempt definitions as follows:

> Networks constitute the basic social form that permits inter-organisational interactions of exchange, concerted action, and joint production. Networks are unbounded or bounded clusters of organisations that, by definition, are non-hierarchical collectives of legally separate units.
>
> Networking is the art of creating and/or maintaining a cluster of organisations for the purpose of exchanging, acting, or producing among the member organisations.

Our main response to these definitions is that, for us, networks also embrace individuals, and that networks are more often informal (unbounded) than formal (bounded). As Jack (1991, p. 3) points out, a network is 'an elaborate, but generally imperfect, system across space or time'.

In an educational context, the distinction between 'unbounded' and 'bounded' networks is important. Our attention here has been largely focused on the latter, but the former are becoming increasingly significant for the promotion of learning partnerships. The prophet in this respect was Ivan Illich who in *Deschooling Society* (1971) envisaged four types of 'learning webs':

- services (such as libraries, museums, theatres, etc.) which facilitate access to formal learning;
- 'skill exchanges' which list and link people with particular skills;
- 'peer-matching' which enables people to find learning partners; and
- 'educators-at-large' who are freelance and mobile resource people.

Some of these webs have a more bounded aspect. But, by and large, Illich saw them as spontaneous and fluid, especially in relation to the learner's world.

Networks and networking have a huge contribution to make to schools and other bodies wanting to become partners in learning. As structures geared to innovation, networks can stimulate schools and their partners to open up and explore their diverse ideologies and approach to education. They can bring more isolated learning communities, such as the home, into a new educational relationship with the wider world. Networks can make learning resources, and what Foy (1980, pp. 118–19) calls 'lively information', widely available and accessible without pressurizing participants to interact at a deeper level or for longer than is functionally necessary.

'Networks are polycephalous, which literally means "many heads"' (Lipnack and Stamp, 1986, p. 7). As such, power is removed from 'steep hierarchies' (Savage, 1990, pp. 72–3) and is distributed across a 'horizontal' organizational structure. This is likely to facilitate a co-operative mode of interaction. In a society where schools are increasingly seeking to establish new partnerships while retaining their own identity, such a structure is a vital resource. Although Alter and Hage (1993, p. 71) believe that networks can still exist even where organizations remain competitors, at least in certain aspects of their relationship.

Many features of networks accord with our communal guidelines (Chapter 5). With regard to all the segments of our social system, networks possess characteristics which are very supportive of external as well as internal community building. Networks are thus a highly significant means of enabling learning communities, including schools, to establish learning partnerships. Nonetheless, we must not mistake the network for the partnership itself, as the former differs from the latter in a number of important respects.

There are at least four major ways in which networks differ from partnerships:

1. The constituency of the former is far more diffuse than the latter. In our terminology, the focal and resource systems are forever changing places, as well as entering and leaving the network. Thus the unbounded nature of many networks make them looser and more ill-defined structures than partnerships.
2. Networks are usually focused on 'like interests', partnerships on 'common interests'. As we have defined these (see p. 35), like interests are shared interests which can be pursued discretely (systems can operate in parallel), common interests are those which require the participants to play complementary roles. For networks to become partnerships, there must be a dovetailing of functions around a clear and agreed focal task which involves each social system dedicating itself to make a distinctive contribution to the whole. In the case of learning communities, this focal task – the glue which holds the partnership together – will be shaped by the principles of a synergistic curriculum code.
3. The communal strength of networks can often be weak and volatile; that of partnerships stronger and more sustainable. Networks can be mechanistic and impersonal affairs; partnerships cannot. Partnerships are permeated by a communal quality which results in developmental exchanges, encounters and engagements of a much more organic kind than characterize networks. Networks can bypass people as people; partnerships cannot.
4. Networks at their best embrace 'a culture of trust'; partnerships at their best embrace by 'a culture of love'. The 'inclusivity' of networks can be a matter of chance or convenience, and of access to the appropriate technology. The inclusivity of partnerships is a more fundamental matter, requiring a shared commitment to a common goal; in the case of learning communities, to learning how to learn together.

THE SCHOOL AS A CONNECTING SYSTEM

Whether the school is engaged in networking or partnership building, it remains a pivotal learning community. It should be a model from which other systems can learn a good deal about both community and education. It should be a catalyst, stimulating these systems to change and develop. And it will be a connecting system (see p. 101) seeking not only to forge links with its own focal and resource systems but assisting others to engage in a similar way with theirs. It is such functions as these which make the school's role so central. To fulfil this role, the school will need to identify and foster a range of new characteristics essential to its entire organizational life.

As a connecting system, the school will require some 'central figure' (whose responsibilities we discuss more fully below) to focus its role. It will also want a 'central team' to help to address particular network concerns. The central figure will need a phone/fax number more than a building, although some kind of open 'meeting room' may be useful. A database of network contacts is necessary, and the circulation to such contacts through an occasional bulletin could be valuable. The networks or partnerships developed may be strengthened by the setting up of small time-limited 'task-focusing teams' (Savage, 1990, p. 183). An occasional gathering (as opposed to formal meeting) of all the participants could help to enhance the communal strength of the partnership.

THE 'SCHOOL AND COMMUNITY' STRAIT-JACKET

For schools to enter into creative partnerships with other bodies (i.e. for them to build community across social systems), the phrase 'school and community' must be confined to the annals of history. This circumscribed interpretation of community as a homogeneous geographical area has had a profoundly negative effect on an understanding of the nature, variety, complexity and spread of other learning communities with which schools might network or enter into partnership.

It is disappointing that even those writers most enlightened in envisaging the school of the future as one among a diversity of learning systems become trapped in the 'school and community' strait-jacket (Sayer and Williams, 1989; Steffy and Lindle, 1994; Townsend, 1994; Atkinson, 1994; Hargreaves, 1994; Ranson and Tomlinson, 1994). All interpret 'community' as the local neighbourhood, the identity of which comes, if at all, largely from a shared residential self-awareness. Such a parochial understanding of community bars the way to the emergence of a learning society made up of networks and partnerships between the school and learning communities, often spread across many sectors and a wide geographical area.

For the primary school, there is some damage limitation simply because the local neighbourhood does encompass most of those learning communities of particular relevance to the very young; notably the home, places of worship, the 'corner' shop and often a number of locally based neighbourhood services (social workers, health workers, the police, etc.). Even here, however, the failure to perceive that the neighbourhood itself is a complex variety of learning communities, some well-equipped as such, others weak and inadequate, leads primary schools to be less discriminating than they might in networking and establishing partnerships. Thus time-consuming connections can be forged with social systems with little to offer in educational terms, while other systems with real potential but to which it is harder to relate are sometimes neglected. Add to this, the inability of many primary schools to break clear of their local neighbourhood as a source of learning partners and the harm done by the 'school and community' strait-jacket is all too evident.

By way of illustration, one might cite white suburban primary schools which seek to form learning partnerships with home and church, neighbourhood shops and one or two local firms. Such partners may provide some cognitive stimulus for topic or theme work, but offer little as lively learning communities embracing the communal and educational riches which we have tried to describe. In such a context, pedagogy can also be denied any linkage with communities of different racial, cultural or religious character, or with systems located in the larger world of industry, health, leisure and government. To 'stay local' has its value (and its logistical and resource justification), but as a means of learning for, about and, above all, through community, it can be highly restrictive.

The 'school and community' strait-jacket is even more damaging when we come to the case of the secondary school. Occasionally, a more explicit break with the locality is suggested, as for example when Steffy and Lindle (1994) define their 'future school' as having two kinds of 'client' (p. 18): 'primary school clients' consisting of 'students and parents', and 'secondary school clients' made up of 'business, government and communities'. Even for Steffy and Lindle, however, 'communities' remain local entities and the range of 'secondary clients' is limited.

It is vital that the secondary, as well as primary, school be transformed if it is to play a catalytic role in future partnerships and networks of learning communities. But many secondary schools will need to engage in a prolonged process of double-loop learning if they are to perceive the massive potential of the many learning communities, large and small, with which they might engage. As yet the secondary school system in this country has only put its toe in the water. It is high time it dived in at the deep end.

It is encouraging that some schools, for example those who have gained a 'Schools Curriculum Award', have taken the plunge. But many more are neglecting the immense and still growing learning potential of a wider society. As long ago as the early 1970s, a London comprehensive school (in which I taught) actively involved its early school-leavers in such external learning systems as local primary schools (Clark, 1973b), FE colleges, families from different social classes, an extensive range of adults speaking about their work, churches, museums, fire and police stations, many businesses and factories, and leisure groups. There were also excursions into the centre of London, visits further afield and camps across the country which brought students into direct contact with a cross-section of wider society. It is good news that such partnerships have become more common, but the quantity and quality of the linkages involved are still far too limited. As Tomlinson (Ranson and Tomlinson, 1994, p. 14) puts it: 'We seem to have imploded the school at the very time when explosion was needed.'

To explode the secondary school and establish a new society-wide context for learning requires that pupils themselves be treated in a very different way. Many young people of secondary school age are still subject to a form of direction and control which will hugely reduce the potential of education in the twenty-first century. One aspect of this explosion will mean more individualized learning in various locations, sustained by a new technology. But it will be imperative to maintain education's communal quality. Here peer and small-group learning (Clark, 1975) remain painfully neglected pedagogic tools, and learning with and from adult role models, along the lines pioneered by Bazalgette (1970) decades ago, a grossly underused educational resource. Alongside such tools for transformation must go 'the negotiated curriculum' and, as the National Commission on Education puts it (*Learning to Succeed*, 1993, p. 92): 'The development of an ethos in secondary schools which allows them to break free of the strait-jacket of set hours and set periods.' Without such a radical shift in our learning culture, all the attainment targets of a National Curriculum and all the competency indicators of National Vocational Qualifications (NVQs) will be a mountain producing a mouse.

INTER-SCHOOL RELATIONS

The partnerships and networks we have so far been exploring have focused on the school and its links with potential learning communities largely outside the formal education system. But as government legislation ensures that the role of the local education authority (LEA) diminishes in scope, the need for schools to link up with one another, and with other institutions of formal learning, will rapidly move up the agenda.

From one vantage point, school focused partnerships would seem the easiest to forge, for schools overall have a similar purpose and structure. But the introduction of market forces into education means that there now exists an ambiguous co-operative–competitive relationship between schools which is making the formation of partnerships a much more tentative affair than might otherwise have been the case. Nonetheless, the strength of common purpose, the need to share concerns and insights and indeed the economic and administrative advantages of co-operation are giving network and partnership building a steadily growing momentum.

Partnerships between schools are described in a variety of ways including 'federations', 'clusters', 'trusts', 'consortia', and so forth. Although most are still in an embryonic stage, they appear to be of three main types: mutual support, geographical links, and curriculum development

Mutual support

Schools are linking to offer each other support in responding to their new responsibilities for local management and the complexity of the administrative tasks they now face. In many cases, these links have been related to more generalist issues but some practical forms of co-operation have boosted contacts, not least in relation to financial management (Levacic and Woods, 1994). The clearest trend in relation to inter-school partnerships (p. 73) is for secondary schools to establish working agreements with their feeder primary schools, although links between groups of primary schools are also growing.

Geographical links

A second context for partnerships is that of the geographical neighbourhood within which the schools are set. Such clusters are easiest to form where the neighbourhood has relatively clear boundaries and where the schools face demanding social and environmental problems. Thus partnerships of this kind are common in inner-city areas of high population density with a strong ethnic minority presence and a good deal of economic deprivation.

But such federations are also appearing in more favourable situations, such as 'new towns' (Cook and Dalton, 1994).

Curriculum development

A third focus, though often producing networks rather than partnerships, is where schools link up for purposes of curriculum development. In this connection, schools, often through a shared co-ordinator (Clark, 1990, pp. 80–1), come closer together in order the more effectively to tap into a wide range of neighbourhood resources. They set up a variety of learning experiences, from trails to reading events, from sports days to public exhibitions, through which their pupils encounter those from other schools as well as the wider world. Such networks are sometimes more specialized focusing on links with sectors such as industry or the health services.

The focal and resource systems involved in these various forms of clustering are very varied. By and large, it is primary schools which find it easier to link up with one another, probably because partnerships of this kind tend to be neighbourhood focused, but links between secondary and their feeder schools are growing. Secondary schools are rather more tentatively linking up with one another as well as with nearby colleges of further education. In the latter case, however, disputes over who should educate pupils at post-16 are beginning to highlight the threat that market forces can pose to partnership building. Furthermore, if schools begin to take increasing responsibility for teacher training, the bonds between schools and institutions of higher education may also become more fragile.

For us, the key question in all this is the extent to which such moves are fostering the development of schools as learning communities. In general, the signs are modestly encouraging. Although many networks and partnerships arise from external administrative or economic pressures, there remains a spin-off into more communal and open educational practice, not least amongst primary schools. There is also a growing awareness that the school has a responsibility not only to itself but to what the Hertfordshire Education 2000 Project calls 'the educative community', and that there is increasing need for 'a comprehensive community dialogue' (Cook and Dalton, 1994, pp. 118–19). Progress is patchy, still more about functional concerns than the development of a synergistic curriculum across schools, but the next decade could see a substantial number opening themselves up in creative and exciting ways through a new era of inter-school partnership building.

BOUNDARY MANAGERS

Partnership and networks do not create themselves. If they are 'a new art form', then they require 'artists' to give practical expression to the principles on which they are founded.

The role of the community educator working across major social systems is essentially the same as that of the person working on a smaller canvas, discussed at some length in Chapter 7. He or she remains what we called there 'a boundary manager', or what Pedler *et al.* (1991, pp. 22 and 27) describe as 'a boundary spanner'. The ten 'A's (see pp. 106–12) still very much apply. But because the scope of community education discussed in this chapter is so much greater, a few words are needed about the approach and skills required in this wider context.

The community educator, working across a larger number of more complex systems, needs to map out with especial care and clarity the constituency with which he or she is dealing. Such a map may have certain geographical limits (i.e. the catchment area of the school), but it is learning systems as potential partners with which he or she is mainly concerned. The community educator's skill lies in identifying qualitative not quantitative alliances. He or she needs to be a person who undertakes this task realizing that (Sayer and Williams, 1989, p. 147) 'the school exercise is to contribute, not to assume the mantle of total education'.

The community educator at the macro level has to be both a skilled maker of contacts and connector of persons. In this sense, Foy's description (1980, p. 120) of 'a spider at the centre of the web' is apposite. Webs are delicate things to create and maintain. So what Handy and Aitken (1986, pp. 121 and 124) describe as 'the human touch', and 'sensitivity rather than power, touch instead of force', are essential.

The community educator as boundary manager on this scale has a major task of communication to undertake, whether this be by spoken or printed word, by old or (increasingly) new technology. Keeping the participants regularly and clearly informed is a communal as well as educational necessity. Here a good database and the ability to communicate information in an appropriate form and manner become all-important.

One other key skill is the community educator's ability to visualize the network as a potential partnership. There may need to be a series of not only educative but communal events which can offer partners a glimpse of a new corporate identity. Such events need to involve students as much as teachers, focal as well as resource systems throughout the network. These happenings are also important to help bond smaller (sub)systems within the whole where, for example, interests are more specialized.

For schools to build partnerships and networks, time and energy are needed. The head's vision is as ever of paramount importance, as well as the ability to manage boundaries on a large scale. But for this wider kind of community building to succeed, it must become the responsibility of far more than just the head. It needs first and foremost to be a team effort, with team members being given special responsibilities to fulfil. But over time the whole school must come to share the vision as well as the action. Governors, too, have their own distinctive role to play in helping the school to build alliances with other partners in learning.

The mid and late 1980s saw numerous local education authorities assisting schools to move forward with network and partnership building. They appointed personnel designated to link schools with one another and with other learning systems of value to them (Sayer and Williams, 1989; Clark, 1990). It was a role of great significance for the future of community education within this country. More recent government legislation has put the appointment and training of such personnel into reverse. The long-term consequences can only be to retard the emergence of a learning society. But what should be quite clear from this change of policy, as well as from a great deal else that has gone before in this book, is that the transformation of education is a political affair. To this dimension of community education we now turn.

Chapter 10

The Learning Society

LONELY CROWD OR GHETTO?

The problem which the whole of this book seeks to address is how humankind can in future decades avoid becoming depersonalized by the lonely crowd or imprisoned in the ghetto of tribalism. On the one hand, our common life is undermined by a 'mosaic of institutions … in which boundaries weaken, edges blur, colours blend, lines curve, shapes fragment; and patterns, though undoubtedly present, are less easily discerned' (Hargreaves, 1994, p. 56). On the other hand, centripetal forces threaten to produce a world of incestuous tribalism founded not only on 'blood and belonging' (Ignatieff, 1993), but on sectarian interests of an economic, religious or political kind.

Our argument has been that the future of our planet depends on a new awareness, appreciation, understanding and ownership of 'community' as the means of holding in creative tension the centrifugal and centripetal forces impinging on our world. Although, in an everyday context, the re-creation of community must interweave with many other tasks, at the macro level of human survival it is the focal task itself. It is a human enterprise second to none, not even the economic. Our thesis, like Boswell's (1990, p. 141), is 'that for economic co-operation to prosper fully, the surrounding culture would need to accord paramountcy to the development of persons through free community'. But our thesis is also that for community to prosper, people must be increasingly open to engage with and learn from one another; 'public co-operation and a reasonably well-educated society appear to be inseparable' (p. 123). Community is as dependent on genuine education as education is on genuine community.

The quest for global communal openness is a daunting task. It is a visionary undertaking. It must occupy 'the summit of our thinking about social ideals' (p. 10). But whence comes the incentive and sustainable impetus to strive for inclusive not exclusive communities, to engage in education and not indoctrination?

There is no easy answer except, as we have done earlier, to point to what we believe are two self-evident reasons for radical change. First, that if we want our children and our children's children to experience an ongoing and ever deepening quality of human life – culturally, socially, economically and aesthetically – then a world committed to the common good and founded on communal openness is utterly essentially. Second, that without such a foundation our planet will eventually self-destruct. As Kingdom (1992, p. 118) puts it:

> The need for a future predicated upon a communal culture goes beyond national economic recovery, the moral claims of egalitarians, the cry for justice by socialists, or even the quest for a good life. It is linked to the sustainability of life on the planet; in a world which believes only the fittest should survive, none will survive.

It is our contention that 'a communal culture' cannot be imposed from above, although it can be fostered or blocked from above. Community building, like every other form of socialization, has to be learnt. Thus the future of our planet depends not on grand plans or quick fixes but on the proliferations of a multitude of genuine learning communities, of all shapes and sizes and across all sectors, from the family to the factory, the church to the business corporation, and not least, as we shall explore further below, at all levels of government itself. In this complex of learning communities – the school, small and at times vulnerable as it may seem – has a catalytic role to play.

Such proliferation and multiplication of learning communities is infinitely more possible now than it has ever been. The 'world-wide web' now expanding at a phenomenal rate is just one strand in a new information flow that can enable even the smallest and relatively isolated community to be part of and contribute to a much wider whole. The synergistic curriculum is now available for increasing billions to pursue.

Yet the vision of networking in itself being the salvation of our world (Ferguson, 1982) needs to be treated with some caution. To engineer networks is not the same as to build community. It does not in itself ensure that we escape the anonymity of the lonely crowd or the sectarianism of the ghetto. As Whitty (1992, p. 110) reminds us there is a grave danger of more fragmentation, 'of political education, development education, multicultural education, peace education, anti-sexist education, and social and personal education, all going their separate ways'. At the same time, access to the intimate attention of millions via personal computer or public media can enable fundamentalists to corral the commitment (and cash) of millions into a formidable range of exclusive pressure groups.

It is not surprising, therefore, that there is a realization that learning communities must spawn learning societies so that the latter can be a stepping stone towards the ultimate and imperative goal of a learning world (Handy and Aitken, 1986, p. 109; Pedlar *et al.*, 1991, p. 21; Ranson, 1993). In our terminology, the learning society must become a learning community of learning communities, just as eventually a learning world must become a learning community of learning societies.

A keen matter of concern is the scale and control of such learning societies. Persuasive arguments are put forward for the city being the most appropriate macro communal system. Handy (1994, p. 252) claims that 'the city is a community on a human scale, the nation state is not'. Yet Boswell (1990, p. 41) asserts: 'For all its dangers, the nation state can still be viewed as a "focus of primary allegiance".' Less convincingly, there are those who still regard the local neighbourhood as the prime unit of a learning society (Hambleton and Hoggett, 1984; Atkinson, 1994). On this question of scale hinges much of the debate about political control, a key issue to which we return.

REFRAMING COMMUNITY EDUCATION

It is in the context of this struggle to fashion a communally open and sustainable world founded on interdependent learning societies, that the concept of 'community education' urgently needs to be reframed. And reframed as one central to the resolution of our present crisis.

That reframing and reinstatement has been the purpose of all that has gone before. We have set out the case for community being rooted in beliefs and values (for us – life, liberty and love) large and inclusive enough to address the challenge of 'the survival of the species' (Palmer, 1987, p. 15). We have argued that community needs to be supercharged with passion (the search for a sense of security, significance and solidarity) if it is to become a force to match the challenges of our age. We have contested that community has to demonstrate the potential to encompass and enrich a diversity of cultures and conditions of 'men', above all the dispossessed and marginalized, if it is to be able to unite us in pursuit of the common good and 'the kingdom of God'. We have argued that community must undergird every aspect of our common life, not least our systems and processes of learning. For education which is not for, about and through community is ultimately fiddling while Rome burns. The hope for humankind rests on the communal transformation of education.

At the same time, we have contended that community building needs education. It requires not simply the processes of nurture, instruction and training, important prolegomena as these may be, but the life and person-centred process of discovery outlined in Chapter 6. We are utterly convinced that for our world to survive in any qualitative sense, community itself must be opened up and transformed by education.

Our thesis is that nothing less than the integration of community and education, in sum a new form of 'community education', can now suffice. The future will continue to embrace a diversity of curriculum codes, but paramount for our world's well-being is the synergistic curriculum, that founded on the parts actively engaging together to create a richer and larger whole. Only if community development and curriculum development transform one another in this way, will there by any ultimate hope for our planet.

Community education has to be 'managed', though 'orchestrated' would come nearer to illuminating the essence of the process. It requires community educators with the commitment, the knowledge and the skills to promote and foster it. In the preceding three chapters, we have explored aspects of such orchestration in relation to the school, which we believe has the potential to be a vital catalyst in this process of transformation. But here the words of the Salford teacher, quoted by Hargreaves (1982, p. 34,) strike a sombre cord: 'How can you make a community in school when there's no community out there?', or, as Hargreaves (p. 130) himself puts it: 'A community education which has lost sight of the nation as a whole as a community is not worthy of its name and can justifiably be condemned as parochial.'

To transform learning communities into a learning society, and indeed into a learning world, we are talking not just about a process of personal self-actualization (though that potentially volcanic thrust from below is immensely important). We are drawing attention to a process that needs encouraging, fostering, promoting and, at times, moving forward in the face of considerable collective resistance (the 'communal dilemma'). Here questions of power and conflict are ever present, and the role of politics and the nature of government, at different levels, become paramount. We shall examine these issues from two complementary perspectives: society as a political community, and society as a learning community.

SOCIETY AS A POLITICAL COMMUNITY

'The politics of difference'

Margaret Thatcher exposed herself to tumultuous political attack when she stated (1987): 'There is no such thing as society.' But she was quite correct when, in the next sentence, she added: 'There are individual men and women and there are families.' She would have been even more accurate if she had gone on to say: 'There are also now a multitude of clubs, pressure groups, single issue organizations, associations, unions and federations forming an ever-changing cultural kaleidoscope beyond.'

Every 'society' now consists of 'a mosaic of institutions', all with blurred edges. But within and alongside these institutions there now exist a multitude of social systems (of every shape and size) focused on: people (gender, age, disability, etc.), environment (the neighbourhood, the work place, the city), interaction (interest groups of all kinds), relationships (family and race), as well as values and beliefs (religion and politics). However, even these categories underplay the variety and fluidity of modern social systems. They also beg the question as to the vitality and strength of these systems as communities.

The mosaic (or, perhaps more appropriately, kaleidoscope) is made even more complex by the fact that these systems have a vast overlapping membership. Outside their families, many people belong to a dozen if not a score of different 'communities', the importance and centrality of which shift as life progresses. In these contexts they will play different roles and have different needs fulfilled. It is this overlapping membership that has led to the generation of 'similarity and difference simultaneously' as Westwood (1992, p. 243) puts it. She is here focusing on the breakdown of a sense of community founded on social class. But she is also depicting a scenario which is affecting all relatively hitherto homogeneous communities, be they rooted in kinship, locality or interest.

The shifting kaleidoscope of forms and formations has been given impetus in all societies by the centrifugal and centripetal forces mentioned in the Introduction to this book. The deconstruction of old expressions of community goes on apace, as rapidly changing role terminology well illustrates. To labels such as passenger, patient, client and member, are now added customer, consumer, 'human resource' or unemployed, not to mention 'yuppie' and 'yob'. With these labels comes not only a new freedom of choice but the fragmentation of identity. At the same time, and often in reaction to the threat of anonymous or powerless roles, many are drawn into associations of protection, protest or vested interest. These social systems, many new, some old but now reconstructed, may be supportive and communal (in our sense of the term). Others, however, threaten to create a ghetto-like and fractious, if not fractured, society.

In a societal as well as global context, therefore, we are faced with an urgent search for sustainable communal forms which can offer people what Handy (1994, p. 100) calls 'twin citizenship', but what might more appropriately be called 'multi-citizenship'. People must be able to find their communal sustenance not just in one but in numerous groupings of differing function and scale. Thus one critical task societies now face is enabling their members to develop and maintain this new kind of citizenship without becoming lost in the lonely crowd or made captive in the ghetto.

The other fundamental question is: how are such pluralistic societies to be governed? Where politics has now become what Westwood (1992, p. 243) calls 'the politics of difference', how can a political community which is able to encompass immense diversity while fostering coherence be fashioned?

The search for sustaining and sustainable forms of community has of course always been one facing humankind. But in our age the population explosion, increased longevity of life, greater affluence and thus choice, the information revolution and the explosion of networking and, not least, the threat of nuclear war or ecological disaster, have all immeasurably raised the stakes. Thus right at the top of the agenda of all societies is the question of how a new political community with any hope of seeing us through the next century can be born. As Martin (1992, p. 6) puts it: 'The project is ultimately to reconstitute the wider meaning of community as society, and to show through our actions that there is such a thing.' In this particular context, our own communal task – that of creating an increasingly strong sense of security, significance and solidarity within and across social systems – becomes not a cross-curricular theme to weave into other focal tasks but the very core of the focal task itself.

It is government in the end which has to manage or, rather, orchestrate this communal task as a focal concern. But the success of such an undertaking depends increasingly on the creation of a political community which, at the level of its participants' beliefs and values, Berger and Luckmann's (1967, p. 110f) 'symbolic universe', is sufficiently coherent and sustainable to make government possible. All nations, internally and in relation to one another, must now engage with urgency in pursuit of this new and sustainable political paradigm.

'The heart of the matter'

If a new sense of political community is to be born, then we have to return to the heart of what community is all about (Chapter 3). We here want to suggest not an 'answer' to the challenge of fragmentation and fundamentalism but a new perspective. If community is rooted in the values of life, liberty and love, and the feelings of security, significance and solidarity, then these must also be the foundations of political community.

'What can be a more fundamental human right than the right to survival?', writes Kingdom (1992, p. 98). For all of us a sense of security is fundamental. The response of the world, albeit half-hearted and unsustained, to the crises of famine and poverty in the Ethiopias and Somalias of our generation indicate that there is at least a glimmer of hope that a political community might emerge which acknowledges, in practice as well as principle, that life and security are due to all human beings by right of their humanity. And there are signs that this right is increasingly acknowledged, as in our Rwandas, even where such insecurity is the direct result of anarchic human conflict.

Beyond these high-profile flash-points on the world scene, political community needs to embrace a more holistic and long-term appreciation of survival. Our planet's physical well-being must form a key part of the communal agenda if humanity is to continue. Here the emergence of 'green politics', however tenuous as yet, has pin-pointed one fundamental principle of community building, that of the affirmation of life and an adequate means of living for all, which must come increasingly centre stage. 'The survival of the species' depends upon it.

However, political community, like all community is not only about survival and a sense of security. Indeed, we have argued, that unless liberty and love, a sense of significance and solidarity, are also present, then our attempts to build ecologically aware and economically sustainable societies will collapse. The bottom line is not the material but the human.

It is in this context that the values of 'the market' have to be set. The market's ideological impact (which underlines the importance of beliefs and values over against the material and the physical) during the past decade and more has been universal and profound. Its human appeal is to our second dimension of community, liberty and a sense of significance. In this respect, it has much to offer which we despise at our peril: personal initiative and fulfilment, social fluidity and mobility have brought and will continue to bring immense benefits to humankind. Without enterprise and effort achieving a dynamic international economy, the kind of political community required for the next century would be impossible.

The problem comes when a market philosophy attempts to colonize those other values and sentiments which underpin community building. If the provision of water, food, shelter and health, and if the care of the environment, simply become a means by which individuals or systems express their own quest for status and wealth, then the search for significance becomes incestuous and poses a major threat to the right of all human beings to life and security. Political community then becomes unsustainable and the state literally 'sold down the river'.

Political community is also threatened where the market infiltrates and subverts the quest for a sense of solidarity and the values on which it is founded. Münch (1992, p. 66) observes that today even 'morality, aesthetics and the search for truth are all subject to market type processes to an ever greater extent'. The freedom of the market promotes competition for scarce resources. This not only sets business against business, but artist against artist, school against school, charity against charity and church against church. Their contribution to the whole ceases to rest on intrinsic worth but on an ability to 'sell' their wares in ways that compel attention. The integrity of political parties and of political campaigning is likewise undermined by the same processes (Mayhew, 1992).

This threat by market forces to a genuine sense of solidarity, and its undergirding value of love, only serves to emphasize how vital yet how challenging a task this search for community really is. It is little wonder that left-wing political parties, which are in theory at least committed to some form of corporate ethic, have found it so hard to retain power for any length of time. To fashion a sustainable communal society on a societal scale out of 'the politics of difference' is the most demanding of all political tasks. That in pursuit of its ideals, the left throughout recent history has resorted to an over-planned economy, offered welfare patronage that has undermined initiative and responsibility, or in some contexts espoused totalitarianism in order to enforce 'solidarity', is thus not entirely surprising.

The good news is that with the collapse of state Marxism and a growing awareness of the acute limitations of a market economy, we are at last beginning to glimpse that the political community of the future has to be a new kind of animal. 'If the quality of human and group relationships really is the basic building block in one's view of the social world, then it is simply not possible to adhere to over-arching cults either of super-collectives, or of individuals as islands, or of an "invisible hand" in social life' (Boswell, 1990, p. 33). The long-term survival of society, not only in terms of quality of life but of sheer endurance, now depends on the emergence of a political community that recognizes the weightiness of each of our three 'L's and three 'S's, but is also able to integrate them into a coherent whole. This will mean new metaphors being honed – the body? the meal? the journey? the human city? – to challenge the hegemony of the market as a paradigm.

Some have called this task the search 'for a communitarian "third way"' (between left and right), even if such is 'still largely amorphous' (Boswell, 1990, p. 9; Etzioni, 1993). Others (Kingdom, 1992, p. 24) have more explicitly termed it 'the social democratic ideal' or (p. 101) 'the social market'. The precise words are unimportant. What is important is that the next century will necessitate the development of a new kind of politics, rooted in a new political philosophy and founded on a new kind of political community, if humankind is to see it through. Such a community will have to emerge not only within societies but between them.

Focal systems and forums

If a new political community is to be built around a more creative synthesis of the values and sentiments at 'the heart of the matter', its scope and operation are likely to reflect, at all societal levels, our guidelines outlined in Chapter 5. This means, for a start, the inclusion of a far broader range of focal systems than has hitherto been engaged in matters political. We are in search of a new form of democracy which can embrace the concerns, interests and resources of a much wider spectrum of public life than has ever been dreamt of before.

This is not just the consequence of new centrifugal forces at work. The shrinkage of our world is also generating centripetal forces already compelling us to hammer out new systems of government. The issue facing societies is not whether the politics of difference will become a reality but how we handle what is already upon us. In this context many systems, such as those embracing the unemployed, the disabled and the single parent, remain relatively weak and, in the light of our guidelines, need to be given hugely greater affirmation, support and authority. But ways now need to be found of enabling all types of social system to develop solidarity with, and find significance within, a new kind of identifiable but open political entity.

The key to this quest is what happens at the boundary of these systems or, as Münch (1992, p. 67) describes it, within the 'zone of mutual penetration'. For though centripetal forces may be turning many social systems in on themselves, centrifugal forces are necessitating complex patterns of external engagement however temporary. Münch writes (pp. 67–8):

> Larger and larger zones of interpenetration are developing between discourses, markets, associations and political decision-making procedures, in which an increasing proportion of events in society take place. At the same time, the subsystems are becoming increasingly interwoven in processes of networking, communication, negotiation and compromise formation. This requires the building up of new institutions with the function of mediating between societal subsystems.

This 'function of mediating' describes what government is now all about. Government has to offer identity and coherence to a society whose future development can only be understood 'in terms of interpenetration, overlaying, communication, networking, negotiation and compromise formation, all of these occurring in ever more wide-ranging zones of an intermeshing fabric of different societal subsystems' (p. 57). It is a task which, on the global scene, now faces challenges such as those typified by 'the internet society' (Kelly, 1994, p. 464) which, 'as its users are proud to boast, [is] the largest functioning anarchy in the world'.

For a form of government to emerge which can promote synergy (Fig. 8.2) rather than segregation or assimilation, the growth of an overarching political community rooted in the kind of views and sentiments outlined above is a *sine qua non*. This means that alongside, as well as within, institutionalized politics, 'connecting systems' with a political role are needed which can forge new links, 'hold the circle' and facilitate a negotiated response to conflict. Sciulli and Bould (1992, p. 260) argue that such a development is 'to break out of the authoritarianism – liberal bifurcation (of Hobbesian centralisation v. normative consensus) altogether and also to abandon the undifferentiated concept of social control', in favour of 'collegial formations ... capable of specifying unambiguously when possibilities of social integration are either increasing or decreasing'. One particularly significant type of collegial formation from our perspective, is the so-called 'forum'.

The concept of forums is not new. They have existed since the days of Rome and well before. What is new is the possibility, in a mass pluralistic society, of once again bringing meaningful and sustainable human scale democratic structures into being. Boswell (1990, pp. 131–40) has begun to delineate some qualitative characteristics of forums which could give them a critical role in the reconstruction of society as a political community.

He stresses that forums must be cross-sectional, encompassing a far wider membership than peers or even market competitors, and genuinely representative of the public they serve. He argues that 'because forums exist in "the economy"' it is quite inadequate to judge them 'by the conventional criteria of economics'. Their key functions are not just the obvious ones of 'information transfer', 'consultation', 'collective research' and even 'group bargaining', but 'quieter, more diffuse and less discussed attributes'. The more subtle but communally more vital functions of forums Boswell distinguishes as 'mutual source surveillance' akin to our guideline relating to mutually supportive accountability (pp. 78–9), 'socio-economic learning' and 'morally extending their members'.

These last two characteristics pin-point the essence of what forums can contribute to the creation of a political community. It is their 'collegial style' expressed through debate, their potential to restructure society through discourse, which offers hope for the future. What matters most, however, is not the quantity of debate and discourse, but the quality, the distinctive nature of such dialogue as portrayed in our own guidelines on communication (see p. 76).

To promote discourse of quality, Boswell (1990, p. 16f) argues for 'organisational transparency', closely related to the 'concepts of "open government" and "accountability"'. For Mayhew (1992, p. 193), the issue is ensuring 'authentic debate within a forum that gives true influence to the public'. Münch (1994, p. 63) believes that such authenticity can only emerge 'if, apart from developing effective strategies to fight economic inflation and recession, [society] builds up corresponding strategies to deal with discursive inflation and recession, and the breakdown of universal public discourse'. This can only be achieved if 'the tokens of public discourse ... the rhetorical symbols of influence' (Mayhew, pp. 198–9) are related to 'true persuasion, unadulterated by threat or by inducements appealing solely to self-interest, [and are] based upon convincing others of common interests' (p. 194).

Forums typified by debate and discourse of this sort are the bedrock of an overarching political community which is so essential if societies are to cohere in the modern world. Forums are gathering momentum, but will need to develop further at all levels of 'government'. They can be seen, often in embryonic form, in such phenomena as neighbourhood committees, area associations, affinity groups, single-issue groups, quality circles, focus groups, tele cottages, teleconferences, and of course across the whole of the media – press, radio (phone-in programmes) and television (informal and formalized debates and discussions of all kinds, with interactive television approaching fast over the horizon).

More institutionalized forms of government will only find a credible communal role in future if they take on many of the features of such forums, and the changing nature of the new political community which they reflect. This requires not only that government, at both local and national levels, commits itself to 'organizational transparency' but that it addresses the reality of an increasingly educated public. One outcome has to be a growing acceptance of the principle of 'subsidiarity', a situation, as Handy (1994, p. 115) defines it, of 'reverse delegation'; where the parts are the ultimate guardians of the rights and responsibilities delegated in trust to the centre, rather than vice versa. And this will demand 'a free political community outside the state to which the state is accountable' (Mayhew, 1992, p. 191).

Such a lateral shift in much traditional political thinking, let alone practice, is very hard for most of us, not least politicians, to make. It requires a huge investment in 'the negotiation of meanings' (Shotter, 1993, p. 118), not least wrestling with how the values and sentiments we have distinguished as the hallmarks of community can be distinctively affirmed yet synthesized, as well as operationalized. It means a much more explicit recognition of the fact that very often 'it is only through compromise that decisions can be made at all' (Münch, 1992, p. 68), and of the primacy of negotiation and the skills to undertake it. It will necessitate much greater weight being accorded to what Boswell (1990, p. 177f) calls 'social monitoring' to encourage 'transparency'. It will also mean much greater influence being given to 'para-intermediaries' (p.130f) who 'exercise leadership by perceiving needs and opportunities for public co-operation, influencing sectional organisations towards it, innovating methods for achieving it, and organising it operationally'.

The political community as a learning community

The politics of difference means that the old landmarks have gone for ever. Centrifugal forces create a pluralistic society and an unending search for 'symbolic universes' which can facilitate community building. Such forces also bring conflict over meanings and purposes, frequent compromise, and the necessity of continuous negotiation. For a new political community to overcome what Berger called (1980, p. 9) this 'vertigo of relativity', it must thus become a dynamic *learning* community. At the same time, centripetal forces are at work which can lead to the domination of vested interests, the hegemony of political ideologies and the corruption of the media undermining emerging forms of political community. The most potent weapon against such potential domination is again an educated and articulate public.

In this context, a reframed understanding and implementation of community education becomes imperative. This will require more than 'education for democracy', though important contributions to the debate have been made under that heading. It will call on all the wisdom and skills we possess to enable society to become a community of learning communities. It will mean our 'rediscovering education's social and political purpose' (Benn, 1992, p. 162).

Community education reframed in this way will set the agenda for all organizations across all sectors of society as they respond to the need to become 'learning organizations', with the characteristics we have explored in previous chapters. It will require us to learn a new language which 'is not that of engineering but of politics, with talk of cultures and networks, of teams and coalitions, of influence or power rather than control, of leadership not management' (Handy, 1990, p. 71). It will need the training of a new type of community educator, networker, negotiator and intermediary with skills drawn from a diversity of professions. Such training few so-called community education courses have even begun to address at any depth.

Community education, if reframed along these lines, will also require what Baron (1989, p. 83) describes as 'a political strategy'. If it is to give impetus to the new political community so urgently required, community education will have to pay particular attention to the political sphere. Here its concerns must be publicly legitimized, here its contribution has to to be nurtured and developed and here its development needs to be adequately resourced. It is, therefore, to the political aspects of the education system that we must turn to see whether our society is grasping the nettle of its future survival.

SOCIETY AS A LEARNING COMMUNITY

In this section, we take a brief look at what is happening to the English education system to highlight ways in which the model of community education we have developed throughout this book is being promoted or hindered by government intervention. All governments need to be involved in transforming education so what more communally important process is there than to learn from one another's failures and successes?

Since 1988, England, with Wales, has been subject to a welter of government legislation for education the like of which has not been witnessed for half a century. The response, in terms of exposition and commentary, has produced a bonanza for educational publishers. But underlying the often complex multitude of changes which have been brought about lie distinctive values and beliefs which shape all social systems, the nation state included.

The government of education

The new conservatism which has given impetus to these changes is now recognized to be an uneasy but potent alliance of old Toryism (with the championing of nation, family, duty, authority and traditional standards) and a revived neo-liberalism (rooted in the values of self-interest, competitive individualism and anti-statism). There is no doubt, however, that the latter has become the driving force of educational reform and has moulded most of the legislation emerging with and since the Education Reform Act (1988).

Major problems relating to such an ideology have already been touched on above. Its failure lies not in its emphasis on the importance of individual liberty and personal significance, but on the devaluing of life and love, security and solidarity in the process. And this communally lop-sided philosophy becomes even more compromised when it takes on an exclusive and élitist tone.

A further problem with the new conservatism is the latent deception (though at times perhaps self-deception) which permeates its more neo-liberal tendencies. This is the frequent appeal to such ideals as the common good, the future well-being of the nation or the 'trickle down' benefits supposed to accrue to all, that in reality produce a highly competitive market culture in which there must be many losers as well as winners. This means that an education system which, in communal terms, should be an inclusive one, is threatened by fragmentation and divisiveness. As Martin (1994, p. 19; pp. 20–1) comments, the 'deconstruction' of education transforms it 'from a public good into a private commodity'.

Nevertheless, despite this divisive market context, education has been communally opened up in two important ways. Internally, focal systems embracing new students have developed apace in range and number. Not only has post-sixteen further education become normative but learning is rapidly becoming lifelong. At one end of the spectrum, pre-school provision is an increasingly important political priority; at the other, access courses for mature students of all ages, especially women and black students have multiplied enormously.

Externally, trends to make schools more open institutions, a process in part fostered by community education over previous decades, have accelerated considerably since 1988. It is to be welcomed that parents have come to the fore as important focal systems. In theory they have been cast as 'consumers' with the right to choose the school to which they wish to send their child. But in practice such choice is continually compromised by the simple fact that the schools parents might choose are not always available where and when they are wanted.

Parents are more than ever before actively involved in the education of their children, through closer contact with teachers, greater knowledge of the curriculum and membership of governing bodies, even if daunting problems of parental availability, time and energy remain. Yet, there is also a deeper issue as to whether parents have enough experience, expertise and time to be well informed and up-to-date in such a complex and rapidly changing educational world.

Schools have also opened up to a wide range of other focal systems, in particular the business world. This is a major gain for education. But two issues remain. One is how to deepen the quality of these new partnerships. There is evidence (Barber, 1993), for example, that work experience for pupils is proving hard to sustain and the honeymoon of school–industry liaison is over. Not only are the demands on curriculum time proving highly restrictive despite belated government attempts to reduce these, but a latent conflict of ideology between education and the business world is sometimes an unaddressed cause of friction.

A related but more far-reaching problem is that community education needs to transform many more social systems into learning communities as such and not merely leave them as the providers of resources. There is an urgent need for a co-ordinated strategic policy that can promote health, social services, business, the arts, leisure services, as well as the education system itself, as learning communities in their own right, but together responsible for the future education of our nation (Barber, 1993). The journey towards a learning society has begun, but only just.

Government has placed a National Curriculum at the centre of its legislation. The question we must pose here is whether such a curriculum, as the focal task of the education system, is adequately communal.

Communally, the most important contribution of the National Curriculum would seem to be that the sharing of experience, insights and resources is facilitated across systems. This is a great gain in opening up an enduring as well as genuinely educational debate about the purpose and nature of learning (far more successful than 'The Great Debate' of the late 1970s).

The communal problems do not lie in the national sharing promoted by such a curriculum. They arise, first and foremost, because this curriculum has been imposed, with 'a determined effort not to consult' (Maclure, 1988, p. 166). Research and negotiation have gone by the board. We shall unfortunately continue to reap the rewards for some time to come. Second, the content of that curriculum remains communally impoverished. The hope that cross-curricular themes (such as citizenship) would help to make it a curriculum for and about community have not been realized (NFER, 1994). Third, if the knowledge content of the National Curriculum remains supreme, 'it must lead to differential levels of attainment ... derived from such irrelevant factors as class, race and, possibly also, gender' (Kelly, 1988, p. 24).

Fourth, and central to our concerns, the National Curriculum is not rooted in a synergistic curriculum code, giving major attention to process and partnership, but follows a traditional approach colonized by important features of a technological curriculum model. Thus, instruction and training take priority over education, as we have defined it (Chapter 6), and the salient features of a community curriculum are, if present anywhere, bolted on to the margins or fitted into the cracks.

In terms of process, many of our guidelines (Chapter 5) are given short shrift with attainment targets and a still overcrowded timetable reinforcing the old and increasingly outmoded transmission approach. Learning through community, and the enrichment which it can bring to the educational task is largely neglected. The class and the school are blocked from becoming genuine learning communities.

The answer to the communally destructive aspects of the National Curriculum is not its abandonment. It is to hone it down to its 'foundation subjects' (English, maths and science), to provide ample time to communalize their so-called 'delivery', and, for the rest, to encourage the development of a school-based community curriculum following the kind of guidelines we have suggested, including active engagement with a wide range of potential learning systems external to the school.

The government's failure to address the consequences of its recent legislation for the process of teaching and learning, has been compounded by an ideological and unresearched attack on teaching styles. The denigration of 'progressive' educational methods has been ill-informed and sometimes verging on the paranoiac. This has meant not only pressure on teachers to return to didactic approaches which have failed many children in the past, but blindness to the fact that the role of teachers in the future must undergo fundamental changes if we are to move towards the creation of a learning society. Government policy, not even more school-based practice, does little to encourage teachers to reappraise their role as the creators of learning networks and a gateway to resources existing way beyond the walls of the classroom.

The local management of schools is, however, one aspect of government legislation which is, in principle at least, communally well founded. It has the value of subsidiarity undergirding it and opens up many opportunities for the enhancement of the school as a learning community (see Chapter 8). It gives schools incentives to create their own distinctive identity as well as new learning partnerships with external focal and resource systems. The head, too, is offered a new role in which he or she assumes the important task of boundary manager in order to enhance learning resources both within and beyond the school.

The problems lie not with the principle of local management or the new role of heads but with the competitive market philosophy which has driven recent Education Acts, and not least the assault on local government. The attempted deconstruction of the education system, not least through the ill-fated effort to establish City Technology Colleges (CTCs) and the golden handshake initially offered to grant-maintained schools, has made it far more difficult than it might have been to build community across learning systems, a *sine qua non* of a learning society.

It is not surprising, therefore, that even where schools have not opted out, competition to survive has weakened many ties and new consortia are proving hard to sustain. Booming management courses for heads seem to be all about total quality management within schools and not between them, and enhancing 'external relations' becomes a competitive rather than a co-operative enterprise, with a consequent waste of human and financial resources (IPPR, 1993, p. 3). The 'island concept of management' (Boswell, 1990, p. 195) is given a new boost, and the development of the school as a learning community again retarded.

The local management of schools highlights the dramatically changed role of local education authorities in England in the 1990s. There is no shortage of suggestions for a new role (IPPR, 1993, pp. 26–7; Barber, 1993; Ranson, 1993; Ranson and Tomlinson, 1994). From a community education perspective, there would seem to be three key functions for them to perform. First and foremost is what Ranson terms 'promoting a vision of the learning society for all throughout their lives'. This means ensuring 'access to a curriculum which empowers learners to develop their capacities and gain the confidence to play their public role as citizens in the development of their society'. But the vision remains paramount. For a local education authority this must mean 'maintaining and enhancing the education of the whole community' (IPPR, 1993, p. 27).

Second, local education authorities should be a key instrument for the promotion of learning partnerships, between schools and between schools and other agencies. Their task is to foster a new collective commitment to education as a universal public service and further the means of attaining this. It is also to ensure that schools and external bodies learn from one another by engaging and interacting in developmental ways.

Here it is important that despite all the financial pressures, local authorities retain and train a task-force of city-wide community education catalysts who are active as 'go-betweens' to network school with school, and schools with external learning partners. The destruction of this developing role, fostered by local authorities in the 1980s, has been a disastrous casualty as far as community education and the growth of a learning society is concerned. Such networks can be hugely productive in terms of the quality of education. It is vital that local authorities are given the chance of reinstating them.

Third, local education authorities should retain a major responsibility for the in-service professional development of teachers and related personnel. There is a great danger at present of in-service training becoming piecemeal and truncated, with the short-term functional needs of the school taking precedence over informed curriculum development and personal career enhancement. There is also a need for local authorities to ensure that such professional development embraces the principles and practice of community education so that every teacher can begin to operate, within and beyond the school, in synergistic mode.

The changes addressed above stem from recent government legislation. From the perspective of community education and the emergence of a learning society, it will be clear by now that all is far from well. We have sought to give credit where credit is due. Recent legislation has contained some communally significant enactments, with the shake -up of the whole education system promoting a strenuous and long overdue debate about beliefs and values as well as organization and management.

However, there is bad news in plenty. The most dangerous outcome of government policy is the centralization of so many powers in the hands of the Secretary of State for Education in a way which provides the constant temptation to divide and rule. Handy (1994, p. 118) is quite right when he argues that subsidiarity requires a centre which is 'strong and well informed'. But, he adds (p. 119), those placed there 'cannot run it [the business], and should be too few in number to be tempted'. A government which seeks to determine, to dominate, to direct and to drive its education system from above will not only lose control, but suck in resources which are desperately needed at the local level to implement a synergistic curriculum code. Such a government will thus undermine the learning process, of which it too should be an integral part, and obstruct the emergence of a learning society as a community of learning communities. If the public is to become an educated community then they must be treated as active partners in the building of learning communities, at every stage and at every level of the political process.

Political and educational connecting systems

A learning society is about transformation: personal, organizational, societal, global. It is a community of a political kind engaged in discourse and debate about beliefs and values. But a learning society as a political community is also concerned with the distribution of power. Finding the means by which power can be effectively and fairly managed for the common good is never an easy task. This is all the more reason why politics and education must go hand in hand if a learning society is not to become prisoner of its own ideological convictions. It is ideological closure which threatens all our futures.

But creating a learning society requires knowledge, experience and skills which have to be delivered by an education system which itself exercises power and influence. Thus, just as the political system needs to be educational, the education system has a political responsibility . The challenge for a would-be learning society is how it integrates the contribution and influence of the political system on the one hand, and that of the education system on the other.

The means of sustaining this creative tension might best be met by the establishment of two major kinds of 'connecting system', one having a more explicitly political and the other a more explicitly educational function. The former would be primarily concerned with the well-being of every citizen. Its political power and expertise may be considerable but educational expertise incidental. The latter would be mainly concerned with the maintenance of more specialized educational organizations and associations. Its educational experience may be considerable but political power and skill more limited.

The political system, as a connecting system, should be concerned with the whole of public life. It must operate at a level where public life can be given an identifiable and sustainable identity. At present this is at the level of the nation state, on the one hand, and at the level of the city and its region on the other. Some, such as Handy (1994, pp. 251f) argue that the city is the future's most viable form of community. It would seem, therefore, communally as well as politically destructive to follow the trend of recent government legislation which diminishes the importance of local authorities. Whatever their precise form and responsibilities, only the latter can represent the general public and the common good in a way that gives at least some power to local people in relation to local concerns, not least in relation to local manifestations of a national education system. Provided local authorities themselves become learning communities and that is a major proviso, there is no reason to be rid of them, and every reason to retain them. Nor should they have to delegate their power to quangos (such as the Education and Training Boards recommended by the National Commission on Education in *Learning to Succeed* (NCE, 1993, p. 350f)) which can only represent a more specialized and elitist public.

It is doubtful, however, whether much political power should, or could, be given to neighbourhood (or parish) councils. The principle of subsidiarity may indicate the right of such councils to control local neighbourhood resources but, as we have argued at length, the neighbourhood can no longer be viewed as an easily definable or self-sustaining community, simply because of the social, physical and cognitive mobility of modern life. This also means that neighbourhood schools and governing bodies cannot claim to represent the general public, even on educational matters. Despite the local management of schools, their political rights relating to educational policy, even at a neighbourhood level, are circumscribed by the social systems they serve.

Thus, in the total political context, we must uphold the importance of both national and local government as the main means by which the affairs of a learning society are shaped and governed. This makes it all the more important that government itself, local and national, learns how to learn. The medium must be the message.

Where then lies the significance of 'the forum' whose praises we sang earlier in this chapter? It will, we believe, become increasingly significant as the prototype of connecting systems of a more explicitly educational kind. In this context, it is likely that in future forums will play a major role, at national and local level, in the promotion of community education and the learning society.

There have been varieties of educational forum in existence for many years. The teaching unions could be said to come into this category. The churches have acted as educational forums, national and local. Parents too, through parent–teacher and parent associations, have networked along these lines. But there is now a pressing need to reconstruct such forums, or create new ones, to represent wider interests and coalitions, with the vision of the learning society much more to the fore.

Steffy and Lindle (1994, p. 13), for example, see their 'future school' as constituted by a variety of forums connecting up legal services, health care, social services, businesses, government, as well as education services and students and their families. Ranson (1993) suggests: 'A stronger democracy suggests the need for community forums with a wider remit to cover all services enabling parents, employers and community groups to express local needs and share in decision making about [educational] provisions to meet them.' But, as we have observed, 'the spirit of corporate management in a really local community has yet to find appropriate forms of management' (Sayer, 1989b, p. 7). We would add 'and a strong common purpose'. It is, therefore, likely that the most valuable educational forums in future will gather people together across a wider area and constituency than the neighbourhood to be channels through which informed educational opinion can enable political decision makers to pursue more enlightened policies on behalf of all. As Maden (1994) puts it:

> It is time to search urgently for ... a structure which ensures that the necessary expertise located in business, in trade unions, schools, colleges, local government departments and so on, is brought to bear on the decision-making processes of those citizens we elect to take [educational] decisions on our behalf.

We urgently need a wide range of educationally articulate forums to be advocates for a learning society. A General Teaching Council would greatly help here. But we also require inter-agency and cross-sector forums of both a macro and micro kind if a reframed and reformed philosophy of community education, and the learning society to which that philosophy points, are to become a reality.

COMMUNITY EDUCATION REFRAMED – THE NEW AGENDA

It is always a great temptation to assume that one lives at a major turning point in human history. But it is more than just a naive judgement that those who have lived through this century have probably witnessed changes as far-reaching and as rapid as any so far experienced in the history of human civilization. In a tiny moment of life on earth, our world has shrunk to a fraction of its previous size, while the number of those jostling for a place to stand has suddenly exploded. All of us are caught between centrifugal pressures forcing us out into the great beyond and centripetal pressures drawing us into social systems which we can still, even if tenuously, call our own. But one thing is certain. We are now 'one world' in a way that previous generations have never been. The name of the game for the century on the horizon is not the survival of some, even the fittest, but the survival of all.

Whatever our particular religious beliefs or political creeds, the search for a way of life, and an ideology to empower it, which can embrace pluralism without destroying identity, is at the very top of the agenda. In our terminology, the search which in the end makes us human beings, is the search for community. Kingdom's words (1992, p. 118) are worth repeating:

> The need for a future predicated upon a communal culture goes beyond natural economic recovery, the moral claims of egalitarians, the cry for justice by socialists or even the quest for the good life. It is linked to the sustainability of life on the planet.

We have argued that our greatest resource in ensuring 'the survival of the species' is community itself; not that vague and unctuous version of community which is used to cover a multitude of sins (and conflicts), but that magnetic power which can hold people together through thick and thin and offer them life, liberty and love. If community is the gateway to a sustainable future, it is only this interpretation of community that will suffice.

All forms of power can be creative or corrupting. Community is no exception. 'Community is a way of thinking and working which contains both radical and reactionary possibilities' writes Martin (1994, p. 25). If community were not such a hugely potent force for renewal, it would not have latent within it such massive powers of destruction. There is always the danger that community will be used to further what Paulo Freire has called 'neophilic' not 'biophilic' ends. This happens when usurpers use religion to turn community into a community of cult, use wealth to turn it into a community of privilege, use the market and the media to turn it into a community of consumers, and use deprivation or immobility to imprison it within a community of place.

In all these cases, the debasement of community is characterized by one overriding feature – that of closure. What should be universal becomes parochial, what should be ecumenical becomes sectarian, and what should be inclusive becomes exclusive. Beliefs, values and feelings are employed to set system against system, for the protection of those within and the denigration of those without. No shrinking planet, no 'global village' can hope or deserve to survive if such distortion and manipulation of the nature of community continues.

If these powers of disfiguration and destruction are to be countered, then we have to put real community education, not the insipid substitute which has gone by that name, at the top of the agenda. We have to discover infinitely more about the rich nature of community itself, not only about its many forms and expressions but about those experiences, values and beliefs which are at the very heart of the matter.

Such learning goes far beyond nurture, instruction or training. It requires education at its richest, at its most profound; education as a challenging journey of discovery into the meaning of being human and the nature of the common good. It requires education as nothing less than transformation. This journey of discovery will be one bringing many surprises, involving many risks, traversing many cultures and continuing over many years. But it is a journey to which it is now imperative that all of us commit ourselves wholeheartedly for the sake of all our futures.

Bibliography

Abbs, P. (ed.) (1989) *The Symbolic Order*. Lewes: Falmer Press.

Alexander, R. (1991) *Primary Education in Leeds – Summary Conclusions and Recommendations*. Leeds : University of Leeds.

Allen, G. and Martin, I. (eds) (1992) *Education and Community*. London: Cassell.

Allen, G., Bastiani, J., Martin, I. and Richards, K. (eds) (1987) *Community Education: an Agenda for Education Reform*. Milton Keynes: Open University Press.

Allman, P. (1987) 'Paulo Freire's education approach: a struggle for meaning', in Allen, G., Bastiani, J., Martin, I. and Richards, K. (eds), *Community Education: An Agenda for Educational Reform*. Milton Keynes: Open University Press.

Alter, C. and Hage, J. (1993) *Organisations Working Together*. London: Sage.

Apple, M. (1979) *Ideology and Curriculum*. London: Routledge & Kegan Paul.

Argyris, C. and Schön, D.A. (1974) *Theory in Practice: Increasing Professional Effectiveness*. San Francisco: Jossey-Bass.

Argyris, C. and Schön, D.A. (1978) *Organisational Learning:A Theory in Action Perspective*. Reading, Massachusetts: Addison-Wesley.

Arias, M. (1984) *Announcing the Reign of God*. Philadelphia: Fortress Press.

Armytage, W.H.G. (1961) *Heavens Below*. London: Routledge & Kegan Paul.

Association of Metropolitan Authorities and Community Education Development Centre (1991) *Looking at Community Education*. Coventry: CEDC.

Atkinson, D. (1994) *Radical Urban Solutions*. London: Cassell.

Bannister, D. and Fransella, F. (1986) *Inquiring Man: the Psychology of Personal Constructs*, 3rd edn. London: Croom Helm.

Barber, M. (1993) *Raising Standards in Deprived Urban Areas*, NCE Briefing No. 16. London: National Commission on Education.

Baron, S. (1989) 'Community Education: From the Cam to the Rea', in Walker, S. and Barton, L. (eds), *Politics and the Processes of Schooling*. Milton Keynes: Open University Press.

Bastiani, J. (1991) 'Home-School Partnership', in O'Hagan, B., *The Charnwood Papers*. Ticknall, Derbyshire: Education Now.

Bastiani, J. and Bailey, G. (1992) *Directory of Home-School Initiatives in the UK*. London: RSA and NAHT.

Batho, G. (1989) *Political Issues in Education*. London: Cassell.

Batten, T.R. (1962) *Communities and their Development*. Oxford: Oxford University Press.

Batten, T.R. (1965) *The Human Factor in Community Work*. Oxford: Oxford University Press.

Batten, T.R. and Batten, M. (1967) *The Non-Directive Approach in Group and Community Work*. Oxford: Oxford University Press.

Bazalgette, J. (1970) *'We are the Writing on Your Wall'*. London: The Grubb Institute.

BCC (1986) *The Seeds of Tolerance. An Account of the Birmingham Experiment in Community Education, 1974–1980*. Birmingham City Council.

Beare, H., Caldwell, B.J. and Millikan, R.H. (1989) *Creating an Excellent School*. London: Routledge.

Beck, U., trans. by Ritter, M. (1992) *Risk Society*. London: Sage.

Becker, H. (1950) 'Sacred and Secular Societies', *Social Forces*, **28** (4).

Benn, C. (1992) 'Common Education and the Radical Tradition', in Rattansi, A. and Reeder, D. (eds) *Rethinking Radical Education*. London: Lawrence & Wishart.

Bennett, N. and Cass, A. (1988) 'The Effects of Group Interactive Process on Pupil Understanding', *British Educational Research Journal*, **15** (1).

Bennett, N., Desfarges, C., Cockburn, A. and Wilkinson, B. (1984) *The Quality of Pupil Learning Experiences*. London: Erlbaum.

Benson, J.F. (1987) *Working More Creatively with Groups*. London: Tavistock.

Berger, P. (1980) *The Heretical Imperative*. New York: Anchor Press/Doubleday.

Berger, P. and Luckmann T. (1984) *The Social Construction of Reality*. Harmondsworth, Middx: Penguin.

Berger, P.L., Berger, B. and Kellner, H. (1974) *The Homeless Mind*. Harmondsworth, Middx: Penguin.

Bion, W.R. (1961) *Experiences in Groups*. London: Tavistock.

Bloom, A. (1988) *The Closing of the American Mind*. Harmondsworth, Middx: Penguin.

Bloom, B.S., Englehart, M.D., Furst, E.J., Hill, W.H. and Krathwohl, D.R. (1956) *Taxonomy of Educational Objectives. I: Cognitive Domain*. London: Longman.

Blythe, R. (1969) *Akenfield*. London: Allen Lane, The Penguin Press.

Boswell, J. (1990) *Community and the Economy*. London: Routledge.

Bottery, M. (1990) *The Morality of the School*. London: Cassell.

Bottery, M. (1992) *The Ethics of Educational Management*. London: Cassell.

Brandes, D. and Ginnis, P. (1986) *A Guide to Student-Centred Learning*. Oxford: Basil Blackwell.

Brandes, D. and Ginnis, P. (1990). *The Student-Centred School*. Oxford: Basil Blackwell.

Brehony, K.J. (1992) 'What's Left of Progressive Primary Education?', in Rattansi, A. and Reeder, D. (eds), *Rethinking Radical Education*. London: Lawrence and Wishart.

Brennan, T., Cooney, E.W. and Pollins, H. (1954) *Social Change in South-West Wales*. London: Watts.

Brett, B., Knightsbridge, J., Marsh, J. and Shilleto, Y. (1989) *Handbook of Good Practice – Community Education*. Waltham Forest: Department of Education.

Brown, R. (1988) *Group Processes: Dynamics Within and Between Groups*. Oxford: Basil Blackwell.

Buber, M. (1958, first published 1937) *I and Thou*, 2nd edn. Edinburgh: T. and T. Clark.

Burgess, E.W. (1961) 'The Growth of the City', in Theodorson, G.A. (ed.), *Studies in Human Ecology*. Evanston: Row, Peterson & Co.

Burgess, T. (ed.) (1986) *Education for Capability*. London: NFER-Nelson.

Burke, J.W. (ed.) (1989) *Competency Based Education and Training*. London: Falmer Press.

Capra, F. (1983) *The Turning Point*. London: Fontana.

Carpenter, E. (1961) *Common Sense about Christian Ethics*. London: Victor Gollancz.

Carr, W. (1993) 'Education and the World of Work: Clarifying the Contemporary Debate', in Wellington, J., *The Work Related Curriculum*. London: Kogan Page.

Carspecken, P.F. (1991) *Community Strategy and the Nature of Power: the Battle for Croxteth Comprehensive*. London: Routledge.

CCC (1990) *Learning Now – The Cambridgeshire Experience of Community Education*. Cambridgeshire County Council.

CEDC (1988) *Home–School Liaison Teachers*. Coventry: Community Education Development Centre.

CEDC (1991) *Community Education and Performance Indicators*. Coventry: Community Education Development Centre.

CEDC (1992a) *School Projects and the National Curriculum*. Birmingham City Council and Coventry: Community Education Development Centre.

CEDC (1992b) *Schools' In-Service Training Materials*. Birmingham City Council and Coventry: Community Education Development Centre.

Chessum, L. (1989) 'A Countesthorpe Tale', in Harber, C. and Meighan, R., *The Democratic School*. Ticknall, Derbyshire: Education Now.

Clark, D. (1969) *Community and a Suburban Village*. Unpublished PhD thesis. University of Sheffield.

Clark, D. (1973a) 'The Concept of Community: a Re-examination', *The Sociological Review*, **21** (3).

Clark, D. (1973b) 'Social Education: An Experiment with Early School Leavers', *Journal of Moral Education*, **2** (3).

Clark, D. (1975) 'Group Work with Early School Leavers', *Journal of Curriculum Studies*, **7** (1).

Clark, D. (1976) 'The Academic, the Interpersonal, and the Role of the Teacher in Social and Moral Education', *Journal of Moral Education*, **5** (2).

Clark, D. (1977) *Basic Communities*. London: SPCK.

Clark, D. (1982) *Community Education for a Multi-Ethnic Society*. Unpublished MEd thesis. Birmingham University.

Clark, D. (1984) *The Liberation of the Church*. Westhill College, Birmingham: NACCCAN.

Clark, D. (1986) *The Neglected Factor – Towards a Community Strategy for Birmingham*. Birmingham: Westhill College.

Clark, D. (1987) *Yes to Life*. London: Collins.

Clark, D. (1989) *Community Education: Towards a Framework for the Future*. Birmingham: Westhill College.

Clark, D. (1990) 'The Model and Guidelines', *The Community Curriculum Project:Birmingham* (1989–1990). Part I. Birmingham: Westhill College.

Clark, D. (1992) 'Education for Community in the 1990s: A Christian Perspective', in Allen, G. and Martin, I. (eds), *Education and Community: The Politics of Practice*. London: Cassell.

Clark, D. and Burgess, H. (1990) 'The Case-Studies', *The Community Curriculum Project: Birmingham* (1989–1990), Part II. Birmingham: Westhill College.

Clark, S. (1994) 'Basic Skills of Model Two'. Unpublished paper.

Cohen, A.P. (1985) *The Symbolic Construction of Community*. London: Ellis Harwood & Tavistock.

Cohn, N. (1970) *The Pursuit of the Millennium*. London: Paladin.

Colomy, R. (ed.) (1992) *The Dynamics of Social Systems*. London: Sage.

Concise Oxford Dictionary, 7th edn (1982) Oxford: Oxford University Press.

Cook, P. and Dalton, R. (1989) 'Schools and Communities: the Hertfordshire Education 2000 Project', in Sayer, J. and Williams, V. (eds), *Schools and External Relations*. London: Cassell.

Coser, L.A. (1956) *The Functions of Social Conflict*. London: Routledge & Kegan Paul.

Cowburn, W. (1986) *Class, Ideology and Community Education*. London: Croom Helm.

Cox, H. (1965) *The Secular City*. London: SCM Press.

Craft, M., Raynor, J. and Cohen, L. (1980) *Linking Home and School*, 3rd edn. London: Harper & Row.

CSV (1988) *Leading out* (1988), video and companion pack. Northamptonshire Education Department and London: CSV.

Curry, P. and Storer, S. (1990) *Developing an Enterprise Curriculum*. London: Industrial Society.

Cyster, R., Clift, P.S. and Battle, S. (1979) *Parental Involvement in Primary Schools*. Windsor, Berks: NFER.

Davies, L. (1994) *Beyond Authoritarian School Management: The Challenge for Transparency*. Ticknall, Derbyshire: Education Now.

Davis, C. (1994) *Religion and the Making of Society*. Cambridge: Cambridge University Press.

DCC (1986) *Community Education in Derbyshire – A Programme for Development*. December 1986. Derbyshire County Council.

Dean, J. (1985) *Managing the Secondary School*. London: Croom Helm.

Delamont, S. (1976) *Interaction in the Classroom*. London: Methuen.

Dennis, N., Henriques, F. and Slaughter, C. (1969) *Coal is Our Life*, 2nd edn. London: Tavistock.

DES (1977) *Ten Good Schools*. London: HMSO.

DES (1989) *Personal and Social Education from 5 to 16*. London: HMSO.

DES (1991) *Parent's Charter*. London: DES. Updated as *Our Children's Education* (1994). London: DFE.

DMB (1991) *A Policy Framework for Community Education in Dudley*. Dudley Metropolitan Borough.

DMB (1992) *A Policy Framework for Community Education in Dudley – First Annual Report. September 1991–August 1992*. Dudley Metropolitan Borough.

Donnison, D. and Middleton, A. (eds) (1987) *Regenerating the Inner City – Glasgow's Experience*. London: Routledge & Kegan Paul.

Dorman, P. (1994) *Economics – For or Against Community?* Unpublished BPhil thesis. University of Birmingham.

Drucker, P.F. (1993) *Post-capitalist Society*. Oxford: Butterworth-Heinemann.

Drummond, H. (1992) *The Quality Movement*. London: Kogan Page.

Durkheim, E. (1933) *The Division of Labour in Society*. Glencoe, Illinois: The Free Press.

Durkheim, E. (1951) *Suicide: A Study in Sociology*, trans. Spaulding, J.A. and Simpson, G.. New York: The Free Press.

Elias, N. and Scotson, J.L. (1965) *The Established and the Outsiders*. London: Cass.

Entwistle, H. (1978) *Class, Culture and Education*. London: Methuen.

Etzioni, A. (1993) *The Spirit of Community*. New York: Crown.

Evans, K. (1993) in NAVET *Papers*, November. Aberdeen.

Ferguson, M. (1982) *The Aquarian Conspiracy*. London: Granada.

Finegold, D. (1993) 'The Importance of the Institution: the Case of the Technical and Vocational Education Initiative', in Wellington, J., *The Work Related Curriculum*. London: Kogan Page.

Fisher, P. (1990) *Education 2000*. London: Cassell.

Fletcher, C. (1984) *The Challenges of Community Education: A Biography of Sutton Centre. 1970 to 1982*. Nottingham University: Department of Adult Education.

Fletcher, C. and Thompson, N. (1980) *Issues in Community Education*. Barcombe, Sussex: Falmer Press.

Fletcher, C., Caron, M. and Williams, W. (1985) *Schools on Trial*. Milton Keynes: Open University Press.

Ford, A., Davern, L. and Schnorr, R. (1992) 'Inclusive Education', in Stainback, S. and Stainback, W., *Curriculum Considerations in Inclusive Classrooms*. Baltimore: Paulh Brookes.

Foskett, N. (ed.) (1992) *Managing External Relations in Schools*. London: Routledge.

Fowler, W.S. (1988) *Towards The National Curriculum*. London: Kogan Page.

Foy, N. (1980) *The Yin and Yang of Organisations*. London: Grant McIntyre.

Frankenberg, R. (1957) *Village on the Border*. London: Cohen and West.

Frankenberg, R. (1966) 'British Community Studies: Problems of Synthesis', in Banton, M. (ed.), *The Social Anthropology of Complex Societies*. London: Tavistock.

Fraser, B.J. (1986) *Classroom Environment*. London: Croom Helm.

Fullan, M. (1991) *The New Meaning of Educational Change*. London: Cassell.

Galbraith, J.K. (1992) *The Culture of Contentment*. Harmondsworth, Middx: Penguin.

Galton, M., and Williamson, J. (1992) *Group Work in the Primary School Classroom*. London: Routledge.

Garratt, R. (1994) *The Learning Organisation*. London: Harper Collins.

Ginnis, P. (ed.) (1992) *Learner-managed Learning*. Ticknall, Derbyshire: Education Now.

Goffman, E. (1968) *Asylums*. Harmondsworth, Middx: Penguin.

Goldman, R. (1965) *Readiness for Religion*. London: Routledge & Kegan Paul.

Gordon, P. and Lawton, D. (1978) *Curriculum Change in the Nineteenth and Twentieth Centuries*. London: Unibooks.

Grey, M. (1989) *Redeeming the Dream*. London: SPCK.

Grey, M. (1993) *The Wisdom of Fools?* London: SPCK.

Gudykunst, W.B. (1991) *Bridging Differences*. London: Sage.

Gunton, C.E. (1993) *The One, The Three and the Many*. Cambridge: Cambridge University Press.

Halsey, A.H. (ed.) (1972) *Educational Priority: EPA Problems and Policies*. Vol. 1. London: HMSO.

Hambleton, R. and Hoggett, P. (1984) *The Politics of Decentralisation*. University of Bristol: School for Advanced Urban Studies.

Hamilton, D. (1990) *Learning about Education*. Milton Keynes: Open University Press.

Handy, C. (1981) *Understanding Organisations*, 2nd edn. Harmondsworth, Middx: Penguin.

Handy, C. (1984) *Taken for Granted? Understanding Schools as Organisations*. London: Longman.

Handy, C. (1990) *The Age of Unreason*. London: Arrow Books.

Handy, C. (1991) *Gods of Management*, 3rd edn. London: Business Books.

Handy, C. (1994) *The Empty Raincoat*. London: Hutchinson.

Handy, C. (1995) in the television programme *Visions of Heaven and Hell*, ITV: Channel 4, 7 February.

Handy, C. and Aitken, R. (1986) *Understanding Schools as Organisations*. Harmondsworth, Middx: Penguin.

Harber, C. (1992) *Democratic Learning and Learning Democracy*. Ticknall, Derbyshire: Education Now.

Harber, C. and Meighan, R. (1989) *The Democratic School*. Ticknall, Derbyshire: Education Now.

Hardy, D. (1979) *Alternative Communities in Nineteenth Century England*. London: Longman.

Hargreaves, D. (1982) *The Challenge for the Comprehensive School*. London: Routledge & Kegan Paul.

Hargreaves, D.H. (1984) *Improving Secondary Schools*. London: ILEA.

Hargreaves, D. (1994) *The Mosaic of Learning*. London: Demos.

Hargreaves, D.H. and Hopkins, D. (1991) *The Empowered School*. London: Cassell.

Harloe, M., Pickvance, C.G. and Urry, J. (eds) (1990) *Place, Policy and Politics – Do Localities Matter?* London: Unwin Hyman.

Harrison, R. (1987) *Organisation Culture and Quality of Service: a strategy for releasing love in the workplace*. London: Association for Management Education and Development.

Haughton, R. (1981) *The Passionate God*. London: Darton, Longman & Todd.

Havel, V. (1990) quoted in *The Guardian*, 20 September.

Hawkins, P. (Autumn 1991) 'The Spiritual Dimension of the Learning Organisation', *Management Education and Development*, **22** (3).

Henry Morris Memorial Trust (1990) *Recalling Henry Morris. 1889–1961*. London: Laserbooks.

Herbert, G. (1963) 'The Neighbourhood Unit Principle and Organic Theory', *The Sociological Review*, **11** (2).

Hewlett, M. (1986) *Curriculum to Serve Society – How Schools can Work for People*. Loughborough: Newstead Publishing.

Hilgard, E.R., Atkinson, R.C. and Atkinson, R.L. (1975) *Introduction to Psychology*, 6th edn. New York: Harcourt Brace Jovanovich.

Hillery, G.A. (1955) 'Definitions of Community: Areas of Agreement', *Rural Sociology*, 20 (2).

Hind, S. (1990) *Work Experience Across the Curriculum*. London: Industrial Society.

Hirst, P.H. and Peters, R.S. (1970) *The Logic of Education*. London: Routledge & Kegan Paul.

HMI (1979) *Aspects of Secondary Education in England and Wales*. London: HMSO.

HMI (1983) *Curriculum 11–16: Towards a Statement of Entitlement*. London: HMSO.

HMI (1985) *The Curriculum from 5 to 16*, 2nd edn. *Curriculum Matters 2*. London: HMSO.

HMI (1989) *Personal and Social Education from 5 to 16. Curriculum Matters 14*. London: HMSO.

HMSO (1988) *Education Reform Act*. London: HMSO

HMSO (1990) *Encouraging Citizenship*. Commission on Citizenship. London: HMSO.

Hoggett, P. and Hambleton, R. (1987) *Decentralisation and Democracy*. University of Bristol: School for Advanced Urban Studies.

Holly, P. and Southworth, G. (1989) *The Developing School*. London: Falmer Press.

Homans, G. (1951) *The Human Group*. London: Routledge & Kegan Paul.

Home Office (1994) *You, Me, Us!* Sudbury, Suffolk.

Honey, P. and Mumford, A. (1989) 'Trials and Tribulations', *The Guardian*, 19 December.

Hull, J. (1975) *School worship – an Obituary*. London: SCM Press.

Hull, J. (1985) *What Prevents Christian Adults from Learning?* London: SCM Press.

Hull, J.M. (1993) *The Hockerill Lecture 1993*. London: Hockerill Educational Foundation.

Ignatieff, M. (1993) *Blood and Belonging*. London: Chatto and Windus.

Illich, I.D. (1971) *Deschooling Society*. London: Calder and Boyers.
IPPR (1993) *Education: A Different Version*. London: IPPR.

Jack, A. (1991) *Networking*. London: The Industrial Society.
Jamieson, I. (1993) 'The Rise and Fall of the Work-related Curriculum', in Wellington, J., *The Work Related Curriculum*. London: Kogan Page.
Jarvis, P. (1983) *Adult and Continuing Education in Practice*. London: Croom Helm.
Jenkins, D.E. (1976) *The Contradiction of Christianity*. London: SCM Press.
Jenkins, D., Jones, E., Hughes, J.T. and Owen, T.M. (1960) *Welsh Rural Communities*. Cardiff: University of Wales.
Jennings, H. (1962) *Societies in the Making*. London: Routledge & Kegan Paul.
Jones, A. (1989) 'Schools, Training and Employment', in Sayer, J. and Williams, V. (eds), (1989) *Schools and External Relations*. London: Cassell.
Jones, P. (1978) *Community Education in Practice – A Review*. Oxford: Social Evaluation Unit, 40 Wellington Square, Oxford.

Karran, S. (1985) 'Volunteer Parent Home Visitors', *Outlines*, Vol. 2, pp. 41–6. Coventry: CEDC.
Keeble, R.W.J. (1981) *Community and Education*. Leicester: National Youth Bureau.
Kelly, A.V. (1982) *The Curriculum: Theory and Practice*, 2nd edn. London: Harper & Row.
Kelly, A.V. (1988) *Damage Limitation: the Challenge of the Education Reform Bill*. Occasional Papers. Liverpool: University of Liverpool Department of Education.
Kelly, A.V. (1989) *The Curriculum: Theory and Practice*, 3rd edn. London: Paul Chapman.
Kelly, K. (1994) *Out of Control*. London: Fourth Estate.
Kelly, K.T. (1992) *New Directions in Moral Theology*. London: Geoffrey Chapman.
Kingdom, J. (1992) *No Such Thing as Society?* Milton Keynes: Open University Press.
Kirkwood, C. (1990) *Vulgar Eloquence – from Labour to Liberation*. Edinburgh: Polygon.
Klein, J. (1956) *The Study of Groups*. London: Routledge & Kegan Paul.
Klein, J. (1963) *Working with Groups*, 2nd edn. London: Hutchinson.
Klein, J. (1965a) *Samples from English Cultures*, Vol. I. London: Routledge & Kegan Paul.
Klein, J. (1965b) *Samples from English Cultures*, Vol. II. London: Routledge & Kegan Paul.
Knowles, D. (1969) *Christian Monasticism*. London: Weidenfeld & Nicolson.
Kolb, D. (1984) *Experimental Learning*. Englewood Cliffs, N.J.: Prentice-Hall.
Krueger, R.A. (1988) *Focus Groups*. London: Sage.

Lankshear, D.W. (1992) *Looking for Quality in a Church School*. London: National Society.
Lawless, P. and Raban, C. (eds) (1986) *The Contemporary British City*. London: Harper and Row.
Lawn, M. and Barton, L. (1981) *Rethinking Curriculum Studies*. London: Croom Helm.
Lawton, D. (1973) *Social Change, Educational Theory and Curriculum Planning*. London: Hodder and Stoughton.
Lawton, D. (1983) *Curriculum Studies and Educational Planning*. London: Hodder & Stoughton.
Lawton, D. (1989) *Education, Culture and the National Curriculum*. London: Hodder and Stoughton.
Lawton, D. (1994) 'Defining Quality', in Ribbins, P. and Burridge, E. (eds) (1994) *Improving Education: Promoting Quality in Schools*. London: Cassell.
Lawton, D. and Chitty, C. (1988) *The National Curriculum*. London: Kogan Page.
LCC (1988) *Review of the Youth and Community Education Services 1986–1988. Summary and Digest*. Leicestershire County Council.
Levacic, R. and Woods, R. (1994) 'New forms of financial co-operation', in Ranson, S. and Tomlinson, J., *School Co-operation: New Forms of Local Governance*. London: Longman.
Lewis, C.S. (1963) *The Four Loves*. London: Fontana.
Lipnack, J. and Stamp, J. (1986) *The Networking Book*. London: Routledge & Kegan Paul.
Long, R. (1986) *Developing Parental Involvement in Primary Schools*. London: Macmillan Education.
Lovelock, J.E. (1979) *Gaia: a New Look at Life on Earth*. Oxford: Oxford University Press.
Lynd, R.S. and Lynd, H.M. (1929) *Middletown*. London: Constable.
Lynd, R.S. and Lynd, H.M. (1937) *Middletown in Transition*. London: Constable.

Macdonald, J. (1993) *Understanding Total Quality Management in a week*. Sevenoaks, Kent: Hodder & Stoughton.

MacIver, R.M. (1924) *Community*. London: Macmillan.

MacIver, R.M. and Page, C.H. (1950) *Society*. London: Macmillan.

Maclure, S. (1988) *Education Re-formed*. London: Hodder and Stoughton.

Macquarrie, J. (1982) *In Search of Humanity*. London: SCM Press.

Maden, M. (1994) 'Blair's Braver Game', *The Times Educational Supplement*, 30 September.

Madge, J. (1962) *The Origins of Scientific Sociology*. London: Tavistock.

Martin, I. (1987) 'Community education: towards a theoretical analysis', in Allen, G., Bastiani, J., Martin, I. and Richards, K. (eds) (1987) *Community Education: an Agenda for Educational Reform*. Milton Keynes: Open University Press.

Martin, I. (1992) 'New times: new directions?', *Community Education Network*, **12** (9).

Martin, I. (1994) *Community Education: the School*. Adult and Continuing Education, Unit 4. Canterbury: YMCA National College.

Mayhew, L. (1992) 'Political Rhetoric and the Contemporary Public', in Colomy, R. (ed.), *The Dynamics of Social Systems*. London: Sage.

McLaren, P. (1986) *Schooling as a Ritual Performance*. London: Routledge & Kegan Paul.

McLuhan, M. (1973) *Understanding Media*. London: Abacus.

McPhail, P. (1972) *Schools Council Moral Education Curriculum Project*. London: Schools Council Publications (Longman).

Meighan, R. (1986) *A Sociology of Educating*, 2nd edn. London: Cassell.

Meighan, R. (1988) *Flexi-schooling*. Ticknall, Derbyshire: Education Now.

Meighan, R. and Toogood, P. (1992) *Anatomy of Choice in Education*. Ticknall, Derbyshire: Education Now.

Merton, R.K. (1957) *Social Theory and Social Structure*, rev. edn. New York: The Free Press.

Midwinter, E. (1972) *Social Environment and the Urban School*. London: Ward Lock.

Midwinter, E. (1975) *Education and the Community*. London: George Allen and Unwin.

Moon, B., Isaac, J. and Powney, J. (eds) (1990) *Judging Standards and Effectiveness in Education*. London: Hodder & Stoughton.

Morgan, D.L. (1993) *Successful Focus Groups*. London: Sage.

Morgan, G. (1986) *Images of Organisation*. London: Sage.

Morgan, R. and Williams, G. (1990) *Industry Comes to School*. London: Industrial Society.

Mortimore, P., Sammons, P., Stoll, L., Lewis, D. and Ecob, R. (1988) *School Matters*. London: Open Books.

Mullan, B. (1980) *Stevenage Ltd. – Aspects of the Planning and Politics of Stevenage New Town 1945–78*. London: Routledge & Kegal Paul.

Münch, R. (1992) 'The Dynamics of Societal Communication', in Colomy, R. (ed.), *The Dynamics of Social Systems*. London: Sage.

Musgrave, P.W. (1968) *Society and Education in England since 1800*. London: Methuen.

NCC (1990a) *Curriculum Guidance 4: Education for Economic and Industrial Understanding*. York: National Curriculum Council.

NCC (1990b) *Curriculum Guidance 5: Health Education*. York: National Curriculum Council.

NCC (1990c) *Curriculum Guidance 7: Environmental Education*. York: National Curriculum Council.

NCC (1990d) *Curriculum Guidance 8: Education for Citizenship*. York: National Curriculum Council.

NCE (1993) *Learning to Succeed: Report of the National Commission on Education*. London: Heinemann.

Newbigin, L. (1980) *Your Kingdom Come*. Leeds: John Paul The Preacher's Press.

Newby, H. (1985) *Green and Pleasant Land? Social Change in Rural England*. London: Wildwood House.

NFER (1994) *Core Skills and Cross-Curricular Initiatives in Secondary Schools*. Slough, Berks: National Foundation for Educational Research.

Nicholls, A. and Nicholls, H. (1978) *Developing a Curriculum*, 2nd edn. London: George Allen & Unwin.

Nisbet, R.A. (1969, first edn 1953) *The Quest for Community*. Oxford: Oxford University Press.
Nolan, V. (1987) *The Innovator's Handbook*. London: Sphere Books.

OFSTED (February 1994) *Spiritual, Moral, Social and Cultural Development*. London: OFSTED.
O'Hagan, B. (1991) *The Charnwood Papers*. Ticknall, Derbyshire: Education Now.
Owen, J. (1992) *Managing Education*. London: Longman.

Pahl, R.E. (1964) *Urbs in Rure*. London: London School of Economics.
Pahl, R.E. (1970) *Patterns of Urban Life*. London: Longman.
Palmer, P. (1987) *A Place Called Community*. Pennsylvania: Pendle Hill.
Park, R.E. (1952) *Human Communities*. New York: The Free Press.
Peck, M.S. (1990) *The Different Drum*. London: Arrow Books.
Pedler, M., Burgoyne, J. and Boydell, T. (1991) *The Learning Company*. Maidenhead, Berks: McGraw-Hill.
Peters, R.S. (1966) *Ethics and Education*. London: George Allen & Unwin.
Pfeffer, N. and Coote, A. (1991) *Is Quality Good for You?* Social Policy Paper No. 5. London: Institute of Public Policy Research.
Phillida, S. (1988) *Psychology for Teachers – An Alternative Approach*. London: Hutchinson.
Plant, R. (1974) *Community and Ideology*. London: Routledge & Kegan Paul.
Plowden Report (1967) *Children and their Primary Schools*. London: HMSO.
Poster, C. (1982) *Community Education: its Development and Management*. London: Heinemann.
Poster, C. and Krüger, A. (eds) (1990) *Community Education in the Western World*. London: Routledge.
Poster, C. and Zimmer, J. (eds) (1992) *Community Education in the Third World*. London: Routledge.
Price, P. (1987) *The Church as the Kingdom*. Basingstoke, Hants: Marshall Pickering.
Pugh, G. (1989) 'Parents and Professionals in Pre-School Services: Is Partnership Possible?', in Wolfendale, S. (ed.), *Parental Involvement*. London: Cassell.

Ranson, S. (1993) *Local Democracy for a Learning Society*. NCE Briefing No. 18. London: National Commission on Education.
Ranson, S. and Tomlinson, J. (1994) *School Co-operation: New Forms of Local Governance*. London: Longman.
Rattansi, A. and Reeder, D. (eds) (1992) *Rethinking Radical Education*. London: Lawrence and Wishart.
Redfield, R. (1941) *The Folk Culture of Yucatan*. Chicago: University of Chicago Press.
Rée, H. (1973) 'Educator Extraordinary', *The Times Educational Supplement*, 2 November.
Rée, H. (ed.) (1984) *The Henry Morris Collection*. Cambridge: Cambridge University Press.
Rée, H. (1985) *Educator Extraordinary*. London: Peter Owen.
Reid, J.A., Forrestal, P. and Cook, J. (1989) *Small Group Learning in the Classroom*. Scarborough, Australia: Chalkface Press.
Reissman, L. (1964) *The Urban Process*. New York: The Free Press.
Rennie, J. (1990) 'Why Community Education?', in Poster, C. and Krüger, A. (eds), *Community Education in the Western World*. London: Routledge.
Reynolds, D. (1990) 'School Effectiveness and School Improvement: A Review of the British Literature', in Moon, B., Isaac, J. and Powney, J. (eds), *Judging Standards and Effectiveness in Education*. London: Hodder & Stoughton.
Ribbins, P. and Burridge, E. (eds) (1994) *Improving Education: Promoting Quality in Schools*. London: Cassell.
Rice, A.K. (1965) *Learning for Leadership*. London: Tavistock.
Riesman, D. (1950) *The Lonely Crowd*. New York: Doubleday Anchor.
Rigby, A. (1974) *Alternative Realities*. London: Routledge and Kegan Paul.
Rogers, R. (1980) *Crowther to Warnock*. London: Heinemann.
Rosenholtz, S.J. (1989) *Teacher's Workplace: The Social Organisation of Schools*. New York: Longman.
Rutter, M., Maughan, B., Mortimore, P. and Ouston, J. (1979) *Fifteen Thousand Hours*. London: Open Books.

Sallis, E. (1993) *Total Quality Management in Education*. London: Kogan Page.

Sapon-Shevin, M. (1992) 'Celebrating Diversity, Creating Community', in Stainback, S. and Stainback, W., *Curriculum Considerations in Inclusive Classrooms*. Baltimore: Paulh Brookes.

Savage, C.M. (1990) *Fifth Generation Management*. Burlington, MA: Digital Press.

Sayer, J. (1989a) 'Issues for Management Training', in Sayer, J. and Williams, V. (eds), *Schools and External Relations*. London: Cassell.

Sayer, J. (1989b) 'The Public Context of Change', in Sayer, J. and Williams, V. (eds), *Schools and External Relations*. London: Cassell.

Sayer, J. and Williams, V. (eds) (1989) *Schools and External Relations*. London: Cassell.

SCC (1990) *Community Education in Staffordshire – A Statement of Good Practice, May 1990*. Staffordshire County Council.

SC/NHP (1970) *Humanities Curriculum Project: An Introduction*. Schools Council/Nuffield Humanities Project. London: Heinemann.

Schön, D.A. (1983) *The Reflective Practitioner*. New York: Basic Books.

Schön, D.A. (1988) *Educating the Reflective Practitioner*. London: Jossey-Bass.

Sciulli, D. and Bould, S. (1992) 'Neocorporatism, Social Integration, and the Limits of Comparative Political Sociology', in Colomy, R. (ed.), *The Dynamics of Social Systems*. London: Sage.

Scottish Education Department (1983) *Education in the Community*. Edinburgh: HMSO.

Sedgwick, P. (1992) *The Enterprise Culture*. London: SPCK.

Senge, P.M. (1990) *The Fifth Discipline*. New York: Currency and Doubleday.

Shotter, J. (1993) 'Psychology and Citizenship: Identity and Belonging', in Turner, B.S. (ed.), *Citizenship and Social Theory*. London: Sage.

Simmel, G. (1955) *Conflict*. Glencoe, IL: The Free Press.

Simpson, G. (1937) *Conflict and Community*. New York: Liberal Press.

Skilbeck, M. (1976) 'Culture, Ideology and Knowledge', *Curriculum, Design and Development*. Educational Studies Unit 3, Milton Keynes: Open University Press.

Skilbeck, M. (1984) *School-Based Curriculum Development*. London: Paul Chapman.

Skilbeck, M. (1985) A *Core Curriculum for the Common School*, 2nd edn. London: University of London Institute of Education.

Slavin, R.E. (1983) *Co-operative Learning*. New York: Longman.

Slavin, R.E. (1990) *Co-operative Learning: Theory, Research and Practice*. London: Allyn & Bacon.

Smart, B. (1992) *Modern Conditions, Postmodern Controversies*. London: Routledge.

Stacey, M. (1960) *Tradition and Change*. London: Oxford University Press.

Stainback, S. and Stainback, W. (1992) *Curriculum Considerations in Inclusive Classrooms*. Baltimore: Pouch Brookes.

Stamp, G. (1992) *Stealing the Churches' Clothes?* CIPL Position Paper G3. Birmingham: Westhill College.

Steffy, B.E. and Lindle, J.C. (1994) *Building Coalitions*. California: Corwin Press (Sage Publications).

TES (1991) 'Unable to Page the Oracle', *The Times Educational Supplement*, 15 November.

Thatcher, M. (1987) in *Womans Own*, 31 October.

Tillich, P. (1962) *The Courage to Be*. London: Fontana.

Timasheff, N.S. (1955) *Sociological Theory*. New York: Random House.

Tönnies, F. (1887) *Community and Association,* trans. and suppl. Loomis, C.P. (1955). London: Routledge & Kegan Paul.

Toogood, P. (1984) *The Head's Tale*. Telford: Dialogue Publications.

Toogood, P. (ed.) (1991) *Small Schools*. Ticknall, Derbyshire: Education Now.

Townsend, T. (1994) *Effective Schooling for the Community*. London: Routledge.

Turner, B.S. (ed.) (1993) *Citizenship and Social Theory*. London: Sage.

UDACE (1989) *Performance Indicators and the Education of Adults*. Leicester: National Institute of Adult Continuing Education.

Vaill, P.B. (1986) 'The Purposing of High Performing Systems', in Sergiovanni, T.J. and Corbally,

J.R. (eds), *Leadership and Organisational Culture: New Perspectives on Administrative Theory and Practice*. Urbana and Chicago: University of Chicago Press.

Vanier, J. (1979) *Community and Growth*. London: Darton, Longman & Todd.

Wallis, J. and Mee, G. (1983) *Community Schools: Claims and Performance*. Nottingham University: Department of Adult Education.

Wardle, D. (1976) *English Popular Education 1780–1975*, 2nd edn. Cambridge: Cambridge University Press.

Warwick, D. (1975) *Curriculum Structure and Design*. London: University of London Press.

Warwick, D. (1987) *The Modular Curriculum*. Oxford: Basil Blackwell.

Watt, J.S. (1989) 'Community Education and Parent Involvement: a Partnership in Need of a Theory', in Macleod, F. (ed.), *Parents and Schools: the Contemporary Challenge*. London: Falmer Press.

Watts, J. (ed.) (1977) *The Countesthorpe Experience*. London: George Allen & Unwin.

Watts, J. (1980) *Towards an Open School*. London: Longman.

Watts, T. (1993) 'Connecting Curriculum to Work: Past Patterns, Current Initiatives and Future Issues', in Wellington, J., *The Work-Related Curriculum*. London: Kogan Page.

Wellington, J. (1993) *The Work-Related Curriculum*. London: Kogan Page.

West-Burnham, J. (1992) *Managing Quality in Schools*. London: Longman.

Westwood, S. (1992) 'When Class became Community: Radicalism in Adult Education', in Rattansi, A. and Reeder, D. (eds), *Rethinking Radical Education*. London: Lawrence & Wishart.

Whitaker, P. (1993) *Managing Change in Schools*. Milton Keynes: Open University Press.

White, J.P. (1977) *Towards a Compulsory Curriculum*. London: Routledge & Kegan Paul.

White, L.E. (1950) *Community or Chaos*. London: National Council of Social Service.

Whitty, G. (1992) 'Lessons from Radical Curriculum Initiatives: Integrated Humanities and World Studies', in Rattansi, A. and Reeder, D. (eds), *Rethinking Radical Education*. London: Lawrence & Wishart.

Whyte, W.H. (1956) *The Organisation Man*. Harmondsworth, Middx: Penguin.

Williams, R. (1976) *Keywords*. London: Croom Helm.

Williams, W.M. (1956) *Gosforth*. London: Routledge & Kegan Paul.

Williams, W.M. (1963) *A West Country Village: Ashworthy*. London: Routledge & Kegan Paul.

Willie, E. and Hodgson, P. (1991) *Making Change Work*. London: Mercury Books.

Willmott, P. (1963) *The Evolution of a Community*. London: Routledge & Kegan Paul.

Wilson, J., Williams, N. and Sugarman, B. (1967) *Introduction to Moral Education*. Harmondsworth, Middx: Penguin.

Wilson, M. (1975) *Health is for People*. London: Darton, Longman & Todd.

Wolfendale, S. (1989) *Empowering Parents and Teachers*. London: Cassell.

WMB (1990) *Community Education Information Pack*, Vols 1, 2 and 3, Walsall Metropolitan Borough.

Wuthnow, R. (1994) *Sharing the Journey – Support Groups and America's New Quest for Community*. New York: The Free Press.

Wright, D. (1971) *The Psychology of Moral Behaviour*. Harmondsworth, Middx: Penguin.

Young, M. and Willmott, P. (1962) *Family and Kinship in East London*, rev. edn. Harmondsworth, Middx: Penguin.

Name Index

Subject Index

access, provision of 110
accountability 78–9
action, facilitating 111
adult education 11, 133, 134
   and community schools 21–2, 23, 25
affirmation 108
agreement, negotiating 109
alliances 107–8
   see also partnerships
alternatives, exploring 110
amorality, and centrifugal forces 3–4
anonymity
   and centrifugal forces 3, 4
   and open learning 7
appraisal 108, 111–12
approaches 107
authority 107, 108–9
autonomous learning 86

beliefs
   and community 48, 53–5, 56, 151, 165
   and school effectiveness 120
   and 'symbolic universes' 104, 105
   symbols and rituals 79–80
boundary managers, community educators as
   101, 114, 124, 126, 128–9, 147–8, 161
businesses, partnerships between schools and
   139–41, 159

centrifugal forces 2–4, 7, 26, 40, 56, 130, 149
   and the communal dilemma 81
   and community education 91, 164
   and learning communities 8
   and political community 152, 155, 157
centripetal forces 5, 7, 26, 40, 56, 130, 149,
   152, 164

   and the communal dilemma 81
   and community education 91
   and learning communities 8
   and political community 155, 157
change
   communal 104–5
   managing 126, 127–9
   and the synergistic code 95, 97
Christianity
   beliefs 53–5
   community movement 38
   involvement of churches in education 135–7
cities, and the learning society 150, 162–3
citizenship 87–8, 152
common good 52, 55, 108, 130, 150, 151, 159
communal dilemma 47–50, 81, 126
   and the churches 135–6, 137
   and focal systems 67
   and the learning society 151
   symbols and rituals 79
   and the 3 'L's 51, 52
   and the 3 'S's 60
communal guidelines
   and the community educator 103–4, 110,
     114, 128
   as gateways for intervention 103–4
   and the intervention cycle 106, 112
   and networks 143
communal task 45, 52, 56, 60, 63, 64, 153
   and appraisal 111
   and community educators 104
   and focal systems 135
   and interaction 74
communes movement 5, 8, 38
communication 113
   and communal guidelines 66, 73, 75–6